VIGNETTES of VICTORY

HEROES · HEROINES
HIGHLIGHTS & SIDELIGHTS

BY PAUL A. MARSHALL

CREST
BOOKS

Copyright © 1997, 2016 by The Salvation Army
2nd Edition, Revised and Expanded

1st Edition Published as *It's a Great Old Army!*
by The Salvation Army, The Central Territory
Printed 1997, Reprinted 2005

Published by Crest Books
The Salvation Army National Headquarters
615 Slaters Lane
Alexandria, VA 22313
(703) 684-5523
sanationalpublications.org

Lt. Col. Allen Satterlee, Editor-in-Chief and National Literary Secretary
Roger Selvage, Art Director
Nick Holder, Editorial Assistant

Available at crestbooks.com

ISBN: 978-0-9913439-4-2

Printed in the United States of America

Contents

"Good Old Army" — Highlights & Sidelights

The Order of the Founder — Our American Honor Roll

The Two World Wars

Touching Lives in Many Ways

Salvation Army Music

In a Holiday Mood

Strictly Miscellaneous

Preface

I would be embarrassed if anyone called this an Army history book. It is not that at all, nor does it pretend to be. Dr. Edward McKinley, in giving us *Marching to Glory,* has done that for us, and done it extremely well. Incidentally, that history is now in its second edition, an edition which is far from being merely a second printing. The changes in the distribution of photographs throughout its pages, the designation of footnotes at the back so as to be found easily, and the content of the book itself have all been improved significantly.

By contrast, the little volume you now hold in your hand was not originally planned to be a book at all. The organization and classification of material which you see now was a later adaptation. Indeed, the question in my mind as I confronted the typewriter month after month was, "What shall I write about this time?"

Consequently, as a history, it would have to be said that it lacks a framework to which everything is tied logically; it lacks flow which would carry the reader smoothly through a long series of events in an integrated, balanced and logical manner; and it lacks consistency or completeness in what it chooses to present. Because of its nature, it jumps over many years without a mention, then suddenly recounts an incident in detail. This is not an apology, but rather preparation for what you are about to read. While it's not history, perhaps you'll enjoy for what it is. It deals with a collection of interesting events and people, often without the lengthy process of placing them in their chronological and social setting

Foreword

As you probably know, nearly all of the following pages appeared on the back cover of the Central Territory's edition of *The Daily Walk* over a period of eleven years. In the first year of my writing, I had a dual assignment: to produce, if possible, something which related to the month in which it would appear, while at the same time keeping to a Salvation Army theme. In the second year, I was given a bit more leeway, since finding material which was both Army-oriented and seasonal would obviously become increasingly difficult as time went on.

The back covers never carried the implication that the material could not be found elsewhere (although some could not, since my sources reached beyond published material). They were set forth month by month to make lively reading, to give the Central's own edition of *The Daily Walk* a touch of Army identity, and hopefully, to cause some to say, "I never knew that."

I have tried to highlight events and facts from Army history which in some cases already appear in books, but often in books which are out of print or not frequently seen by most Salvationists. Take for example Harold Begbie's unabridged biography of William Booth. Two or three of my columns came out of that two-volume set. Yet when people ask me, "Where in the world did you find that?" The answer, I admit, seems pretty prosaic.

As for my sources overall, I would group them into three categories. The first source, as I have indicated, was from Salvation Army books. The second, from Army periodicals, where such items appear once and often are never seen again. Many shouldn't be so easily forgotten. My bringing them once again to view through the instrumentality of

The Daily Walk may have served a good purpose, but when the study booklets are eventually discarded, those nuggets will again fade into virtual oblivion, since for most readers they will be inaccessible. It is hoped that this book may prolong their life. Let me add that the limitations of space on the *Daily Walk* cover naturally made it impossible to credit the original writers. I hope that does not make it seem as if I "cribbed" their material.

The third source has been from my personal experience and observations, and from acquaintanceship with Salvationists, some of whose careers went "a long way back," not to mention my own family, with grandparents, both maternal and paternal, whose officership went well back into the 1880s.

As you will observe, there are no footnotes. The fact is, the book contains at least a couple of rather humorous stories "told out of school" by officers who served in high places. For obvious reasons those sources were not footnoted! But their stories are, after all these years, harmless enough; they fall into the "now it can be told" category, and perhaps can serve as illustrations of the fact that we're all human, from the General on down!

I must mention the many distinguished Salvationists who have been admitted to the Order of the Founder. Every American who has been thus honored was given at least one *Daily Walk* back cover. So here they are, the first time all such American honorees have been brought together in one book.

There are a number of people who deserve acknowledgment, but let me trim that list to three. Ken Romin has been unfailingly patient and good-natured for all these eleven and a half years in turning my little offerings into print, first for *The Daily Walk,* now for this book. Then there is my daughter Julia, who spent many late evening hours at her computer, correcting proof pages. Many thanks, Ken and Julie!

Let me conclude by paying tribute to Philip Collier, my mentor, who wrote a brief biography of every Order of the Founder inductee in the Southern Territory. Tragically, he did not live to see his book published. I am grateful to Mrs. Millie Collier for sharing the proof pages regarding the last couple of honorees, since I was having trouble learning much about them.

It would seem that I am having almost as much trouble concluding this preface as Beethoven had in concluding his Fifth Symphony! There is one more thing which needs clarifying. Since this is a reprinting of articles published in past years, obviously some of those featured are no longer living. In some cases, it would have been next to impossible to discover whether they are living or not. So I have followed the policy of leaving the text as it appeared when the articles were originally published.

"GOOD OLD"
ARMY
HIGHLIGHTS & SIDELIGHTS

The Look-Alike

A century and a half ago, a boy died shortly before he entered adolescence, leaving behind a grieving mother and father. One day as the parents walked near their home, another boy caught their attention. He was perhaps twelve years of age and remarkably similar in appearance to the son they had lost.

Let the historian who recorded this incident tell it in his own words. The bereaved parents, passing the boy while he played in the streets "would turn so often to look at him that at last he became aware of their interest. He would look up at them as they appeared, and watch them as they passed on, wondering what it was that caused them to regard him so affectionately. One day, they stopped and spoke to him, the gentleman asking how he was getting on in school. The lady then made it clear why they were interested in him. Her eyes filled with tears as she told the boy that he greatly resembled the son whom they had lost.

"After this a friendship sprang up between the old people and the boy, They asked him to their house, treated him with the greatest kindness, and would even have adopted him. They were Wesleyans and, with his parents' permission, began taking him to chapel. This was his first introduction to Methodism."

As for the boy's own parents, they were too preoccupied with financial woes to pay much attention to him. Worse, the father was absolutely irreligious. The boy did occasionally accompany his mother to her church, but he found the worship cold and perfunctory. "Church" held no attraction for him—that is, before he was taken to the Wesleyan chapel. Soon the word took on a new dimension; he felt at home there.

But in all too short a time, he was obliged to move away, and he lost touch with the people who had befriended him. The story could have ended there—but it didn't. The couple who had taken him to their church did far more than they ever knew; they had opened wide the doors of a vital, relevant Christianity to this boy. Once settled in his new city, he sought out a local Methodist church. When a visiting evangelist, known for his powerful preaching, visited that church, the young man was saved.

It's a story to ponder. One boy's life was cut short, but hardly wasted! His death paved the way for the conversion of his lookalike: none other than William Booth!

Was This His Day of Destiny?

On a summer day in 1865, a tall, bearded preacher strode down Mile End Road. William Booth had left the Methodist New Connexion to be a full-time evangelist. After a time, his denomination closed their doors to his ministry. Obliged to preach in smaller and smaller chapels to poorer congregations, his desire to reach the unreached masses grew while his opportunities seemed to dwindle. Through a process often painful, the Lord was directing him to new fields.

He was asked to preach in a tent on an old Quaker burial ground for a week. The week stretched into six, and every day he walked through the same blighted area, teaming with masses of lost humanity. A serious problem confronted him: a tent was all right for July and August, but what of the winter ahead? Where could he gather crowds needing to hear the Gospel? Lost in thought, he came face to face with a professional boxer bound for a match.

Many years later the boxer, Peter Monk (by then a longtime convert), described his encounter:

> "I was walking toward the public house, but on the opposite side of the way, just strolling along with my hands in my pockets, when I came across General Booth for the first time in my life. Something in the man's external appearance took hold of me then and there. I stopped dead in

the street, looking at him; and he stopped too, looking at me… I could see he was a minister…. After he had looked at me for a long while, says he very sadly, 'I'm looking for work.' I was taken aback. I got hold of some coins in my pocket, and was just going to offer them to him, when he pointed to 'the boys' outside the public house just opposite, a great crowd of them, and says he, 'Look at those men! Why should I be looking for work? There's my work over there, looking for me. But I've got no place,' says he, 'where I can put my head in.'

"'You're right, sir,' I said. 'Those men are forgotten by God and man, and if you can do anything for them 'twould be a great work.'"

Soon afterward (some think that very night) he declared to his wife, "I've found my destiny!" And no wonder! In the depths of his depression, God gave him an electrifying new vision.

Persecution and Persuasion

The year 1882 was a year of incredible contrasts in The Salvation Army's history. The mission which four years previously, just thirteen years after its inception, had changed its name from a mission to an "Army" to emphasize its militant evangelism, was repeatedly being attacked in the streets by ruffians. Before it would end there would be martyrs, people killed while proclaiming God's word on England's streets. Such extreme incidents were rare, but they did happen. In some districts and cities, the police not only ignored extreme (and illegal) violence against the Salvationists, they actually arrested the victims, presumably because they were the cause of the disturbance. The police were "keeping the peace."

This topsy-turvy "justice" did not end with the police. There were judges who sentenced Salvationists to jail for telling of Christ's love. Were these judges carrying out some sort of British national policy? Not at all.

As a matter of fact, something quite different was taking place behind closed doors at this very time. It involved the Church of England, which derived its authority directly from the British throne. Today, as then, the reigning monarch is the church's temporal head, with the prerogative to appoint its archbishops, bishops and other offices.

Top-level representatives of the Church of England were meeting to ask that this new organization become an integral part, a militant arm, of the Queen's own Church of England! Some of their clergy had tried conscientiously to reach the masses who, for the most part, seemed unreachable. They had to admit that their efforts paled before the remarkable success of this new Army. So it was that a committee of five had been appointed to work out an arrangement whereby The Salvation Army, with its aggressive, militant, and highly effective evangelism could in some way be grafted into the authorized church, thus adding a new dimension to its efforts.

It began early in 1882 with a letter to William Booth from the Archbishop of York, who said he was writing at the request of some of his clergymen. From this initiative followed the consultation. Most people today, if they know anything about this bit of Army history at all, fail to realize that this was not just another committee appointed to "look into" a matter. This committee was really serious about negotiating a merger, and its members were absolutely top-drawer.

Keep in mind that only a few Anglican clergymen have the distinction of being made bishops by the Queen, and that at any one time, two will occupy the highest offices: the Archbishops of York and of Canterbury. Let it be noted also that, of the two, the Archbishop of Canterbury occupies the highest position in the Church of England.

One could hardly expect that august personage to wait upon William Booth, trying to persuade him to join his rag-tag forces with the Church of England! The Archbishop would be too busy, for one thing. But he did the next best thing: he entrusted this mission to Dr. Randall Davidson, Dean of Windsor. Another committee member was Dr. Benson, Bishop of Truro. What stature did these men bring to the committee? Suffice it to say that each of them in turn was later appointed Archbishop of Canterbury. Another member was Canon Wilkinson, who was subsequently Bishop of Truro, then Bishop of St. Andrews.

But the two who, even today, loom large in the minds of serious New Testament scholars are not revered simply because they climaxed their careers as bishops, but because of their contributions to biblical scholarship. Personally, I was electrified when I learned that Bishop Lightfoot sat on that committee, dealing directly with William Booth. It is true that Dr. Lightfoot was Bishop of Durham. But today we remember him, not as a bishop but as a towering figure in the field of New Testament scholarship. For many years, because of his definitive studies on the apostolic church, and particularly on St. Paul as set forth in his commentaries, he was widely regarded as the final authority in those areas of knowledge.

And lastly there was Canon B. F. Westcott of Westminster, and of the University of Cambridge. Later he became Bishop of Durham. In addition to his major scholarly works regarding various areas of New Testament studies, he contributed many articles to William Smith's *Dictionary of the Bible*. By the time the committee met he had spent more than a decade as professor of divinity at Cambridge, had played a major role in the reorganization of the Divinity School there, and had just completed eleven years on the committee which produced the Revised Version of the Bible.

Westcott was a man who never limited himself exclusively to the proverbial ivory tower; indeed, he was later influential in bringing about the settlement of a major coal strike. His social awareness led to his being elected president of the Christian Social Union, a position he held until his death. Doubtless for him, it would have been a joy to be associated with William Booth.

But of all his many accomplishments, his name reverberates today in the words "Westcott and Hort," the universally recognized "short-hand" designation for *The New Testament in the Original Greek* which he and F. J. A. Hort produced after a period of twenty-eight years of joint research. Although he spent his earlier years as an Anglican clergyman, Hort was not on the committee because he had given up that life to return to Cambridge as a scholar and full time professor. Those on the committee were all clergymen.

So there they were: two future Archbishops of Canterbury, another high-ranking bishop, and—most striking to us today—Lightfoot and Westcott, altogether a most prestigious quintet committed to wooing William Booth and his Salvation Army into some sort of organic, practical working relationship with the Church of England. To readers who have known nothing of this, it must seem nearly unbelievable.

What was the outcome? Well, the committee asked too much of Booth. They wanted him in effect to give up leadership of his Army, while he wisely perceived that, with him removed from the vanguard of his ranks and replaced by an Anglican clergyman (or committee!), The Salvation Army would soon lose its independent spirit, its holy daring and the other characteristics to which it owed its phenomenal growth and effectiveness.

One committee member in particular feared that if Booth were allowed to continue his leadership of the Army, it might be inevitable that he would one day "become a high ecclesiastic in the Church of England," as Bramwell Booth stated it. To this member that was unthinkable.

After some time had elapsed between their occasional meetings and before an understanding could be worked out, the committee member most committed to bringing about the merger died. Without the influence and impetus of this large-spirited man, subsequent meetings saw little progress, while the impasse remained regarding William Booth's role in the new union. Eventually the proposal quietly expired.

But that was not quite the end of it. Later that same year, after it became clear that a merger or a formal alliance would not take place, some of the church's leaders, in hopes of infusing some of the fire and spirit of the Salvationists into the Church of England, put a new plan into action. If The Salvation Army could not be grafted into the Church of England, they would have their own army of salvation! So, before the close of 1882 they inaugurated the Church Army. It had some military trappings, and its representatives were dedicated to carrying out an Anglican social ministry among the poor and disadvantaged, and by humble Christian service at the level of greatest need, to make the message of salvation appealing to those needing it so badly.

This Church Army was no ephemeral "consolation prize." The new organization not only became a reality in England but crossed the Atlantic to become an arm of the Protestant Episcopal Church in America as well. It is still in operation in some major American cities today, and its statement of purpose is something to which Salvationists can wholeheartedly say "Amen!"

The "Army Father"

If ever a man could be excused for being too busy with worthy causes, too pressured by financial need, or too harassed in a hundred other ways, that man was William Booth in the years when his children were young and his East London Mission was taking shape. Yet even in those difficult days, he set a pattern as a father that is worth pondering.

Miss Jane Short, an early member of the Mission, became a boarder with the Booths in 1867. Long afterwards, she retained her vivid memories of the experience, which she shared with Harold Begbie as a source for his biography of the General:

> "To tell you the truth," she said, "I was terribly afraid of going to live with these dear folk, because I had been so often disappointed in religious people. It seemed to me that the Booths could not possibly be in their home life what they were in their preaching. I loved them so well that I shrank from finding my hero-worship an illusion."

But she was not disappointed. She was soon "Sister Jane" and became a beloved member of the family. She recalled that William Booth made it a rule, so far as possible, to give the children a part of his evenings at home. They would come charging into the room for a romp with their father with no set game, although "Fox and Geese" was a favorite. Still, a tussle of some sort was the usual amusement. The Rev. Mr. Booth would lie full length upon the floor, and the smaller children would try to pull him up.

He loved to be tousled; he would sit reading a book with complete absorption while one of his children sat upon the arm of the chair, rubbing his head:

> "One evening," said Miss Short, "his daughter Emma, then about six, amused herself by putting his long hair into curl papers. She worked away until his whole head was covered with little twists of paper. Such a sight you never saw in your life. And when she had finished her work, the door opened and a servant entered, announcing a visitor. Up sprang the General, and was all but in the hall when the children flung themselves upon his coattails and, screaming with laughter, dragged him back. You can fancy that when the General looked in the glass, he laughed too."

The Founder was almost obsessively concerned with the needs of mankind; it may be said that he was the most serious of men. But he knew better than to take himself too seriously, and he knew how to show his children the love he felt for them.

Cherish People, Not Things

During Evangeline Booth's long tenure as Commander in the United States, she visited England a number of times. On one of those visits, she greatly desired to see the room in the Methodist chapel where her father had, at age sixteen, flung himself down at a small table and offered "all there is of William Booth." An officer was sent ahead to the chapel where the incident had taken place. His mission: to forewarn the minister and custodian that the Commander was coming and of her desire to see that particular table, probably to kneel at it herself and renew her own vows. Naturally, they would want it dusted and not piled high with hymnals, etc.

The minister and custodian held a frantic consultation. "Where is that table?" To which the custodian replied, "I don't know; I've never heard of it. One thing is sure; there's no table of any sort in that room now." To which the minister replied, "Well, find one. Find a table somewhere; any table."

After a mad scramble, a table of suitable size was found and placed in the room. (Remember: this was being done eighty to ninety years after Booth's consecration.) The table incident, it must be borne in mind, was not done to deceive posterity; it was done so as to avoid disappointing a loving daughter as she strove to retrace her father's steps. Afterwards, no one said anything about it. It would only have hurt the Commander. Besides, maybe they did find the right one. Who knows?

When it was decided that The Salvation Army should have a sizable exhibit in the Hall of Religion at the 1933-1934 Chicago World's Fair, the question naturally arose: what should be the centerpiece of the exhibit? The National Commander, Evangeline Booth herself, had an idea: that table, her father's place of consecration, surely an object of historic significance.

There is no doubt that a tangible object of some sort was needed as the focal point. It is difficult to find a suitable object of any size which can "speak" to thousands of people of all types and persuasions in a way that might touch them, conveying a significant and lasting message.

It must be understood that only a small handful of junior officers at International Headquarters knew about the table. A spirit of kindliness had kept them from gossiping about it, even though they found it rather amusing. Now it was entirely too late to tell the Commander that her feelings had been poured forth at the wrong table, a plain table with no known history!

And so it was shipped to Chicago, where it served its intended purpose. Thousands stood in a moment of silent contemplation as they gazed upon it. I know; as a boy ten years of age, I was one of them. More than thirty years later one of those young British officers, by that time a commissioner stationed in Chicago, told the story to a few associates. One point was clear to all: the identity of the table, a mere object, was unimportant. What really mattered was Booth's consecration.

Miss Liberty and Mr. Booth

July 4, 1986 went down in American annals as the day when "Liberty Enlightening the World" (alias Miss Liberty), 100 years young and thoroughly rejuvenated, was rededicated. This benign colossus, her torch shining some thirty stories above the pavement, doubtless has given rise to more intense emotion in more people than any other statue on earth. Millions, crowding the rails of incoming ships, gazed upon her as they awaited the moment when they could disembark and begin a new life in the New World.

The words of Emma Lazarus, inscribed on the base, say it all:

> "Give me your tired, your poor,
> Your huddled masses yearning to breathe free,
> The wretched refuse of your teeming shore.
> Send these, the homeless, tempest-tost to me,
> I lift my lamp beside the golden door!"

Great ideals! But how to make them a reality for those "huddled masses" who couldn't afford to ride across town, let alone pay passage across the ocean? William Booth had a plan, to be carried out through The Salvation Army. The third great emphasis of his Darkest England Scheme of 1890 would mean transporting the unemployed from the slums of London to thinly populated areas of the British Empire and America. Salvationists would screen the applicants, make contacts with employers overseas, provide passage, even hire ocean-going ships for Army use, accompany the emigrants, and see that they were established before the books were closed on their cases.

But it was not easy. Early on, New Zealand's top leaders all favored the idea and hoped to set aside 10,000 acres for the Army's farm colonies. But those with less vision feared the entry of "undesirable persons, the paupers and criminal scum of the alleys and byways of Great Britain," and in the end their hysteria prevailed. Elsewhere, Booth was told he should try his hand with the down-and-outs already in Australia before "emptying the refuse of Europe" onto those sunny shores.

Again the word "refuse"! It was thrown in Booth's face, but he had already dealt with it. The poetic license of an Emma Lazarus could not be the credo of a truly practical visionary. He had written, "Neither do I mean the exportation of the class more or less composed of the refuse of the community, whether they be vicious, criminal or wastrel."

Eventually the Army sent and placed more than a quarter-million emigrants. Less than one percent failed or returned home. In Christ's name, the Army helped the "huddled masses" to "breathe free."

Our First Presidential Booster

Perhaps it's not surprising that the first American President to seek contact with William Booth was Theodore Roosevelt. Actually, they met not once, but twice. The first meeting, in 1903, was a dinner with various cabinet members, along with a guest who was interested in "some kind of slum settlement" in New York; and the famous portrait painter John Singer Sargent (who was there to "do" President Roosevelt). And, of course, there was the Chief Executive himself. General Booth sat next to Roosevelt, who showed "much interest in our Criminal operations, the efforts for the rescue of the poor Lost Women, and the Colonization of the land." (All quotations are from Harold Begbie's biography of William Booth.)

The second dinner took place in 1907, at which time Evangeline Booth sat next to the President while her father, the old Founder, sat at the right hand of Mrs. Roosevelt. The first dinner had been an all-male affair, but at the second, evidently out of deference to Evangeline, a number of wives were present. In a letter to Bramwell, the General opined: "Whether their company made the interview more profitable or not, it certainly did not render it any the less agreeable." Writing of the President, the Founder seems to have captured the spirit of the popular Teddy" in a few words: He "came in with a nice little friendly bounce, and shook hands all round."

A sort of pictorial footnote to these visits showed up in the Central Archives. A posed photograph of the hundreds of Salvationist delegates to the 1914 International Congress who went on a particular ship showed them crowded together on deck, with the Chicago Staff Bandsmen, in their distinctive new Congress festival tunics and cowboy hats, near the center.

Seated in their midst was Teddy Roosevelt, obviously enjoying himself and his fellowship with these people whose work he so admired.

In a sense, he began, for Americans, the recognition and moral support from those in high places which has helped to make our work effective. Let us do all we can to be sure the Army is ever worthy of that confidence!

Stewardship of Our Days and Hours

Considering Catherine Booth's rich and multifaceted life, it is difficult to select one facet or incident for a brief vignette. Bearing in mind the fact that she lived a mere dozen years after the Christian Mission became The Salvation Army, let us focus on a single aspect: her remarkable use of time. Always in "delicate" health, she began her teen years by spending seven months lying face down on a special contrivance to treat a spinal problem; then she was confined to bed for nearly two additional years. Repeatedly throughout her sixty-one years she suffered serious illnesses, culminating in terminal cancer.

What sounds like a recital of endless woes simply formed the background against which Catherine lived a rich, full life. Hers was not a life dominated nor soured by illness; she worked around it, through it, and in spite of it. Times of enforced physical inactivity only heightened her intellectual and spiritual activity. During those long months of lying face down, she would prop a book beneath her and read whatever was available in her family. They were all serious books, "heavy" books which would normally be considered "too old" for a mere girl. These helped develop her powers of thought, her grasp of logic, her analytical evaluation of current theology, preparing her for a work she could not have imagined at that age.

Later Catherine became a speaker of note, yet never neglected her eight lively children nor her restless, energetic and visionary husband. Let one incident illustrate. Elizabeth Swift (later Mrs. Brengle) and two other American girls traveled Europe and met the Army. Later, visiting the Army mother in her home, Elizabeth ("Lily") was shocked to find Catherine in a shabby looking sitting room, sewing a large patch on a gray flannel shirt, and to hear a motherly voice say, "I hope you don't mind my working while we talk." After a time of answering questions on Army doctrine and methods, Mrs. Booth set aside her sewing and offered prayer.

Later, when Lily voiced astonishment at the lowly surroundings, her friend said, "What did you expect? Someone on a throne with a halo?"

"Well, not exactly," mused Lily, "but I didn't expect to find the greatest woman preacher of the age patching her husband's shirt."

The Swift Sisters

Elizabeth ("Lily") and Susie Swift came from very old American stock whose ancestors, both maternal and paternal, had set foot on these shores less than ten years after the landing of the Pilgrims. The third girl we know little about. In Glasgow, Scotland, they met The Salvation Army for the first time. Susie and the other college chum, eager for any new thrill, insisted on going to one of the meetings, but Lily refused, convinced that "the better type" of people didn't go there. The two girls knelt at the penitent form, and from that moment Susie lost interest in everything except the Army.

Going to London, the three girls sought out Headquarters, and as they began to learn more of the Army, Lily also accepted Christ as her personal Savior. Their visit to the home of William and Catherine

Booth took place at that time, and they talked to the "Army mother" while she patched one of William's flannel shirts.

The third girl had to return home, but the Swift sisters stayed on in London and interested themselves in the work of the Army. Lily spent her days at the Clapton Training College where Emma Booth put her to work teaching the less educated girl cadets. Susie was assigned to help edit *All the World.*

In May 1885, the two sisters returned to America as Army zealots. They held meetings, visited and prayed with the poor, and talked with their fashionable friends about their souls. At summer's end, Susie returned to London, resumed her work on *All the World* and became an officer. Elizabeth became an officer in America. Later she married Samuel Logan Brengle and, as they say, the rest is history.

As for Susie, she edited *All the World* for some years. But there was increasing feeling that the magazine was too elitist, that it was not reaching the rank and file of Salvationists. In truth, this was Susie's concept: a report of the Army's worldwide work for supporters of that work, many of whom were not Salvationists but were Christians anxious to support a ministry they felt their own churches were not undertaking. To remedy what was perceived as a shortcoming, a gifted officer who had a great understanding of the human heart was brought in to breathe new life into the magazine. A rather surprising sidelight regarding this replacement was that she was a member of the British aristocracy, and her father was a good friend of the Prince of Wales, later King Edward VII.

Susie served in other capacities, sometimes expressing her deep spiritual feelings in poetry, such as song 510 in our present song book ("Mine to rise when thou dost call me, lifelong though the journey be"). But apparently she had increasing misgivings about the Army's way of doing things. Her spiritual pilgrimage took her from the Army to the Catholic Church, where she became a nun and later the Mother Superior of a convent.

Mrs. Commissioner Brengle and the Mother Superior—a surprising ending to a "Salvationist" story of two sisters, but one which points, perhaps, to the need for great caution in criticizing others for their spiritual perceptions and consequent decisions.

You Don't Have to Be a Genius!

In 1882, a studious-appearing man sat attentively through a number of Salvation Army meetings at the Chalk Farm Corps, notebook and pencil in hand, ready to jot down anything of interest. Had the simple folk of the corps known his background and the reason for the notes, they might have felt very uncomfortable. After all, who wants to be studied like a bug in a bottle?

A professional musician, widely read in the fields of philosophy and science, he had made something of a name for himself (and a tidy income) as a lecturer espousing atheism. He was at the corps only to "study character when under the emotional stress of religion."

As a member of the Royal Albert Hall Orchestra Society, playing first violin under conductors such as Sir Arthur Sullivan, he knew success. Yet success had not brought peace. Atheism satisfied his reasoning powers, he told himself, but his spiritual and moral needs were disquieting.

One evening he tried another corps, a onetime dancing saloon. When testimonies were called for, a servant girl stood and said, "My missus says she believes I am saved because I sweep beneath the mats, and I didn't before I was saved."

Whereas other testimonies had amused or intrigued him, "this testimony came as a flash of divine lightning that struck my soul," wrote Richard Slater later. He began to listen in earnest, and within weeks had surrendered his life to Christ. Army historians unanimously call Lt. Colonel Richard Slater the "father of Salvation Army music."

"Many Avenues of Service"

Will J. Brand had spent all of his teen years wanting to be a Salvation Army officer. After being employed at International Headquarters for a time, he applied to enter the Training College. But the officer in charge of his department, knowing the young man's lifelong state of delicate health and assuming from his appearance that he must be tubercular, turned back his application. Young Will was kindly told he could never stand the rigors of officership, and that his chances for a long life were not at all good. Disappointed? Of course!

Taking brisk action to use the years remaining, whether many or few, young Will hired on with a firm of refrigeration engineers, studied so as to specialize, and stayed with the company forty-two years. Meanwhile he was faithful in the corps, always a songster, sometimes adding to this other tasks.

At first poetry had no part in his life. His first efforts were simply humorous verses written to younger relatives. But as his gift emerged, he began to work at it, putting deeper truths into meter. None of his work was seen by officers outside his corps until he was middle-aged. But quite suddenly he gained recognition and was called upon to write for specific occasions and for the Song Book then in process (which contains fourteen of his poems). At one point during his long life, 140 of his works had been accepted for publication by the International Music Board.

The officer who, fearing for Will's health, would not back his application for officership, wrote forty-six years later to congratulate his former employee on his work for the Army. Will's response to the letter speaks volumes: "God has many avenues of service. Hallelujah!" We all know that youthful dreams may never see fulfillment; circumstances may sometimes be harsh; yet somewhere, somehow, there is a place in God's service for every sincere Christian. With Will Brand we can say, "Hallelujah!"

Out of Tragedy, Triumph

If Will Brand had grounds for disappointment in his life, George Marshall had grounds for utter devastation. A native of South Shields, England, he was one of nine children, the son of a coal miner who was also a talented musician, a man who toiled underground six days a week and on the seventh served as organist for the Methodist Church.

When George was twelve, he obeyed his father's dictum and went to work in the mines. Two years later he was converted in an Army meeting where his mother took the children. His inherited flair for music began to flower in the corps band.

Despite his distaste for mining, George continued the work which his father saw as a family tradition. This did not keep him from playing a trombone, composing Army songs and marches which were quickly published, and becoming a bandmaster at a youthful age. In due time, he became a foreman in the mine. When at age thirty George married the lovely young Salvationist who had written lyrics for some of his music, their future looked extremely bright.

A mere four months after they were married, disaster struck. George was bending over some work in the mine when a section of the tunnel collapsed, half burying him in rock, breaking his back in two places, and paralyzing him from that point downwards. Terribly injured, he was given two hours to live by the doctors. But many were praying for him! He clung to life. Much later a famous consulting physician declared he could not live more than a few months at most.

Yet for thirty-eight years this man lived on, a paraplegic, never free from pain for a day. Nevertheless he held fast to his faith, and from his invalid chair he poured out a torrent of joyful music. Often his compositions were "ahead of their time," and he did much to bring our Army music to its present high standard.

If a man could turn such tragedy to victory through faith, how much more should we live victoriously!

Handicaps Are Hurdles, Not Walls

An inquiry among Salvationists revealed that very few had heard of Frank Maxwell and his association with Mahatma Gandhi. For those who have missed it, here's the story.

Maxwell, a native of North London, moved to his grandfather's farm in Northern Ireland when he was thirteen years of age. Two years later a serious case of pneumonia left him with a weak, high pitched voice that could hardly be heard a few yards away. His outstanding mechanical ability marked him as a likely candidate for an engineering career, but the family did not have the money for such an education. So he joined his brother in operating a bicycle shop.

To demonstrate the merits of their product, Frank raced bicycles, repeatedly carrying off top honors and gaining fame among cycling fans. He joined the YMCA and was present when a Salvation Army officer came to address the men. Afterwards, he talked to the officer and accepted Christ as his Savior and Lord.

Frank applied for officership, but his weakened voice, which precluded public preaching, delayed his acceptance for many years. Some of that time he worked for the Army, bringing about marked improvements in the operation of Hadleigh Land Colony. Again at age thirty-six he applied for Training and was accepted.

After Commissioning, he said he would serve anywhere. "Anywhere" turned out to be India. He was told of the plight of Indian weavers; their looms were awkward and slow and their production pitiably meager. After long study and experimentation, Maxwell designed a new loom that authorities called "one of the few radical innovations in the improvement of the textile machinery." The Army built an Indian loom factory so weavers could make a decent living.

Mahatma Gandhi, who was most friendly to Salvationists, asked to see Maxwell about using this loom in his *swadeshi* (home industry) movement. All was going well when suddenly he exclaimed regretfully, "No! I can't do it after all. Ours is an all-Indian movement and I could not use a loom invented by a European."

"But Gandhi," replied the inventor, "the looms are made by Indian craftsmen and the wood is all Indian-grown."

"All the same," said Gandhi, "the cotton is grown by us, spun by us, woven by us…" But Maxwell, having noticed something on the way in, added, "…and sewn on a Singer sewing machine?" Gandhi sat silent. At last, looking up with a smile, he said, "I never thought of that."

So it was that a Salvation Army officer's loom aided Gandhi's plan to raise his people's standard of living.

Showdown!

Many years ago, a real-life scene was played out in a remote part of the world. It would have been a natural for a movie or TV script. All the elements were there.

Consider: there was a rather smug in-group preparing to make mincemeat of a newcomer who was asking for admittance to their exclusive association. True, the applicant was taking this step only so he could more fully serve poor and outcast people. But some of those who belonged to this cozy group had forgotten that their association had no other reason to exist than to serve mankind better, and they were interested mainly in preserving the status quo.

Enter the Salvation Army officer, a doctor whom they had thus far prevented from practicing medicine as a licensed physician— even from prescribing medicine for his penniless patients. Somehow the sight of his uniform made them doubt his qualifications. And so this little showdown had been arranged.

The questions began, and when the examiner couldn't comprehend the applicant's answers, his findings were declared to be wrong. He was washed out—rejected—through!

But the officer, in true Christian humility and self-restraint, simply asked if there were a higher authority who could be called in to adjudicate. Yes, there was, and (thought some of the examining board) why not play out the farce to the end?

While waiting for the Major-General (for this was the rank of the doctor being called in), the Salvationist gave himself to prayer and on a large blackboard skillfully drew diagrams of the three cases concerning which the examiner said he knew nothing. To the board's surprise, the medical authority at once recognized the validity of the petitioner's diagnoses and the surgery he recommended. The board had no choice; the negative decision was reversed. As a matter of fact, his examiners should have felt humiliated. Here was a doctor direct from Europe who possessed all the latest medical data, while at least some of them had been content to drift into an "island mentality," perhaps lulled by the tropical climate and their isolation from the progress being made elsewhere.

This in brief is the true story of Dr. Vilhelm A. Wille, eye surgeon from Denmark who had become a Salvation Army officer and, finding himself forced into this confrontational situation, toppled the opposition in Java. He brought up-to-date surgical procedures to a group of men on a distant shore who had been cut off too long from firsthand contacts with the latest European technology. Let it be said that they realized their error and made things right. It should be added that Dr. Willie's graciousness and humility made it easy for them to do this, and to welcome him into their fellowship.

Dr. Wille brought more than technical expertise. He brought the message of salvation, and he was always more excited about winning a person to Christ than the saving of a patient's eyesight. His years in Java were many and fruitful.

Can we accept "knocking about" with true Christian love and patience? Add Dr. Wille to your roster of examples!

Honored by Two Monarchs

It would be unfortunate to leave the impression that the highlight of Dr. Wile's work was that he overcame attempts to exclude him at the onset of his ministry in Java. That incident, though representative of some of the prejudice overcome by early-day Salvationists, was, in his case, greatly overshadowed by what followed.

But perhaps, before reviewing some of his accomplishments, it would be well to add that the aforementioned examination before the medical board lasted for six days. By the end of that time, the board's initial skepticism about this uniformed Salvationist had given way to unqualified admiration. In the years which followed, some of those same doctors referred particularly difficult cases to him, knowing of his unusual ability and broad knowledge of tropical diseases.

Although he began by treating the poor who had nowhere else to turn, soon his remarkable cures attracted European patients of all classes. Commissioner Carvosso Gauntlett, whose younger son would one day also become a medical missionary, wrote of Dr. Wille, "If some well-to-do business man, who paid full fees (to the hospital), complained that he was not given preference over some poor person, the doctor would courteously reply: 'Sir, I quite understand. But you, too, must understand. You are able to pay any of the medical men practicing on the island, while these (with a gesture towards the miserable beggars and others) have no one else to whom they can go. I shall be happy to do my best for you— if you will be good enough to await your turn.'"

Over the years, in addition to his tireless medical work, especially eye-surgery, so often among patients who could afford to pay nothing, he continued his research. Thus he was the first to diagnose xerophthalmia, which had robbed thousands, particularly children, of their sight. Not only did he diagnose it, but he achieved notable cures by a special diet, and he showed how new cases could be prevented. This was published in the leading medical journal of Europe.

His was a long life of service in Java. Captain (Dr.) and Mrs. Wille arrived with their four small children in 1907. He turned sixty-five in 1927 but continued in his appointment. Finally, in 1931, Lt. Colonel Wille retired from the charge of the Army's hospital in Semarang, a hospital which he had been responsible for bringing into being. But he remained in Java, maintaining a private practice. Still, his favorite patients were his old Salvation Army comrades and "society's step-children."

His contributions to medical journals went on, even after retirement. *The International Index-Catalogue* shows articles were published in 1921, 1927, and each year from 1933-1938.

As always, he loved evangelistic work, and Sunday after Sunday the by-then-famous surgeon would take part in the Army's open-air meetings, witnessing to large gatherings of Javanese, Chinese and others of Christ's redemptive power—right to the day when the Japanese occupation forces stopped the Salvationists' public activities. He died in 1944 at the age of eighty-two.

Many spoke and wrote of Dr. Wille's humility and his childlike faith, but perhaps three instances of "official" recognition will serve as a fitting conclusion to this brief review. He was in the first group of admissions to the newly-created Order of the Founder in 1920. The following year Queen Wilhelmina of the Netherlands appointed him an Officer of the Dutch Order of Oranje-Nassau, and in 1937 King Christian X of Denmark made him a Knight of the Order of Dannebrog.

Royalty Sought Her Out

Back in the early years of the twentieth century, when Britain's royal carriage—easily recognizable by the royal crest emblazoned upon its door—was repeatedly observed at the curb alongside The Salvation Army's International Headquarters, no one seems to have made much of it. Perhaps it was because, for the Salvationists who comprised the IHQ staff in those early years, the policy of complete confidentiality was so ingrained that they kept any private speculations to themselves.

But, you might say, surely some newspaper reporter who noticed these recurring visits, often a couple of hours in length, would have tried to unlock the secret. But remember: it would have been easy to assume that some member of the royal family was consulting with General Booth on a particular aspect of a social problem; hardly sensational news.

There's no need to remind readers today that the attitude of "the man in the street" toward royalty was far different in the early decades of the century. The reason those once highly confidential visits can now be mentioned is twofold: first, over the decades they have faded into history. Secondly, the visits have already been mentioned in an Army publication—but just once.

At the center of the story is Commissioner Mildred Duff, a woman richly endowed with the attributes of a sympathetic ear, a capacity for deep and perceptive understanding, and great wisdom. But why, you may ask, would royalty come to a Salvation Army officer in a tiny office in the editorial department at IHQ? Although it skirts the main question, one answer is that others of nobility also sought out Mildred Duff. One of these was the Queen of Wurttemberg, a country whose identity has been swallowed up in Europe's political convulsions. The Queen was a zealous Christian who would slip out from her palace to distribute gospel tracts to the rough coachmen, who were considered dangerous to approach. They received her with scowls, but she would say it was "done for God."

At one time Queen Olga of Greece, who had stayed in England for five months after her husband's assassination, sent a telephone message that she would like to see Mildred Duff at Marlborough House. The two spent an uninterrupted hour together. The Queen was very depressed and in great fear regarding her return to Greece. They prayed together, and afterwards Commissioner Duff told the officer who traveled with her on the bus across town that she felt she had been able to help her. The commissioner was more than a listener, however. The other officer later wrote that "in the bus on the way home she wept and wept" over the Queen's sorrows. Mildred Duff was a person who really cared.

But why would royalty seek her out? Perhaps because they felt she could understand their situation far better than most. Mildred Duff came from nobility, yet served in very difficult appointments in the pioneering days of the Army in Sweden and Finland, as well as spending time in Russia. She could have had a life of luxury. Her father had been on intimate terms with the Prince of Wales before he became King Edward VII. Later the King said of Mildred that she was the most beautiful young society woman of her year. Commissioner Duff was not only of noble birth, but of noble spirit. Her sensitivity and remarkable empathy made an indelible mark in the lives of many.

The Work of a Kindly Providence

The great Commissioner Gunpei Yamamuro wanted to be sure this story was not lost to posterity, so he wrote it himself and sent it to the insurance department at International Headquarters following the great Tokyo earthquake of 1923.

When our splendid headquarters building in Tokyo was completed a few years ago, International Headquarters wrote us saying that an earthquake insurance policy should be taken out. We had never heard of such a thing, but we obediently made inquiries in the City. The insurance people there seemed as ignorant of such an arrangement as we were, so we wrote to IHQ saying that earthquake insurance policies were not issued in Japan. We thought that the matter had ended with the writing of that letter, and our surprise was great when, some time later, we received another communication on the earthquake insurance proposals.

Our surprise became tinged with something between chagrin and annoyance when the letter was read, for it contained the news that IHQ had found someone in London willing to issue an earthquake policy, and that forthwith one had been taken out in our name for which IHQ was charging us £200 as the first premium.

"Why, why, why?" We said. "They haven't even asked us about it, and this £200 was badly needed for other purposes. Even then, £200 once would not be so bad, but a premium of £200 a year! It is a great burden!" Nevertheless, we faced the situation like loyal Salvationists, and told ourselves there must be some good in it.

Before twelve months elapsed the great earthquake laid Tokyo in ruins. Thousands of buildings were destroyed, and among them our new Headquarters. As soon as we recovered from the shock of the disaster we remembered the earthquake policy, and then we learned that among all the splendid buildings that were thrown down to destruction in Tokyo, ours was the only one insured against damage by earthquake.

When the newspapers heard of this they discussed it at length. One of the most influential said, "If there is anything in Providence, as the Salvationists believe, surely this is the work of a Kindly Providence."

We who knew that with the £20,000 insurance money such a new building could be erected as The Army would not otherwise have seen in Tokyo for many, many years, realized that what we thought to be "rather cool conduct" on the part of Headquarters was in reality the leading of God.

Since then arrangements have been made to issue earthquake policies in Japan, the Companies basing their premiums upon calculations culled from the fact that earthquakes in Japan do not occur in the same place more than once in every sixty years or more.

Soon earthquake insurance will doubtless be as common in Japan as Comprehensive Policies in this country, but The Army will retain the distinction of being the first to test its value, and the test is convincing enough seeing, by the farsightedness of IHQ, the full value of the policy was received before the payment of the second premium.

We Japanese Salvationists believe in the leadings of God, and this incident is to us but another example of His control of our business affairs.

Greater Than Mother-Love

At midpoint in the nineteenth century, France set up a system of exile for her worst criminals, sending them to sweltering French Guiana in South America. The worst feature was *doublage,* which meant that, when a man had served his term, he had to remain in that remote land for a time equal to his original sentence.

Men in *doublage* were known as *libérés:* free men, a sorry joke for one not free to leave, where even the food and shelter of prison were not available, where most of the few jobs were virtually slave labor.

Some *libérés* would kill for a man's few belongings. Malnutrition and tropical diseases shortened many lives. Hopelessness bred suicide If one lived to finish his time, how would he then get home? He had to earn his fare, then find a way to keep it safe while surrounded by thieves and murderers. Nearly impossible! Hemmed in by shark-infested waters, many *libérés* saw alcohol as their only means of escape. But of course the "escape" left them worse off than before.

Into this scenario of living death, The Salvation Army entered in the late 1920s, first in the person of Ensign Charles Péan, later followed by a number of other officers whose work was nothing less than heroic. Before Péan had a chance to see the situation at first hand, the plan might have been to alleviate the sufferings and injustices which befell the *libérés* almost daily, through providing housing for those liberated, by giving them a safe place to save money for the hoped-for trip back to France, and through other provisions which the Salvationists might find practical, once they had seen conditions at close range. But (to get ahead of the story) once Ensign Péan saw the horrible conditions, the goal became nothing less than to persuade the French government to abolish such barbaric punishment, to close the colony forever, and to return the prisoners to their homeland. Eventually the Army succeeded, but it took years of crusading to get the Chamber of Deputies to pass the necessary legislation.

Meanwhile, young Salvation Army officers, some single and some with families, went to French Guiana to provide hostels for *libérés*, to live among them and to assure them they had not been forgotten. Out of this practical demonstration of love came opportunities to share the gospel.

A captain, with his wife and baby, ran one such hostel. One lodger, from a background of wealth, had had a child by a maid in his father's employ. To conceal his misdeed, he committed a far worse one; he had drowned his baby. Yet the man was a gentle, sensitive person. In the day room of the hostel, he was serving cold drinks to the men when the wife of the captain was called to help her husband with something upstairs.

Her child was sleeping in its pram; she did not want to waken it. After a moment's hesitation, she said to the onetime murderer, "I leave my baby to your care." Some minutes later she returned. The *libéré* was on his knees in front of the baby, gazing intently at the child, his face bathed in tears, "What a wretch I am!" He sobbed. The overt recognition of his guilt led him to better things—and all because a mother's love was transcended by the love of Christ.

The Cancer Called Devil's Island

What Charles Péan and his comrades accomplished both in French Guiana (which included "Devil's Island") as well as in France is a story every Salvationist should know. Commissioner Péan's own account: *The Conquest of Devil's Island* (1953) may be very hard to find, but you should have more luck with Richard Collier's *The General Next to God*, in which the author chose this story as a fitting climax to the whole book. His Devil's Island account is brief but exceedingly well told.

Although most of us have some knowledge of "the Devil's Island story," few realize how long Salvationists labored to bring their crusade to a successful conclusion, or how hard-fought the struggle was. Let us look at some of the facts presented by Richard Collier. I trust he won't mind if I reorganize them for our use, and perhaps add an observation or two.

The plight of the 10,000 exiled French prisoners had haunted Commissioner Albin Peyron from 1910, prompting him to contact top French officials asking that The Salvation Army be allowed to send workers there to do something to ease the hopelessness of the prisoners, and to try to stop their all-too-frequent slide into the lowest depravity. The commissioner began his efforts in 1910, but it was to be thirty-five years before he and his successors succeeded completely. Thirty-five years!

That thirty-five-year span was not in any way caused by the lethargy of Salvationists, once they set foot in French Guiana. It was caused by the reluctance of the French Chamber of Deputies to close the penal colony and authorize the repatriation of all prisoners, or at least the *libérés*. They feared public opinion and what a vote for closure might mean to their chances of reelection! Tragically, when such legislation was finally enacted, the outbreak of World War II brought all repatriating efforts to a standstill.

By contrast to that thirty-five-year figure, it should be pointed out that Ensign Charles Péan, only eight years after he made his first fact-finding visit to the colony, was escorting the first group of returnees to France; men who had earned their passage honestly through projects set up by the Army, and with the Army's safeguarding of their savings until they had accumulated enough for a ticket home. What happened in those eight years "could fill a book," as they say. In fact, it did fill much of Charles Péan's book.

Perhaps some clarification is in order. Devil's Island was a seventeen-acre site, fortified in the 1890s to imprison Captain Alfred Dreyfus. It was only one of many convict settlements which stretched for more than a hundred miles across French Guiana, but because its name so eloquently described the whole sorry situation, it came to be a sort of shorthand designation for the entire penal colony.

Enter the Salvationists

Commissioner Peyron did not sit and wring his hands when he learned something of the situation in France's penal colony in Guiana. From 1910 onwards he wrote letters to successive Ministers of Justice, but his appeals all fell flat, and many of the commissioner's letters were never even acknowledged. One might have thought that, after 1918, following the remarkable work of Salvation Army Red Shield workers in France during the World War, French officials would have turned a sympathetic ear to proposals for some kind ameliorative action on our part. After all, they had to know something of our work as we helped in a war defending their own country—and on French soil, at that. They had to know how Salvationists had served in so practical and effective a way under the most adverse conditions. Their top generals had paid the Army high tribute. Yet their bureaucrats continued to turn a deaf ear for another ten years after war's end.

Finally, in 1928 a chance contact with the Minister of Colonies had caused the door to be opened a crack. Peyron wasted no time. He summoned Ensign Charles Péan, a young bachelor who could speak English as well as French. Péan realized that his most effective weapon would be facts, so for three months he traveled from settlement to settlement in a *pirogue*, a narrow tree-trunk canoe, filling notebook after notebook with his observations. Conditions were absolutely appalling, but the most appalling thing he found was the system of *doublage,* or double time. Nearly 3,000 of the men were worse off than the prisoners. They had served their time, but by law had to serve an equal time as *libérés,* or so-called free men. No longer were they housed, nor even fed the miserable fare provided by the government. Many soon discovered that being a prisoner on a work gang, brutal as it might have been, was better than being turned out to make it on their own. The civilian population wanted nothing to do with them, and only a tenth of them could find work. Even then, much of that work was little better than slavery, since they were at the mercy of plantation owners or other businessmen who could hire them on their own terms.

When Ensign Péan returned to France to report his findings, 300 *libérés* gathered at the dock, some pressing notes to family into his hand, some weeping, all begging him to come back as soon as possible. He did plan to return soon, but the corruption so prevalent in the colony nearly cost him his life and delayed his return for two years. While he was in Guiana a sharp attack of malaria had landed him in a hospital where he was given the standard treatment for that tropical fever, injections of quinine. But the convict-nurse had stolen the quinine and sold it, covering his crime by filling the containers with unsterilized water. As a result, Péan suffered recurring internal abbesses for which he underwent major surgery three times. He was rendered a semi-invalid for two years and could in no way leave France for a return trip to the prison colony.

The one bit of hope for these men was to earn enough to buy a return ticket to France after their *doublage* was served. But how to safeguard that money? Many of their fellow *libérés* would kill for money, and when dead bodies turned up in the jungle or isolated fields, often with nothing but a skeleton left by the ants, who could know who they were? For that matter, who cared? Thus too many men were murdered with impunity, and the hope of ever getting home was very faint indeed.

At the risk of getting ahead of the story, let it be said that one of the first things the French Salvationists, under the leadership of Ensign

Péan, accomplished when they arrived was to set up a system for the men exiled there which gave hope—a tangible, realistic hope—of a return to their homes in France.

Faithful to the Last

The Salvation Army's campaign to help the *libérés* did at last get underway in spite of Ensign Péan's protracted illness. While the Army in France, armed with the ensign's fact-filled description of unspeakable conditions, worked tirelessly to get the Chamber of Deputies to abolish the colony, Salvationists sent to Guiana began a vigorous campaign to help the *libérés*. Housing was erected, and a pineapple plantation, citrus and banana groves were cultivated, with a fruit-packing station to market the produce. The free men built a henhouse, and they created a fishery by netting off a creek and collecting the fish at low tide. A carpenter shop was set up to construct benches, chairs and folding beds.

Not everyone was happy about the Army's efforts, however. The receivers of stolen goods, rum peddlers, prostitutes, and corrupt prison guards saw Péan's crusade to win the minds of men as a potent threat to their graft. Often Péan opened his morning mail to discover anonymous threats. Salvationists were waylaid at night by tough-muscled assailants. One lieutenant's jaw was broken in three places.

But the work went on, and slowly converts were won, many because of the trust Péan placed in them. He also gave them hope in a most tangible form—hope of going home in the foreseeable future. He set up a coupon system so that men were not left to try to safeguard their cash savings in some desperate way. The Army ran a sort of a banking system. Twenty months of continuous work earned a man enough to buy a third-class ticket to France. Once there, Salvationists would feed him, clothe him, and find him work.

In 1937 a bill finally came before the Chamber of Deputies to abolish the prison colony, but it was June 1938 before its abolition became official. This victory, however, was soon swallowed up by a bitter irony as World War II began, and all repatriation ground to a halt. With all shipping pressed into service to get military equipment and food to Europe; with the Atlantic swarming with German submarines, the "free men" were marooned in their prison colony, along with their Salvationist friends.

In occupied France the Nazis forbade the wearing of Salvation Army uniform. Péan took up work in Paris among abandoned children. However, unknown to him, General de Gaulle's governmental-exile was implementing most of his plans. In 1946 the Minister of Colonies set aside a large sum for the repatriation of free men and convicts. Charles Péan and The Salvation Army were chosen to carry out the work. Péan was appointed the only non-government member of the High Council of Penal Administration.

With the war finally over, Péan was able to return to French-Guiana, hardly knowing what he would find. What of the officers and their families stranded there, in some ways no better off than the *libérés?* He found them faithfully carrying on just as had they prior to 1939.

Later, on his return trip to France he took a long detour though the United States speaking in a number of places. He told of going by motorboat a long way up a river to the most remote of the Army's centers. No one knew he was coming. It was Sunday evening. He walked silently to the little Army hall and listened at an open window, out of sight. He said the officer told of the Savior's love and sacrifice with as much fervor as he did before the long years of delay caused by the war. The officer's invitation to the men was as heartfelt, as urgent as ever. When Péan looked in, he saw the officer's uniform was spotless, as neatly pressed as if he were preaching his inaugural sermon to a new crowd.

In spite of being cut off from all supervision and all encouragement, the Salvationists had kept their standards high, their purity untarnished. They had continued to represent their Savior and to preach Christ crucified as faithfully as ever!

Commissioner Péan, as one would fully expect, was admitted to the Order of the Founder. But he always felt that his faithfulness was, if anything, exceeded by that of the Salvationists unexpectedly exiled in that faraway tropical prison colony for all those years.

Perhaps an editorial I wrote for the January 29, 1972 issue of *The War Cry* will serve as a suitable conclusion to this all-too-brief summary of the Devil's Island story.

From New York to Philadelphia

It has been pointed out how quickly William and Catherine Booth responded to the report of the Shirley family's success in Philadelphia and their request that the General take command of The Salvation Army in America officially. Booth did not hesitate; an expeditionary group was chosen with George Scott Railton as its leader.

His middle name, Scott, was his mother's maiden name, and perhaps he continued to use it as a part of his name as a tribute or sort of memorial to the mother who had died heroically so early in his life. Probably there was no personage in the early Salvation Army more dedicated, more fearless, and more unpredictable than he. As for the title of Commissioner, it had no military equivalent in that day, and still hasn't. A commissioner was, and is, generally speaking, a government official in charge of a bureau or department. When William Booth assigned that title gratuitously to Railton, it had no parallel in the military establishment, and thus no clearly defined level of authority. He was the only commissioner in the embryonic Salvation Army, an Army yet without a rank system.

Railton was not an organizer. Dr. McKinley, in describing his activities in his earliest days in America, said of him, "Even in a settled command with regular procedures, Railton took a cavalier view of record-keeping. Now a pioneer with a dozen things to do at once, flying around the city like some wild evangelical bird, he kept no records at all. Nor did his lieutenants, stalwart women with great hearts but little ability; none of them could even read competently, and they had no interest in details." One must understand that McKinley said this kindly; he was not writing an exposé, and his account is always a happy combination of objectivity and sympathy.

Railton as well as Catherine Booth were committed to the concept of utilizing women in positions of usefulness and leadership in religious work. According to McKinley, it was Railton who hit upon the idea of forming a group composed entirely of women, with himself as leader. This would show what they could do! So it was that Railton and seven women, hastily assembled, were actually aboard ship two short weeks after the news had arrived from America. That haste was evident, however. McKinley also says that because of their functional illiteracy, their first testimonies were memorized and seemingly had no more effect than a memorized recitation. Only one, Emma Westbrook, was an officer. She "opened fire" in New York's No. 1 Corps and handled the roughs of the area most effectively.

After the cold reception experienced in New York, Railton and his group moved, in just two weeks, to Philadelphia, where they were to present, on behalf of Catherine Booth, her handmade Army flag as part of a planned-for event (previously described). And what an event it was! Railton never forgot it. That meeting spoke volumes about the pioneering work of the Shirley family, and it confirmed Railton's decision to establish the Army's first American head-quarters there.

HCJB: The Raders and the Army

To my knowledge, The Salvation Army has never published a book, nor even an article, about the two brothers from the Army's Chicago Temple Corps who were responsible for the founding of HCJB, the world's first missionary radio station. Now as it approaches its ninetieth year of continuous operation, HCJB continues to be the most powerful radio voice in the world for the proclamation of the gospel.

The story, which began with two Salvationists, expanded far beyond the Temple Corps. We need to go back in time for a brief look at the seeds of the "Army spirit" engendered in the two brothers, Clarence and Howard Jones. Their parents, Captain and Mrs. George Jones, had been officers in a day when Salvationists in America were sometimes physically persecuted. Once, in Duluth, a saloon keeper, mad with hate, came dashing down the street with his team of horses, determined to crash into the Salvationists and break up their open-air march. But Captain Jones grabbed the reins of the horses and held them back. Infuriated, the man took his whip and lashed the captain repeatedly across the back, cutting his uniform until the blood flowed. But the captain held on until his group had passed to safety. At a later time the captain resigned his officership but remained an active Salvationist, serving as sergeant-major of the Chicago Temple Corps. The two sons spent their teen years taking part in corps activities, including open-air meetings. They both learned to play brass instruments, Clarence taking a turn at everything except tuba. They became very proficient, Clarence on trombone, Howard on cornet.

In 1918 Clarence tried to enlist in the Navy but was rejected because of his eyesight. Some time later he accepted an invitation from his neighbor, Richard Oliver Sr., father of his best friend, Richard Jr., to visit the Moody Tabernacle. Where evangelist Paul Rader was conducting a most effective ministry. (Rader was a member of the same family as our former general, a great-uncle, I believe.) Mr. Oliver, who had been a bandsman in the Chicago Temple Corps band, had been offered the post of music director at the Moody Tabernacle, which he had accepted. Later Mr. Oliver asked if Clarence would like to join the Moody band, where in the meetings he would be playing for thousands. Clarence said he would give it a try. Later in a missionary conference, Clarence, inspired by the challenge, realized he was not adequately prepared to be a missionary. He enrolled at Moody Bible Institute for three years. He graduated in 1921 as class president with top honors. The next day he left to travel with an evangelist through the coal-mining areas of West Virginia, his first step toward foreign missions work which was to become his life's work.

Paul Rader left Moody Tabernacle in 1922 to be an international evangelist, but there was such a demand for him in Chicago that by 1925 he had a new tabernacle built on the north side. His new staff included many of the same men. Several, including Clarence, wrote gospel songs which were compiled in a song book. Of the seven composers pictured on is frontispiece (in addition to Rader himself) five had been Army bandsmen.

From Temple Corps to Ecuador

The very first broadcast on Christmas Day of 1931, which thus began a whole new chapter in proclaiming the gospel worldwide. To initiate that ministry on the very day set aside to celebrate Jesus' birth was a particularly happy milestone for Clarence Jones in his journey from Chicago's Salvation Army Temple Corps to the mountains of Ecuador, and we have seen his faithful efforts to obey the command he received from that clearly audible voice.

But was this story of the broadcast the true climax, since it was heard on only sixteen radios? No, you'd want to know much more, such as how the listenership was soon expanded by dedicated distributors who, with little profit to themselves, imported and sold radio sets at the lowest possible cost. One of these distributors was the same Eric Williams who had built the first little 250-watt transmitter in his own garage in Chicago.

As the station grew, progressively more powerful transmitters were added in order to increase broadcast ability. The pair of eighty-foot tall eucalyptus tree trunks, between which the original antenna wire was stretched, were later replaced by steel towers. Today, this area contains so many transmission towers that employees refer to it as "the forest". HCJB's requirements for electricity later outstripped what the city of Quito could supply, so the mission built its own hydro-electric plant.

You would also want to know about the worldwide scope of the station after it began to broadcast additionally in short wave, and expanded by buying other stations, such as the one in Panama City, which was placed under the management of Howard Jones, Clarence's younger brother.

Thanks to Clarence's learning experience from his original four-nation trip (plus a great deal more which he learned later), added to the missionary experience and enviable reputation of Reuben Larson, the two men established some farsighted agreements with the Ecuadorian government. For example, the station would give twenty percent of its air time to government representatives, including the president himself. In return, the station would be exempt from payment of any duty on goods brought into the country for use of the station or its personnel. Government officials would be free to say whatever they chose during their time on the air (within the scope of common prudence, of course). As for the missionaries, they made it clear that their gospel message would never be critical of the Catholic Church; it would be totally Bible-based. In addition they would provide dependable local and world news, free of political commentary. As for music, it was their intent that it would be "live" rather than recorded. (One might observe that back in 1931 phonograph records had little of the sound quality we expect in our day. "Canned music" could never be mistaken for live music.)

By such careful planning and farseeing provisions, the foundation was laid for a lasting institution.

On to St. Louis

One of Railton's characteristics was his unquenchable optimism. Whatever goal was in his sights at any point in his labors for Christ was always envisioned as bright and shining, with little concern for any circumstance which might confront him before he could begin to attain that goal. As for failure, that possibility never seemed to enter his head. For example, in February 1880, just before their ship was to leave England for America, Railton scribbled a last-minute note to the General, declaring that they would "shake America," and that "all that lies between us and that result is marvelously insignificant." Forget jeering crowds, antipathy, and an "insignificant" 3,000 miles of water! But once in New York City, he found the same problem so often found in England; Mayor Edward Cooper forbade the Salvationists to hold religious services on the streets. What to do? Railton had already seen men won for Christ in their indoor meetings in New York, but the climate did not augur well for establishing a national headquarters there.

So after a mere two weeks in New York City, he moved to Philadelphia. After a search, he found a place for his "headquarters" at 45 South Third Street, where he had a large sign placed across the front of the building. But the only place occupied by the Army was a "dank and dirty basement," where he actually lived and worked. He commenced a newspaper, *The Salvation News*. The first edition, published July 3, 1880 was sold out in a few hours, but Railton admitted he could not offer "any regular terms" for the *News;* it was "merely a pioneer of our American *War Cry* which, hopefully, would soon appear. During the summer of 1880 he embarked on long train trips to find likely places to open the work. He traveled light and left almost no record, so we do not even know how many cities he might have visited, or the cities' names. All that we know is that he traveled 4,200 miles and spoke 80 times, scouting the terrain for future attacks. The variety of races and languages comprising the populace of this new "melting pot" prompted him to write to Booth, "If I can get the Americans, Germans and Africans all fairly started, I hope by stirring such up to hearty rivalry to keep them all at full gallop." One may well wonder how he could have imagined such racial and national "rivalry" as a valid motivating factor in their labors for the Lord.

For reasons which remain unclear, Railton decided in November to transfer his headquarters to St. Louis, Missouri, a distance of 959 miles by railroad from the rest of his troops. In a sense he was correct in considering the location of St. Louis a logical place to serve as a "gateway to the west." Oddly, the fact that the Army was entirely unknown there did not seem to trouble him. He arrived with virtually no money, but once there, as in so many other places where he opened fire, he found encouragement and support, and gladly acknowledged these "good folk" and "sympathizers." He would have suffered actual want if a Mr. and Mrs. George Parker had not taken him in for the winter simply because he was a Christian worker.

The Voice

In the life of Clarence Jones in his progression from a bandsman at The Salvation Army's Temple Corps, to inaugurating the world's first missionary broadcasting station, there were a number of definitive events. We have room for only two of them on this small page.

In 1922, soon after he finished his three-year course of study at Moody Bible Institute, Clarence was hired as part of Evangelist Paul Rader's staff of nineteen men. Among his duties was playing in a brass quartet: two cornets and two trombones, highly versatile and mobile, useful to Rader on many occasions. Soon there came a call from Chicago's Mayor William Hale Thompson: "We need musicians to help us on our new radio station." Rader jumped at the chance. "Sure, we'll come," he told the mayor. Rader was elated; to his staff he said, "We'll take our gospel songs right into the homes, the hotels, the saloons, even the bawdy houses—every place where there's a receiver. At last we're going to fight Satan on his own territory—the air!" On a windy June day in 1922 Rader and his quartet climbed to the top of the old City Hall in downtown Chicago. The station's call letters were WHT, the mayor's initials. What they saw was a smallish booth constructed of rough pine boards with no roof on it, and a small hole cut out on one side. "Point your instruments at that hole, and when we say 'play,' you play," they were ordered. A hand pushed an old telephone through the hole. "Play!"

"And we blew our heads off for several numbers, then Rader preached. We were scarcely able to hear ourselves above the noise of the wind and the traffic below." But all across the city, on those first little crystal sets, they were heard. This was the crude beginning of what was to be a major force. "Radio grew by leaps and bounds," said Jones, "and so did our vision."

With Clarence as program director, soon the Gospel Tab was broadcasting fourteen hours every Sunday over five stations, and from 7 a.m. to 8 a.m. daily on the CBS network. The mail poured in— thousands of letters weekly. Lance Latham, a key staff member, said, "Clarence was always coming up with new gospel songs, new ideas," and Latham remembered especially his flair for interesting program introductions.

Soon new opportunities and possibilities began unfolding. For Clarence the most significant happened at a missionary conference in Camp Maranatha at Lake Harbor. The Lord spoke to Clarence in a voice so clear that he was sure it had been audible all around. It was only four words: "Go south with radio." Later, in discreet questioning, he found that no one else had heard anything. It was a message for him alone!

Clarence took it very seriously as a command from the Lord. But the initial message was so brief! It would require a lot of subsequent direction along the way. How far south? In the U.S.? the Caribbean? Or Central or South America? Perhaps most men would have dismissed it as imagination or a fluke, but not Clarence. His tenacity, plus the help of Christians he had not yet even met, led ultimately to an entity as yet beyond his or anyone's imagining: "The Voice of the Andes."

God's Plan Unfolded One Step at a Time

Let's review some of what we've learned. Clarence Jones grew up in The Salvation Army, where his values were formed. His disappointment in not being asked to join the Staff Band may have played a part in his responding to an invitation from a former corps member to visit Paul Rader's ministry. He was soon pressed into service, then felt the need for more study. He completed a three-year course at Moody Bible Institute enabling him to teach in Rader's Tabernacle day school, where he came to know another teacher who left for missionary work, married another missionary, and went with him to serve in Ecuador. Meanwhile Clarence came to know Eric Williams, a brilliant but cynical young engineer who was sent from Columbia Broadcasting System with responsibility for the broadcasts emanating from Paul Rader's new Chicago Gospel Tabernacle. It was through Clarence's counsel that Eric accepted the Lord, which turned out to be a life-changing experience.

During a summer at Rader's newly acquired conference center, over which Clarence was given full responsibility, he slipped into their missionary meetings whenever he could spare the time. It was in such a meeting that a voice with no visible source spoke clearly to Clarence with the unmistakable words, "Go south with radio." He took it very seriously, but what could be the exact meaning of "south"? On the basis on this command, Clarence was given a grant to travel south to four nations, seeking a place where he could set up a Christian broadcasting station. What he found was four heads of state fearful of having an independent radio voice in their land, and Protestant at that! In each instance, the proverbial door was slammed in his face. Clarence was puzzled, not to mention embarrassed, at having spent two thousand dollars on a seemingly fruitless tour, and no more idea of what the word "south" could indicate. He went back to his Tabernacle assignment confused, and for eighteen months he had no clue as to what the Lord's plan could be. But he was honing his skills. At the end of that discouraging time, his former schoolteacher friend, with her husband, came to Chicago on their missionary furlough. It was logical to ask Clarence if he knew of a suitable place to rent. At that moment there was one vacant apartment in the same building which could serve as their "base of operations" during breaks in their series of meetings in various states.

During this time, Clarence and his wife heard much about an ideal country to the south which he had not considered: Ecuador! A short time later, when a second missionary couple from Ecuador followed their friends to Chicago, Clarence met two people with much greater experience, a man whose far-reaching innovations had won considerable favor with the country's top leaders, including the president himself. Doors would soon open for the hoped-for radio station!

And we can't leave out Eric Williams, the CBS radio engineer who was saved at the Tabernacle. Not only did he build HCJB's first transmitter in his garage in Chicago, but he and his wife went to Ecuador as a part of the team!

Thinking Outside the Box

Commissioner William McIntyre's becoming the territorial commander of the Central Territory coincided, more or less, with the onset of the Great Depression. At about the same time, Will Rogers, a lassoo-twirling cowboy became a famous show-biz personality when he went on the stage. It wasn't just his lassoo that made him a national figure; it was his seemingly unrehearsed, off-the-cuff patter regarding current events and noted personalities as he demonstrated his skill. Not only could he be funny, but his running commentary was so on-the-mark that people just loved it and somehow took him into their hearts. Soon radio stations clamored to have him on their shows, obviously not for his rope tricks, but because he had become sort of a spokesman for the common man.

One of the companies bidding for his wit and wisdom was the Gulf Oil Co. The problem was that the series they wanted him for was on Sunday nights. Even after an offer of $50,000 for the series (something like seven weeks) did not tempt him to violate his personal standard regarding Sabbath labor. Evidently someone persuaded him it would be alright if he did not do it for personal gain; he could give it all to put food on the tables of the desperately poor families. Then the clincher: Think of the hungry children he could feed just by doing radio shows! That did it! As for how to put the money to its intended use? Well, he would give it all to the American Red Cross and The Salvation Army, $25,000 apiece.

As for the Army, they would divide it equitably among the four territories by a set formula. The Central Territory's share was $7,000. Remember: it was meant to feed the hungry. If seven families were chosen to receive twenty dollars a week for groceries, (not much for a family, even at depression prices), the money would be used up in less than a year.

But McIntyre came up with a brilliant plan. He would use the $7,000 to build a Scout and Guard camp! At first glance it seemed as if he were way off base, using it for one of his pet projects. Wouldn't this leave the twenty families high and dry? Not on your life! If he could tie it into the Government's new WPA (Works Projects Administration), the U.S. would provide for the needs of more than 20 families of unemployed workers while the fathers worked at the camp for as long as it took to build it. Some of this could continue for considerably more than a year, while all that time families would have food on the table, clothing for school, etc. The Salvation Army would provide the empty land (which, I think, we already owned), plus the building materials, adequate year-round housing and all the meals for the workers. We had to supply the lumber for all the cabins, plumbing equipment for washrooms, etc. As for that lumber, you'd be amazed to know what $7,000 could buy in the early 1930's, when lumber yards were hopelessly overstocked, due to the unfounded optimism of the late 1920s. New homes simply weren't being built. Rather than feeding seven families for one year with that $7,000, and "*thinking outside the box*", the Army was able to help far more people much longer. The Commissioner's "brainstorm" was indeed a boon to many!

Personal Glimpses of the Founder

As was common at that time in England, the Booths took a boarder to supplement their income. One such a person who lived with the Booth family was Miss Jane Short. She had followed Booth's ministry for some time when the opportunity presented itself for her to board with the family. In later years she said, "to tell you the truth, I was terribly afraid of going to live with these dear folk, because I had been so often disappointed in religious people. It seemed to me that the Booths could not possibly be in their home life what they were in their preaching. I could not imagine that it was possible for them to live their ideals. You see I loved them so well that I quite shrank from finding my hero worship an illusion." But Jane learned that her fears were unfounded.

Although the General was terribly serious about his ministry, he could be quite a different person when he was with his family. At times it seemed essential for him to get away from the terrible conditions in the slums and take his family into the beautiful surroundings of the countryside.

"He was like a schoolboy directly he got away from London, laughing, singing, and joking nearly all the time. But mind you, he never went away without his Bible in his pocket, and I think he hardly ever passed by a gipsy without speaking to him about his soul." Miss Short continued, "William Booth made it a rule, so far as his engagements would allow to give (his family) a part of his evenings at home; the children would come charging into the room for a romp with their father. Sometimes he would lie full length upon the floor and the smaller children had to try and pull him up. He delighted in having his hair ruffled; he would sit reading a book with complete absorption while one of his children sat upon the arm of his chair rubbing his head. One evening, his daughter Emma, then about six, amused herself by putting his long hair into curl papers. She worked away until his whole head was covered with little twists of paper; such a sight you never saw in your life. When she had finished her work, the door opened and a servant entered announcing a visitor. Up sprang the General and was all but in the hall when the children flung themselves upon his coattails and dragged him back, screaming with laughter. You can fancy that when the General looked in the glass, he laughed too."

The Empty Stable

The beginning of The Salvation Army in the U.S. was hardly a triumphal entry. It was mother and daughter who took the brunt of the burden. The "man of the house," Amos Shirley, was kept busy six days a week as foreman in a silk factory, so it was up to his wife, Annie, and daughter Eliza to search the streets of Philadelphia for a suitable building, and to prepare it for use. Everything they paid out: rent, furnishings, posters, etc., had to come out of the pocket of Amos, and as a workingman, his pockets were not all that deep. They had no smart uniforms to identify themselves as Salvationists. As a matter of fact, the word "Salvationist" would have meant nothing, coming from the lips of these ordinary immigrants with the funny accent. Who had even heard of this "Army"?

While Amos worked long hours at the factory, Annie and Eliza trudged through the poorer neighborhoods looking for a good-sized building they could afford. Why poorer neighborhoods? They wanted to carry their message of salvation to the sort of people that the Army was reaching in England. They finally found what they were looking for: an empty building which was large enough for the crowds they anticipated. But it was a *mess*. Our mental image of the "disused chair factory" we've read about is probably too nice. What we are not likely to know, unless we study our history carefully, is that, after the chair factory moved out, the horses moved in; it was turned into a stable. The building had no real floor; only dirt. When you consider what horses do when left stabled all night, you can begin to imagine what the atmosphere in the building must have been like. All the scrubbing in the world couldn't restore a dirt floor to pristine condition!

Mother and daughter slaved away at cleaning it up; patching holes in the roof, whitewashing the walls, covering the floor with sawdust, and building a platform of low-grade, unplaned lumber. This exhausted the family's small savings, leaving nothing to pay for the lumber needed to build benches for the expected crowds. Now what? You couldn't expect people to come in and stand during a whole meeting. Without benches, it didn't even *look* like a meeting hail. There was no Community Fund or generous foundation to which they could appeal. They didn't even represent an organization that was known in the United States.

But they went ahead and calculated what the lumber would cost to do the job. It was at this point that something happened which doubtless gave them the unshakable faith to persevere, in spite of any future disappointments or setbacks, the firm knowledge that the Lord was behind their efforts, and He would see them through. As Edward McKinley wrote, "The Shirleys, in perfect faith, petitioned the Lord for the exact sum necessary to purchase lumber to build benches to hold the expected crowds. When a man arrived with the very sum in hand——he informed the rejoicing Shirleys that God had told him while at prayer to carry such a sum to this address——the cheerful militants naturally took this as further proof of the righteousness of their crusade. Nothing could stop them now!"

A Tale of Two Children

I want to tell you two true stories, the first a cautionary one, the second with an ending as different as day from night. John, a young Indiana boy, was sent to Sunday school by his parents. (Evidently they sent him, not took him.) The youngster was overly full of energy, impishness and mischief. Obviously this boy needed someone to channel that energy, someone with the wisdom of Solomon, someone to perceive his quick mind, lively imagination, and considerable ingenuity. Possibly the boy's defiance of adult authority might have hinted at youthful, albeit misdirected, fearlessness. But the good folk who tried to deal with him couldn't see it that way. They were entirely out of their depth. His first Sunday school teacher was completely flummoxed and said in short order, "Take him out of my class. He's beyond me." However there was another teacher with a similar age group. John was moved to that group, but the outcome was the same. Neither wanted to see him again—ever. So that's what the boy was told: don't ever come back. He didn't. He never darkened the door of a church again. His name was John Dillinger. If you are too young to recognize the name, think of "Public Enemy Number One". Think of bank robberies and reckless murder. John himself was killed in a hail of bullets.

But our story is about a young girl named Delores, living in a small Minnesota town during the Depression. Her hardworking parents were determined to stay off welfare. The mother managed a cream station for a local dairy, while the father farmed just outside town. They made sure their little girl went to Sunday school, first at a German Lutheran church, then at a Presbyterian one. At about that time a boy, a schoolmate, invited her to "the Army" without including the word "Salvation," not surprising for a seven-year-old. She thought he said "the Armory", where she knew there was roller skating, as well as games, and so on. She later wrote, "Boy, was I surprised when I found out that it was another Sunday school."

The officers made quite an impression on her. She says, "They showed me Christian love and taught me about the Lord." She was enrolled as a Junior soldier. Some time later she attended her first youth councils in Minneapolis. For the trip she got to ride in the rumble seat of a Model-A Ford. Of the councils, as well as of the succeeding years she says only, "I don't remember too much, other than that I continued attending the S.A., became a Corps Cadet and a bandsman. Learned to play the cornet at school."

In early adolescence her life became unsettled. She ran away from home. Twice she spent time in foster homes, but then chose to return to her own home and to the corps. But, she acknowledges, she had become "a mean little kid." Although she had loved the first corps officers, the two single women then stationed there couldn't cope with her. She recalls, "they told me to 'get out and don't come back.'" To which she said, "O.K., I won't." And she never returned to that corps. But she was no Dillinger. The Lord had her firmly in His hand. One day she would become Major Delores Rivitt, Order of the Founder!

Easter Revisited

If a creative writer were to set his hand to compose a dramatic fictional version of the events of that weekend, he might have Jesus bursting forth from the tomb, leaving the grave clothes in disarray and speeding straight to the Temple grounds, (or wherever He found the biggest crowds) to proclaim His triumph over death, and to confound the Jewish leaders. Instead, He chose to appear without fanfare to three small groups of His grieving followers: the three women who went to the tomb early in the morning; two men on the road to Emmaus, and ten of His disciples—all except Thomas—in a room behind a locked door.

Now think back for a moment to Jesus' temptation in the wilderness before His public ministry even began. Satan suggested that Jesus make a huge impression by leaping from the pinnacle of the Temple and landing unhurt on the pavement below, thus establishing His reputation as the Son of God. Jesus refused, just as He refused to confound the crowds after His resurrection by demonstrating that He had conquered death itself.

There is also the question of Jesus' scarred body. If we believe that Jesus was restored completely after His crucifixion, why did He still have scars? These were not wounds that were still healing; otherwise Jesus would not have told Thomas to put his finger into the nail prints and his hand into His side. These marks were unmistakable identifiers. His followers could see immediately that it was not someone who looked like Him. The prints gave incontestable evidence that it was the Savior Himself. This was what prompted Jesus to say, "Reach hither thy finger, Thomas, and behold my hands; and reach hither thy hand, and thrust it into my side; and be not faithless, but believing." To which Thomas answered, "My Lord and my God.

This irrefutable, living evidence called forth the strongest of declarations.

The Haze of History

In looking back to past events of significance, we often see their eventual success, while tending to overlook the discouragement and seeming futility which dogged them at the onset. Case in point: The Salvation Army's beginning in America. Amos Shirley, by then a foreman in an American silk factory, was as anxious as his wife and daughter to see the Army's ministry commenced in the U.S. He was inspired by a vision of what could be done for the Christless masses in Philadelphia. But he, tied to his job six days a week, had to leave all the hands-on work to Annie and Eliza. Last month we looked at the tough job they faced in transforming a stable into a usable meeting-hall. There were seemingly endless hours of patching, cleaning, and generous applications of whitewash. A platform of rough lumber took the last of their savings. Then providentially, a stranger arrived with the money to buy a suitable grade of lumber for all of the benches!

Meanwhile the Shirleys conferred with other Christians before their first meetings, recruiting twelve of them to join them on the platform. Amos had plastered the neighborhood with posters announcing the meetings. Ironically the posters urged, "Rich and poor, come in crowds." Crowds?

When the "Salvation Factory" was ready, the three Shirleys conducted their first open-air meeting on the corner of Fourth and Oxford, to announce the indoor meeting to follow. Edward McKinley had this to say: "No unprejudiced observer can fail to be touched by it: these obscure and unimportant people, favored by nothing in this life, unknown and unsupported even by their distant comrades, possessed of nothing but a love for God and their fellow sinners, held up the Cross of Christ over the manure and cobblestones of a Philadelphia gutter in 1879." Apparently none of the three played a musical instrument, which might have helped. Reminiscing about the event 46 years later, Eliza could not recall if anyone stopped to listen to them, as their unamplified voices sought to compete with the din of traffic. Nor is there any mention of anyone being attracted to the first indoor meeting.

Since the first street-corner meeting was a failure, the courageous trio next sought a corner frequented by more people, namely Five Points. Here the opposition was worse, accompanied by a "shower of insults, mud and garbage." Few followed them indoors except a handful of sympathetic Christians. The Shirleys decided it was time to appeal to the mayor for police protection. But he frowned on their unorthodox ways and told them they could not meet on *any* street, since the crowds obstructed traffic. What they needed was a vacant lot where people could gather around. However, the only one they could find was a discouraging eight blocks away. And after trudging there from the factory, few listened. Probably it was even hard to see them. (At best there might be gas lights. The light bulb was not even invented until the next year, and only the main streets would have had arc lights.) No listeners followed them to the empty hall, where even the original twelve "Christian friends" began to wonder if it was a lost cause.

A Change of Heart

The tragic story of John Dillinger's being ejected from Sunday school and told never to come back may not seem relevant to the case of Delores Rivitt, but it does show the vital importance of dealing sensitively with young people. It's probably true that exclusion from church was not a decisive factor in Dillinger's later life of crime. But we don't *know* that. In Delores Rivitt's case, we naturally see the ejection of a little girl from a Salvation Army Sunday school as inexcusable.

But the Lord had plans for this little girl who, admittedly, had become hard to handle at about the age of twelve or thirteen. What about her being told to stay away from the corps? The solution to that problem came about through a decision of her parents, whose hard work had yielded a combined income barely above the subsistence level. They had a close relative in Seattle, WA, who urged them to come west. The family made the trip by train. But Delores could not go with them because of school exams. She stayed with friends until her exams were finished, then took a train by herself. The kindly conductor, who she learned was a corps sergeant-major in a Montana corps, took special care to see that she was all right.

Her parents were living in a hotel downtown until they could find a place to rent. Meanwhile she found a corps a short distance from the hotel. In spite of having told herself she would *never* go to the Army again, curiosity led her there. She attended a few times before her parents found a house near Lake Washington. That could have meant "end of story," but the Lord was just beginning! She writes, "Was I surprised when a retired Colonel appeared at the door of our house. He came to see if I would be interested in working at the Evangeline Residence. I was! I worked for a couple of years and attended Seattle

51

Citadel—played in the band, etc. Later the corps officers asked me to help in the corps and in their home. When they farewelled to Bellingham, WA, I went, too. It was there on Nov. 16, 1948 that I surrendered my life to the Lord. But not to go to Training School. That came later!"

At the time when she made her crucial decision, there was a poster on the bulletin board that bore some familiar words: "Love so amazing, so divine, demands my soul, my life, my all." As to the message on the poster, she writes, "That did it! I applied for Training and was accepted as a cadet in the Standard Bearers Session, 1949-1950."

At the end of the session came another significant step in the Lord's plan for her. She later said, "My secret desire was to some day visit Alaska, so imagine how I felt when a week before Commissioning I was called to the Principal's office, and he said, "How would you feel about going to Alaska?' I don't remember anything else he said." It was so unexpected and sudden that, when she tried to put it into words more than 50 years later, she confided that she had later asked herself, "Did he really say what I think he said? Did I dream it?" But it wasn't a dream. It was the beginning of a lifetime of devoted service for Major Delores Rivitt, Order of the Founder.

Allow Me to Digress

It seems difficult to omit any mention of the human element in telling of our beginnings in India, The Salvation Army's first mission field. This is especially true because I mentioned the Booth-Tuckers in March, but gave little more than their hyphenated name. Among the many ministries the Army has established in India is that of hospitals.

That brings us to the poignant account of the boy whom the Booth-Tuckers took with them. He was not a relative, nor was he an orphan in the usual sense. His mother, Mrs. Andrews, was a stranger to the Booths. She died in bearing her eighth child. Perhaps because of some physical problem, she had had a strong feeling that she might not survive this birth. So she had talked to seventeen-year-old Bramwell Booth, who was trying his hand at hospital visitation. Could his family, she hesitantly asked, adopt the baby if she didn't survive? She could see that her hard-working husband, a foreman in a paper-box factory, with very long working hours typical in those days, could scarcely be expected to cope with eight motherless children. The tenderhearted Bramwell promised on the spot that his mother and father would certainly take the baby into the bosom of their family! We can safely assume that young Bramwell discovered it was far more difficult to inform his parents of his promise than it had been to respond so quickly to Mrs. Andrews.

It was also painfully true that William and Catherine Booth, with their own eight children, already had their hands full, managing to care for their own brood. But a promise is a promise. Their daughter Emma eased the situation by taking chief responsibility for the boy. He was never "adopted" in the sense that he took the Booth name, but young Harry Andrews found himself in the midst of a loving family. Much later, when the Booth-Tuckers went to India, they responded to Andy's pleas that he could go as well. It turned out wonderfully. A kit of dental instruments, sent to the young teenager as a gift, brought to light his own gifts. His compassionate heart was moved at some of the things he saw about him. Many people had deplorable dental problems. Often their teeth, having never been properly cared for, were in a state of advanced decay. Well, Andrew now had the means to deal with that. When the Booth-Tuckers were appointed to a small hospital, Andrews was given one room to be used as a sort of clinic. He strove tirelessly to alleviate pain. There was a great need for qualified workers in several fields. Andrews took training in nursing, but more was needed. He went to London and trained to be a dresser. But what was really needed was a bona-fide medical director to run the hospital. So Andrews devoted years of study to become an M.D. Centralites will be interested to know that his advanced study took place at the University of Illinois Medical School in Chicago, Illinois! Not only did Dr. Andrews develop the Catherine Booth Memorial Hospital into a first-rate institution, but he did it all again, establishing a second fine Army Hospital in South India.

The Not-So-Empty Lot

If you have studied the beginnings of William Booth's evangelistic work in England after he began to minister independently, you know that he faced some cramped, drafty, dirty and seemingly unpromising meeting-places. Unpromising? Perhaps a better word would be *impossible* or so it seemed at the time. It must have been extremely hard for Booth to take, having been a minister ordained in a major denomination, who had preached with such force to many large crowds, until petty politics and jealousy worked against him. The Shirley family's circumstances were different, but equally discouraging. They were trying to preach in a disused livery stable with a dirt floor. When you think of horses housed all night, night after night, with that dirt floor, you are faced with a mental picture that, in our day, we don't even want to think about. Scrubbing could do little to alleviate conditions, and it's not likely that the sawdust which the Shirleys spread on the floor improved things very much. Perhaps the best we can say is that, in that day, people were used to such things.

After the mayor of Philadelphia forbade the Shirleys to hold any meetings on the street, they had searched for a vacant lot where listening crowds wouldn't block traffic. The nearest lot they could find was eight blocks from their "Salvation Factory." Eight blocks! At the outset at least, the outdoor meetings were necessary to attract people to the indoor meetings. But can you imagine crowds following them for eight long blocks to the announced meeting place? Well, they didn't. It was one thing to pass by and hear the unamplified voices of people who were barely visible. But why would anyone walk a long eight blocks on a dark street to hear more from the same three people? The Shirleys couldn't even promise a musical treat, since it seems that none of them played an instrument.

For four long, fruitless weeks, the Shirleys faithfully persevered, night after night, with few if any following to the hall. And what of the twelve Christians who at first gave support by joining them on the platform? Understandably they had not foreseen taking part in such a barren ministry. One by one they stopped coming. Historian McKinley says that by the end of four weeks, the Shirleys were returning to an empty hall, with not even any Christian support on the platform.

Yet they kept on, perhaps sustained by the remarkable visit of the man who, while at prayer, had been directed by the Lord to come to that address and give a specific sum of money. It was that visitation which had provided the seating for the crowd. *Surely* the Lord had some plan in mind! And the Shirleys were resolved to be prepared for the crowd when it finally came.

After four discouraging weeks, it happened, suddenly and unexpectedly. As with such lots today, theirs was not entirely empty. It contained unwanted junk which people had dumped there, simply because there was no one to stop them. One item was a partially filled barrel of tar—unwanted perhaps, but useful in the Lord's hands as an instrument for Kingdom-building!

What Ever Became of...?

When Commissioner George Scott Railton received the cable January 1, 1881, summoning him back to England after less than a year in America, he virtually ignored it. It arrived just after Railton had finally found another meeting place and was commencing a series of evangelistic meetings. Later, when Booth sent a second cable, Railton reluctantly obeyed, but not too quickly. In that same year Eliza Shirley returned to England where she married Capt. Philip Symmonds. In the meantime, Captain Amos Shirley, Eliza's father, was left nominally in charge of all the work. It was the only recognition the pioneer captain ever received. When Major Thomas E. Moore arrived to take over in June, he made Amos his aide-de-camp, but Amos quarreled with Moore for reasons now unknown, and he resigned after a month (it should be noted that Major Moore was the man who later caused a split, incorporating a separate Salvation Army of America). Despite Amos's resignation, his wife continued as an officer.

In 1884, while swimming in the Atlantic at Asbury Park, NJ, Amos was caught in the undertow and drowned. Later his widow, Annie, married an English officer, Major John Dale, and together they served in America for years. In 1885 Eliza, now Mrs. Captain Symmonds, returned to America with her husband. Widowed early, she remained an active and successful officer until her retirement. (A personal note: our family has a photo of a corps songster brigade in Minneapolis, in which my father, at that time a teenager, was singing. Sitting front and center was the corps officer, Mrs. Eliza Symmonds, flanked by two of her daughters, soon to became officers as well. Later, one of those daughters was the wife of our corps officer.)

In the Central Territorial Archives is a letter from Eliza to a granddaughter, written not too long before her death. Interestingly, a good part of the letter was about the Chicago Cubs, whose fortunes she followed as a real fan. She mentioned the manager by name as well as some of the players. When she died September 18, 1932, just before the end of the baseball season, her passing was observed by a moment of silence in Wrigley Field. Not only was she honored because of her unique part in bringing The Salvation Army to America, but she was such a fan of the Cubs—an irresistible combination in Chicago!

While the aforementioned daughters became officers and served their entire lives in the Central Territory, another daughter was among the first Salvationists to serve as doughnut girls in France during World War I. Three grandchildren later became officers, and a great-grandson is now an officer.

As for Emma Westbrook, the only officer among the seven women who came over with Railton, she served faithfully and was honored during the 50th anniversary celebrations in 1930. There is in the archives a photo of Army dignitaries in an open touring car as they drove past the Central Territorial Headquarters on Chicago's State Street. Seated in that car with the top dignitaries was Field Major Emma Westbrook (Ret.).

A Surprise Reunion

This column has dealt with the story of Delores Rivitt, since her first encounter with The Salvation Army in Crookston, Minnesota. A seven-year-old boy, just about her age, invited her to attend "the Army," by which she thought he meant the Armory, with its roller-skating rink and other attractions. But Delores liked what she saw and kept attending. For a considerable time she found it a wonderful experience, thanks to the loving and understanding ministry of the corps officers and their assistant. But some years later, by the time she was twelve, two single women had been appointed there, the assistant (whom we will call Ruth, not her real name) was right out of Training College. The officer in charge seemed unable to relate to Delores, who later described herself as having become a "mean little kid." True, at that time she was very unsettled, to the extent that twice she ran away from home and spent time living in two foster homes. Later she voluntarily returned home, as well as to the corps.

However, things did not go well between Delores and the C.O. who was obviously out of her depth in dealing with such a youngster. We can only say that the officer's response was inexcusable; she told Delores to leave the corps and never come back. For Lieut. Ruth, new and inexperienced as an officer, this was appalling. But she, feeling she had no authority to interfere, said nothing. As time went by, she moved to other appointments, while the officer who had dealt so harshly with Delores resigned her officership, perhaps suspecting she was not cut out for such a ministry. As for Ruth, she was haunted with the feeling that she had utterly failed in one of her first crises as an officer. Worse, there was no way to make it right. She later learned that Delores and her family moved to the West Coast, leaving no forwarding address. All Ruth could do was pray that in some way the Lord would take care of this girl whom she had failed.

A great many things happened to Delores after she moved to Seattle. For one thing, she was truly saved. But although now a Christian, she dismissed the thought of officership as "not for me." Later the words from a song, printed on a poster on the corps wall went straight to her heart: "Love so amazing, so divine, demands my soul, my life, my all." As she later wrote, "That did it!" How could she do less than offer herself for officership if the Lord wanted her? So it was that she was in the next session of cadets, training for the very calling she had once brushed aside as not for her.

We saw how Delores was sent to Alaska, beginning a long and fruitful ministry, particularly among the many Indian tribesmen who worship in Army corps. After thirteen years she was sent as a delegate to the National Brengle Institute in Chicago. Ruth, the former assistant in Minnesota, was now stationed at Territorial Headquarters, so of course Delores went to see her. Imagine Ruth's utter astonishment to see standing in her doorway this uniformed officer, this answer to her prayers for a girl she feared had been lost!

The Burning Barrel

In their attempts at an outdoor ministry, the Shirleys apparently lacked two things: people who would stop in their tracks and really pay attention to their vital message; and potential hearers who would recognize their own hopeless condition and be truly receptive to the promise extended by the Shirleys. They saw no results at their vacant lot, and worse, the indoor services were being held in an empty hall. There is no better way to express the situation than in the words of Edward McKinley in his *Marching to Glory:* "Four weeks passed, with the Shirleys' hopes for the future of their mission sinking daily lower. Penniless, friendless and discouraged, they prayed for some sign from the Heavenly Commander that He favored their dying crusade and would yet bless it.

"Arriving at their dark and lonesome lot one evening, the trio were amazed to find flames, smoke, noise, and—most dazzling of all prospects to their hungry hearts—a crowd! Several boys had set fire to a barrel of tar in 'their' lot, and the horse-drawn fire engines had arrived. Fire was a desperate threat in the crowded, wooden, gas-lit American cities of the late nineteenth century; fear, along with the self-important clang and bustle of fire engines always drew large crowds to fires. The Shirleys were certain the fire was providential and threw themselves on the startled crowd with thankful hearts, singing, 'Traveler, whither art thou going, heedless of the clouds that form?' Their curiosity aroused, the crowd stayed to listen to Amos's brief, simple homily on the grace of Christ. At the end of it a drunken, rumpled man, who proved later to be a notorious local known only as 'Reddie,' struggled forward to ask, in his bewilderment, if such Good News could be for the likes of him. Tearfully the Shirleys assured him that it was, and embraced the man, bearing him off to the Salvation Factory....The crowd, now thoroughly amazed, followed the quartet into the hall. Reddie was allowed to sleep while the Shirleys sang, prayed, and spoke to the crowd, which now occupied all the seats and filled the hall to overflowing. Reddie was revived, and in the presence of the large and enthusiastic crowd—Eliza remembered the number to have been over eight hundred—he was soundly converted. Sobered by his experience, Reddie promised to come again the next day to explain in his own words what had happened to him....Many in the crowd had been deeply affected by all that had happened—that Reddie was suddenly a changed man none could deny—and they promised to return to hear him. The Shirleys took up a collection and raised enough to carry on for a few more weeks. Though exhausted, they were overjoyed; the work was saved. The Salvation Army had been launched in the United States after all."

The divinely directed investment in lumber for all of those benches had suddenly proved to be a spectacularly sound one; the benches were filled, and the Shirleys had their first convert, as so often in the following days, a seemingly hopeless case. It was the crucial turning-point, marking the true inception of The Salvation Army in America.

A New "Uniform"

Many years ago, when I was stationed at Territorial Headquarters, we were approaching the Easter weekend when I received a call. Would I be available for emergency flood work? All the corps officers were tied up with special Good Friday and Easter services in their own cities, and some of the headquarters staff were committed to being special speakers. In short, it was difficult to find officers who were not committed somewhere for the weekend. Heavy rains had caused a river in northern Wisconsin to overflow its banks, endangering a town of some size. They had plenty of volunteers to keep up the sandbagging around the clock, but they were depending on The Salvation Army and the Red Cross to serve hot food to those workers, night and day. The town itself was not yet flooded; that's why the sandbagging was essential: to win the battle against the rising water. (Yes, they succeeded.)

There were Army vehicles there from neighboring cities, all black in color, as required by the then-current Army regulations. They were being pushed to their limit to transport large containers of beef stew, bakery goods and coffee to the men sandbagging along the section of the river endangering the town. Driving through the clinging mud put a strain on the cars and station wagons. (As yet we had no SUVs or vans, not to mention cars with four-wheel drive.)

In order to coordinate the services of the Army and the Red Cross, the area had been divided into two sectors, one for each organization. No vehicle or person could enter those areas unless authorized by one or the other, so as to prevent spectators from interfering with a vital task.

The city had a large Catholic convent. Early on, they telephoned and offered their services if they could be of any help. At the moment such help was not needed, but their offer was gratefully accepted, with assurance that we would call on them if needed. That help was suddenly needed when one of our hardworking station wagons burned out its clutch. We didn't have even one spare vehicle; all were needed through the entire night. A garage mechanic kindly promised to work through the night to have the clutch repaired or replaced by morning. But we needed a car right then. Time to call the convent! When called, the mother superior was delighted to help. She immediately sent one of their cars, a black, four-door Chevy sedan (just like Army regulations). One of their nuns was to drive it. But since nuns did not travel alone, there were two of them, both dressed in their habits (slightly modernized by that time). A uniformed Army officer—in this case me—was to ride in the back seat.

We loaded a large container into the trunk and set out. When we reached the workers, the three of us served the stew. But on the way we came to a national guardsman, keeping out curiosity seekers. The nun opened her window and said, "It's all right. We're from The Salvation Army." The guard probably never saw me in the back, but waved us on. As we drove on, she chuckled and said, "I wonder what he thought when he saw my habit, and I assured him that we're from The Salvation Army."

Fishers of Men

When I was young, there was still a good deal of "fishing" (as in Matthew 4:19) going on in many of the Army's salvation meetings. Officers as well as lay members—whom we call soldiers—used to walk quietly and slowly up and down the aisles during the "invitation" (or altar call), observing the faces of hearers who might show signs of being "under conviction" or in some other way responding. The person doing the fishing would quietly ask the one they had observed if he or she were truly saved, or some other question such as "how is it with your soul?" We kids hated it when a person came near us, since we hardly knew what to say in response. And, let it be said, not everyone attempting to do the "fishing" was adept or effective, and in some cases were more of a liability than an asset. So for a number of reasons, the practice dwindled away and today is likely to be found only in youth councils.

But in our early years, a good deal of it bore fruit. I know the story of a young man, a Presbyterian, who was thus approached in a meeting by a woman officer who asked him if he was a Christian. "That's my business," he snapped. "It's a pity that you can't mind your own business. A girl like you would be better at home under your mother's care." The girl was crushed. She wept. The young man left the meeting feeling uneasy. He realized that the Army officer was more interested in his soul's salvation than he himself was. Soon afterwards he responded in the way she had hoped for, and he was truly saved. Thanks to his response to that faithful fishing he soon heard God's call to become an officer. Later one of his five officer-children, and still later a grandson, served as National Commanders. Let me hasten to assure you that I am not foolish enough to believe that the ultimate mark of success is becoming National Commander! But as the old saying goes, "you never know." What if no one had dared to deal with him personally after that initial rebuff? As it turned out, his response and his true conversion bore great fruit. He and his wife, plus his children and their spouses, and his grandsons and their spouses, plus granddaughters who became officers: this immediate family totaled 25 officers, all because of the fishing of a young woman officer.

I really started out to tell of an older woman who, in 1947, continued this practice faithfully and was able to sense when she should really persist. She dealt with a fine looking young man who was a stranger to our corps. He attended that single meeting to fulfill a promise he had made to a Salvationist while in Germany. It was a real challenge, since he had been brought up a member of another denomination where, to him, the way of salvation had not been made plain. But his church membership had convinced him that he must certainly be a Christian.

I saw his face when, after some intense counseling, he really saw the light, and when he rose from the altar a changed person. I later became his roommate in a Christian college and saw his life transformed into that of a pioneer missionary and a lifetime Bible translator. A remarkable story which began with "fishing" in our corps!

Railton and Mrs. Booth

Early in 1880 there were several factors which helped to hasten the progress of the fledgling Salvation Army in America. In January the Shirleys opened a second corps in Philadelphia, even before the letter reporting their first victories reached London at the end of January.

Meanwhile in England, George Scott Railton's longstanding relationship as Booth's "lieutenant" was fading as William's son Bramwell was given the title "Chief of the Staff," second only to Booth himself. What of Railton, who lived in the Booth home for 11 years and, as of 1873, had been designated General Secretary of The Christian Mission? Catherine Booth shared similar thought processes with Railton and, at 20 years his senior, was the nearest thing to a mother he'd had since he was orphaned at age 15. She could see that Railton was in an increasingly frustrating position—on the "outside" rather than at the very heart of consultations and decisions, as he had been previously. Bramwell was demonstrating marked administrative ability, and his father was happy to place many matters in his son's hands. Catherine was not blind to the virtual unanimity between her husband and son, while Railton differed sharply in his views on many policies. She saw that he would inevitably grow increasingly unhappy as he was by-passed. There is evidence of this in the way Railton signed his letters. He had long been "Your faithful Lieutenant," but he had by that time given that up. Catherine could see that he needed a meaningful, responsible post away from London, perhaps in some new country, where he could begin to fulfill his vision of a worldwide Army.

In order to summarize Railton's contributions, let's take a paragraph from Bernard Watson's excellent biography. "The official records show Railton as the Army's first Commissioner, better educated than the norm among his colleagues, a linguist, a prolific writer, and leader of the Army's first official invasion overseas…. He is known to have framed many of the movement's Orders and Regulations, to have helped set out its first doctrines and to have made radical and highly successful contributions to Salvationist tactics." Add to this some words of Dr. John Kent of Bristol University, who wrote, "Railton was the most important influence in the Army, after the Booths themselves. He has been adjudged the most important and influential Chief of the Staff the Army has ever had, even though he was never officially given that title."

When the reports of the success of the Shirley family in Philadelphia reached William Booth January 31,1880, coupled with a request for reinforcements, Railton and Mrs. Booth were ready to make it happen. They decided that all members of the "invading force" (except for Railton) should be women; seeing this as a logical step, since they both strongly favored granting women a much greater part in the "Salvation War."

Emma Westbrook, a dependable, sturdy officer, was selected as leader of the women. The other six, hurriedly chosen, were not yet officers, nor really trained. They sailed for America February 14, 1880, a mere two weeks after the Shirleys' letter arrived in London.

The Pawnbroker

It is hard to imagine William Booth, later to become the founder of a worldwide evangelistic movement, spending most of his teen years employed in a pawnshop. Yes, it seems incongruous, considering that we are looking at a future soul winner of great influence. But of course he had no choice at the time, and those years gave him the wrenching experience of seeing great numbers of fellow human beings who were at wit's end and in great distress. Doubtless it crystallized his lifelong compassion for the "submerged tenth," having been compelled to witness at close range their despair as they parted with their most treasured belongings. Many of them finally had to part even with necessities in order to put some semblance of food on the table for their families. Certainly it tore at his heart to be thus involved. But he was contractually bound to stick it out for a specified period of time.

William's father had been a builder, but apparently not a good businessman. Finally, the calling in of a mortgage precipitated his ruin. William, at age 13, was taken out of school and apprenticed to a pawnbroker. Harold Begbie, a major biographer of Booth, found in his research how much the boy shunned the work. Begbie says, "In all his writings I can find no direct reference to the nature of this employment. He speaks always of 'a business' or of 'a trade', but never once can he force himself to say outright that the business into which his father apprenticed him was a pawnbroker's. Until this time, his parents had tried to hide their poverty from their neighbors, as though their neighbors were respectable and prosperous and they alone were poor and struggling. But now he learned that many other people were fighting against poverty, and grew to know that suffering and sorrow, deprivation and shame were like an immense dragnet in a wide sea of human misery."

We may wonder why his father chose this particular business. But much later William explained it in his own words: "Because he knew no greater gain or end than money." His father had a talk with him, holding forth to the boy the allurements of money. He told him that it was a business where fortunes could quickly and easily be made. He counseled his son to keep ever before him the prospect of setting himself up in business and of avoiding partnerships. But reality soon set in; it was a small pawnshop in the poorest part of Nottingham.

William had been in that work for less than a year when he was summoned to the side of his father who was dying. The Sacrament was administered. A small group sang "Rock of Ages" around his bed. His was a deathbed of repentance. William later wrote of it as a "skin-of-the-teeth sort of business of getting to heaven, to be in no way recommended." Yet, at the time when he was still virtually unchurched and had no proper understanding of the gospel, William had hopes that he would meet his father in heaven. At about this time he began to be more interested in religion. But the darker side of pawning one's belongings to stay alive was to leave a lasting imprint on the heart of our future Founder.

A Double-Barreled Story

In what may be seen as a strange coincidence, a barrel played a key part not only in events leading to the Shirley family's first convert in America, but also in the case of Railton's as well. Both were plain old oaken barrels, one burning, the other freezing. But in each case the barrel was essential to bringing a man to the feet of Jesus. In the Philadelphia story, as already related, it was a barrel of burning tar which brought the fire engines, as well as the ensuing crowd of curiosity-seekers, including the bleary-eyed "Reddie," whom the Lord saved that very night. That was the night the Shirleys' ministry "caught fire" in a glorious way.

In Railton's case it was the almost legendary "Ash-Barrel Jimmy" who became his first American convert. There are two versions regarding that barrel; no one now knows which is the most accurate. For sake of completeness, historian Edward McKinley recorded them both. One is that James Kemp, in a somewhat drunken condition, toppled head-first into an empty barrel and was unable to extricate himself. He was found soon afterwards by Salvationists and carried, barrel and all, to the meeting place, where they managed to fish him out and take him indoors to the meeting. During that meeting he was truly saved.

The other version seems to indicate that Jimmy showed more determination than we might credit him with having. "He was a homeless alcoholic who had earned his nickname when he was found by a policeman drunk in a barrel" on a frigid night, having been there long enough for his long and unkempt hair to freeze into the standing water-turned-ice in the bottom. He "was dragged thus encumbered to the police court. The magistrate was in a jocular mood: he ordered James Kemp to attend The Salvation Army act at the Variety (Theater). Ash-Barrel lacked the twenty-five cents admission (the theater's charge, not the Army's) and thus was turned away. But he dutifully—and drunkenly—found his way to the Hudson River Hall the next night. After making several efforts to get past the policeman in front of the hall, Ash-Barrel was finally gathered up in Railton's loving arms and carried over the threshold. Kemp was soundly converted—a turning point in more lives than his own. Ash-Barrel was a well-known local hard case, and word of his 'getting saved' brought crowds. Enough money was collected by the Army pioneers to rent a hall of their own, the Grand Union on Seventh Avenue, which became the 'Blood and Fire New York No. 1' corps, for which Catherine Booth's flag had been destined."

Through these incidents we see one great fact which stands out in those early days of The Salvation Army in the U.S.A.: the highly original methods sometimes employed by those Salvationists to get a hearing from an otherwise unheeding public could have been dismissed as nothing more than outrageous clownishness, unbecoming when practiced by people claiming to be representatives of the Christian gospel. But there was no dismissing the remarkable transforming power taking place in the lives of well-known, even notorious, "hopeless cases." It was the power of this gospel that brought the crowds.

Cousin Margaret

Margaret Metzger was a teenager in Evansville, Indiana, when a new family moved next door. The newcomers, who were Salvationists, soon became good friends with the Metzgers and invited them to visit "the Army." Within a year, daughter Margaret, better known as Marge, had become a soldier and leader of the young people's string band. The youthful musician witnessed for Christ in open-air meetings on downtown street corners of Evansville. In due time, she sensed a call to officership which was so compelling that she applied for the upcoming session of Training college. This meant some sacrifice on her part, because she had already been offered a college scholarship. Leaving the matter in the Lord's hands, she forfeited the scholarship and became a cadet. Although she might have felt she was sacrificing personal ambition in order to carry on the work of the Lord, she would later find that the Lord's plan included both Army service and a degree from a prestigious university. But that came later.

After Training College, she was kept on as a sergeant for a year, then was made a captain and was appointed to the command of Chicago's No.8, a skid row corps on the then-notorious South State Street. A year later she was transferred to DeKalb, IL, where she remained until her appointment to the chief secretary's office. However, it wasn't just a "desk job," because she was asked to write weekly for *The Young Soldier*, responding to letters from young readers to "Cousin Margaret," her *nom de plume*. Not only did she answer the letters, but added words of guidance and encouragement. This opened the door to the field of writing which, before becoming an officer, she had envisioned as her future calling. She was even able to take evening courses at Northwestern University!

Four years later, she married John Troutt, a tall, lanky officer with a strong southern accent and a country boy demeanor. Although some might have perceived them as an oddly assorted couple, their marriage proved to be one of those often described as "made in Heaven." An extension of her corps work was helping with the summer camping program at Shagbark. Marge, determined to "do things right," familiarized herself with authentic American Indian culture, which was being stressed in our Scout and Guard program at the time. (Her Indian princess outfit was the envy of many.) The Troutts served in Chicagoland corps until war clouds loomed over the country.

In June 1941 they were appointed to the newly-formed USO, and were among the earliest of our club directors. Because they demonstrated such rapport with the servicemen, they were sent to England when the huge buildup of American forces there called for an "American presence" in The Salvation Army's British Red Shield clubs.

After the war, they spent their remaining active years in Men's Social Service Centers. This gave Marge time to write, not only for Army publications, but for other Christian magazines as well, and once for the *Reader's Digest*. It was she who wrote the book on the life of Tom Crocker. But her *magnum opus* was *The General Was a Lady*, the painstakingly researched, definitive American biography of Evangeline Booth.

God Calling

It is true that God can communicate with us in any way He chooses. After all, the Old Testament tells us that God actually spoke at crucial times to chosen people, sometimes audibly. What about today?

Millie was a young woman apparently suffering from depression so severe she was on the verge of suicide. With a bottle of pills near at hand, while she was trying to write a note which, hopefully would explain her seemingly rash act, she stopped to pray a desperate prayer, telling God, "I really don't think I want to do this," then adding to herself, if only she could talk to that kindly minister she had sometimes watched on television! The Rev. Ken Gaub, a TV evangelist, had at times given her great comfort, seeming to zero in on her own needs. But she couldn't just tune in and hear him right now. That was impossible. She had no clue as to how to reach him. Actually, it was worse than she knew; he was on the road, more than 2,000 miles from his headquarters.

As all hope drained from her, she turned again to the note. But as she wrote, one number, then later another, then another, began to invade her mind and take over her thinking. Because of their persistence and clarity, she finally began jotting them down, just to get them out of her head. After ten digits, they ended. Puzzling over them, it occurred to her that there are ten digits in all phone numbers, with the area code. Then a seemingly wild thought: "Wouldn't it be wonderful if I had a miracle from God, and He has given me Rev. Gaub's phone number?" In what might have seemed an irrational act, she lifted the phone, knowing that there was only once chance in millions that her call would reach him. But she did one very logical thing: she made it a person-to-person call.

As for Ken, that evening in the 1970s, he with his wife and grown family drove their two ministry buses, down I-75 just south of Dayton, Ohio. He wondered silently whether his ministry was doing any real good and wished he could have some sign of approval.

"Hey Dad, let's stop for some pizza!" One of his sons suggested. Still lost in thought, Ken turned off at the next exit onto Route 741, where they saw the usual string of fast food places. Ken's son and daughter-in-law quickly turned their bus into a pizza parlor's lot, and Ken followed suit. They went in, but he decided to stay outside to stretch his legs, saying he wasn't hungry. Soon a persistent ringing from an outdoor phone booth broke into his thoughts. No one answered it even after ten or fifteen rings. Finally, thinking it might be an emergency, and irritated that the man working nearby continued to ignore it, Ken answered it himself.

"Long-distance call for Ken Gaub," came the voice of the operator.

"You're crazy!" He said. Then realizing his rudeness he tried to explain, adding, "But it is true that I'm Ken Gaub."

"Are you sure?" She asked.

At the other end, Millie, hearing and recognizing his voice, said, "That's him!" Puzzled, he took the call, and there followed one of the most remarkable counseling sessions ever.

The James Jermy Story

The year 2005 marks the 125th anniversary of the year when The Salvation Army officially "opened fire" in the United States, so perhaps this significant event deserves mention in this column before the year has slipped by. Eliza Shirley and her parents really began the work in Philadelphia 126 years ago. But William Booth did not receive the letter telling of their first real success until early in 1880, when Railton was dispatched with reinforcements.

But did you know there were two beginnings even earlier in the 1870s, when co-workers in Booth's cause crossed the Atlantic, bringing the Christian Mission's message with them? They were James and Ann Jermy and later, the Rev, and Mrs. James Ervine. Yes, they planted churches, Jermy no less than five. The problem was that Booth had no thought at that time of extending his mission work here; he had his hands full with what was going on in England. When we look carefully at his objectives, and at the problems facing him, we'll have to agree that his attitude at that time was understandable.

Let's take a look at this seeming blank spot in Salvation Army history. After all, the Jermys and the Ervines were one in spirit with Booth; indeed, their work was in reality an extension of his efforts in a new and promising field. The information regarding the Jermys appeared in an article in *The Officer* by Commissioner Edward C. Carey in September 1979, and was included in a book by Commissioner John D. Waldron entitled *Pioneering Salvationists*.

The Jermys were, in Carey's words, "the first of a long line of pioneers who carried Booth's principles and methods to the far corners of the earth, and surely were instrumental in preparing the Founder to respond to subsequent appeals for help that reached him from America ... and many other places, and ultimately carried the Army flag around the world." James Jermy was an ardent Christian layman who had been closely associated with William Booth from the earliest days of the East London Christian Mission. He was mentioned a number of times in the *East London Evangelist* and later, with the Mission's change of name, in *The Christian Mission Magazine.* Though he earned his living as a cabinet-maker, he gave his evenings and Sundays to preaching the gospel and promoting the expansion of Booth's work. After the first mission station was established, he helped open a station in Croydon and is also credited with opening a station in Old Ford, London.

Evidently his cabinet-making business was not doing as well as the Mission's work, and Jermy had five children and his wife to support. So, as he noted in his personal journal, "there was much talk of Canada." A decision was made to emigrate, and Jermy reports that Catherine Booth took a great interest in the family, helping them with their preparations, particularly with the acquisition of furniture to take with them. A farewell meeting was held in Bethnal Green on May 23, 1870, and the family set sail for Canada, where they stayed for only a year. In 1871 the American saga began.

Railton's Early Years

The story of George Scott Railton's part in the official commencement of The Salvation Army in America has already been partially dealt with. It is true that undue emphasis upon him and his part can only lead to an unbalanced story, since there were others who also had a vital part in it. However, so much about him was unusual that we don't want to see him as "just another name" in our early Army history. (Of course, there is no substitute for reading the whole of *Soldier Saint,* Bernard Watson's careful biography of Railton. Railton was a major influence in our history, truly dedicated but quite peculiar!) True, he was not a systematic, patient administrator; he was sort of an adventurous knight-errant, brandishing a spiritual "sword and shield," never for personal glory, but always for the Kingdom of God and the salvation of souls. Not only was he ready and willing to "endure hardness" for the gospel's sake, he seemed to seek out all that was difficult for himself, as if trying to outdo St. Paul in carrying out the apostle's exhortations as well as his example.

Let's go back to his boyhood and try to trace possible sources of his unusual, often self-sacrificial life. His Scottish parents had met and married in the West Indies as young missionaries. George grew up in pastorates in Scotland and the North of England. When at age ten he was hard hit by flu, he was sure he was going to die. It was during this crisis that he had what he always considered his conversion experience.

George was sent to Woodhouse, a school open only to the sons of Wesleyan ministers, a strongly evangelical institution with a strict, almost monastic atmosphere and lifestyle for boys. One of the dividends of his life there was his grounding in Greek and Latin, which revealed a marked aptitude for foreign languages. While he was at school his parents were serving on the Isle of Man, just west of England, where a severe epidemic, probably of cholera, broke out. Both parents nursed those who were too poor to afford medical care, and both contracted the disease and died six hours apart, leaving George an orphan at age fifteen.

Already past the normal age limit of fourteen for the school, he was obliged to leave, virtually penniless, as well as homeless and jobless. His elder brother, a Wesleyan minister, found him a place in a London shipping company, where he soon astonished his employers and himself with the ease with which he learned Spanish, enabling him to take over much of the company's correspondence in that language. Yet he was restless, feeling that he should be doing great things for the Lord. But how—and what? Around Limehouse he tried out his new-found linguistic skill, distributing tracts to seamen from Spanish ships, talking to them personally whenever one was willing to stop and listen for a moment. But his efforts to convert Catholics to Protestantism were a dismal failure.

Perhaps it was at this point that he began to see his aptitude for language as a possible key to carrying the gospel to other parts of the world. Ignorance of the English language need not be tantamount to ignorance of the gospel.

Beginnings in America

We began the story of James and Ann Jermy, faithful members of The Christian Mission. Financial considerations led to their sailing for Canada, hoping to find it a land of opportunity for a cabinet-maker. In this they had the blessing of William Booth, their close friend, and the practical help of Catherine. After the farewell meeting at Bethnal Green on May 23, 1870, they departed, settling first in Hamilton, Ont., and subsequently in St. Catherines. Although they stayed only six months in each of these towns, Jermy found abundant opportunity for Christian witness, conducting one-man open-air meetings, and later helping at a "Colored" Methodist church in St. Catherines, where he said he had his happiest times.

In a letter to William Booth, Jermy wrote, "Brother, I cannot live on good meetings now and then, I must see souls saved. So I prayed about it and said to my wife, 'I must go to the States.'" Thus after a year in Canada the Jermys, now with a sixth child, arrived in Cleveland as "strangers and with no one to welcome us." In his personal journal, which was later made available to Salvation Army archivists, he did not even mention the challenge of having to find housing for a family of eight as well as a job, and of getting his four elder children established in school. But he did write, "By faith and prayer, the way soon opened for God and souls." Later in a letter to the Founder he wrote, "When I got here I found thousands going the way of death. Some parts of the city looked like Whitechapel. Here, human nature is the same, with drunkenness and every other sin. Mission work is very much needed." As for his secular employment as a cabinet-maker, which was his means of support for his large family, he made little mention of it in his journal.

He immediately sought an avenue of ministry. He tells how, on his third Sunday (probably in July 1871), he chanced upon a little hall and read a sign which said, "Christian Chapel—The Poor have The Gospel Preached to Them." He entered the hall and found a few African-Americans who asked him if he would be willing to preach if their own minister, a young Methodist named James Fackler, didn't come. Evidently Jermy preached, because it wasn't until the next Sunday that he met Fackler. When he told him of William Booth and the work of The Christian Mission in England, Fackler responded, "Brother, this is what I have been waiting for." The two men soon opened a second hall with "good attendance and great power."

Later Jermy wrote a letter to Booth with the heading: "Unfurling the flag of the Christian Mission in America." In concluding the letter Jermy asked, "Will you acknowledge us, the Mission flag is hoisted!" In his answer Booth acknowledged the American branch as part of The Christian Mission. To William Crow, a friend and confidant, he wrote, "Our flag has been unfurled, and a branch started in Cleveland, Ohio." James Jermy went on to open five mission stations in Cleveland, a work commenced within six years of that at Mile End Waste!

Learning Through Failure

At the time the Suez Canal was being built, North Africa was in the spotlight. The nineteen-year-old George Scott Railton, with savings of 20 pounds in his wallet, decided to journey to Morocco to win the Moors for Christ. He didn't know that St. Francis of Assisi had tried this very thing and failed. George failed too. He tramped through Morocco and Tunis, carrying a flag inscribed REPENTANCE—FAITH—HOLINESS. With his mission a failure and his money gone, he had to go to the British consul. When asked, "Why did you come here?" Railton told the consul, "Because God sent me." He was allowed to work his passage home as a steward, and his elder brother had to provide for him when he arrived. The whole thing seemed to have been a complete fiasco, but he later said he had learned much, and the Lord had kept him safe from many dangers.

He returned to the home of his brother, Launcelot, but felt he could not continue to impose upon him. So he decided to walk to Cornwall, where there was work to be had in the lead mines. Later he wrote, "On arrival at Bridport (sic), I sank exhausted by the wharf, every penny gone, and no idea how to get any further. Then I remembered that I still had a pawnable overcoat, and the proceeds carried me to a lead-mining village not far from Exeter." The people there were Bible Christians (one of the early breaks from Wesleyan Methodism). He found work, and at the same time learned a lot about common people, discovering "how much kindness can be shown to a tramp, how much patience with his incapacity, how much readiness to help him in every way." He also learned the value of lay participation, of eccentric and sensational tactics, and the worth of women preachers, and began serving as a local preacher.

All of this ended when Launcelot found him "more suitable" employment with an uncle who ran a shipping company. George was 21. Soon he was promoted to a larger Middlesbrough agency, but he had his heart set on being a minister. After appearing before a board of examiners he became a local preacher there, with prospects of soon joining his brother in the Wesleyan ministry, even though he lacked his brother's formal education.

During that time Launcelot visited a "hydro" in Matlock, a place frequented by Methodist ministers with health problems. There he met the Rev. William Booth, who was suffering from nervous exhaustion, frustrated by disorganization and confusion within his Mission. (It was at the very time when James Jermy wrote from Cleveland, Ohio, trying in vain to get reinforcements for his thriving Christian Mission work.) Booth needed a manager of details, a chief of staff for the business for which he had neither time nor inclination. He listened with keen interest to Launcelot's account of his younger brother's exploits, particularly George's single-handed invasion of Morocco. Booth too had known both audacity and failure. Later, Launcelot told his brother of his meeting with the leader of the East London Mission and indicated that Booth needed an assistant. George bought a six-penny booklet in which Booth described his work, and found it a trumpet call to action.

The End of the Beginning

James Jermy's early evangelistic work in Cleveland, Ohio, can hardly be viewed as an unauthorized incursion into a new country. William Booth, in correspondence with Jermy, as well as in a letter to a friend, gladly recognized it as a part of The Christian Mission. In January 1873, *The Christian Mission Magazine* reported the news and asked for prayers for "God's continued blessing upon The Christian Mission in America." Published in the same issue was a further letter from James Fackler, Jermy's co-worker, saying they had six or seven preachers belonging to the Mission, and four indoor preaching stations. In his reply Booth gave pages of sound advice and wrote, "So you have raised the banner of The Christian Mission in Ohio. Amen!" In another letter to Booth, Jermy rejoiced that in the very first meeting at one of the new stations, fifteen seekers came to the Mercy Seat.

The year 1873, however, brought problems. Fackler, for reasons of health, moved south, leaving Jermy to struggle with the expanded Mission program. This was also a year of a large-scale financial panic in the U.S. The resultant depression led to a drying up of work for Jermy as a cabinet-maker, so he resorted to opening a butcher shop.

The extremes of temperature characteristic of America's climate, so unlike that of London, proved a hardship to both the Jermys. Nevertheless Mrs. Jermy supported her husband in his ministry, sometimes walking four miles, even through snow and bitter weather, to their newest post. In January 1873 the temperature dropped to as low as 20 degrees below zero. Jermy, feeling the pressure of supporting his large family while trying to keep five mission stations going, wrote to Booth, appealing for someone to help. But Booth, who had serious problems of his own, did not respond. He had suffered a nervous breakdown and was out of action for six months in 1872. Added to that, Catherine was now suffering from angina.

In 1873 Jermy wrote to Booth about the progress of the work and told of their new opening on "The Broadway," with "souls being saved every night." He also requested a copy of the rules of The Christian Mission and purchased a set of Christian Mission Song Books for use in Cleveland.

But the many responsibilities were almost too much for one man. In 1875 Jermy wrote in his journal: "The way opened in the providence of God, for us to return to the land of our birth." He was given a personal welcome by the Founder in October 1875 and was invited to ride with Booth in his "chaise" as they visited some of the mission stations. He accepted "specialing" assignments and, when the Mission became The Salvation Army in 1878, he donned the uniform, serving faithfully as a very active soldier of the Clapton Congress Hall Corps. He was an ardent open-air warrior until a few weeks prior to his death in 1929 at age ninety-two.

It is fitting that both James and Ann Jermy are buried at Abney Park cemetery in London, very near the graves of William and Catherine Booth, their revered leaders.

A New Team, a New Name

Launcelot Railton told his brother George of his meeting with the Rev. William Booth, the leader of the East London Mission, who indicated he needed an assistant. In a short time (in 1872), George sought out Booth, and soon they formed a bond: the young idealist Railton and the seasoned campaigner Booth. The young man was a guest in the house of the Booths, and as it turned out, this was to be his home for the next eleven years. The Booths, about twenty years older, were like parents to him, and Catherine, whose thought processes were so like George's, became a sounding-board for his views, perhaps much as his mother might have been had she not died.

George was tired of "pale and quiet religion," as Bernard Watson expresses it, and yearned for a more aggressive evangelism. This coincided with events across Europe and in England at that very time. After the Franco-Prussian War of 1870, when the German peasant conscripts routed the professional French forces, England's government under Prime Minister William Gladstone hastened to reform the British military establishment. The purchase of commissions was abolished, promotions were to be based on merit, and for the first time, short-term enlistments were allowed. There would now be, as Watson says, a people's army, an army of the common man, instead of an army of career soldiers. The newspapers were full of this at the time the partnership of Booth and Railton began.

Back in 1865, the year which saw the beginning of Booth's Mission, the Rev. Sabine Baring-Gould, an Anglican, was asked on short notice to compose words for a song to be sung in a procession of Sunday school children on Whit-Monday. He hastily dashed off a set of words for use on that occasion. As a children's song, it was not intended to be taken very literally. It was originally sung to "St. Albans," a rather slow melody taken from Haydn's Symphony in D, hardly militant in mood, but in 1871 this tune was superseded by Sir Arthur Sullivan's "St. Gertrude," and a classic was born: "Onward, Christian Soldiers." Some of the lines of the new hymn resonated in Railton's head: "Like a mighty army moves the Church of God."

From the start, Railton referred to Booth as "General." Perhaps earlier, some had called him "General" as an abbreviation for General Superintendent. But in January 1873 young George addressed a letter to him as "My dear General" in what clearly was meant to be seen as a military term. At the close he signed himself as Booth's future "faithful Lieutenant." In the Mission, a growing militancy simmered unofficially for six years.

Then Railton, who did much of the writing for Booth, set forth the Mission's 1878 report. Bramwell and Railton, living in the same house, were called to William's bedroom to review the report before it went to the printer. It stated, "The Christian Mission is a volunteer army of converted working people." In the British army, volunteers were held in rather low esteem. It was William who put his pen through "Volunteer" and above it wrote "Salvation." Thus began The Salvation Army.

First Impressions

The tribute to William Booth came from the pen of a man whose first impression of the Founder was something radically different from what it came to be over many years. William Begbie began as a newspaperman in the 1890s in England, then published a book of his of his poems said to rival that of Kipling's patriotic appeal. He then began writing very popular novels, and later developed a keen interest in social issues, resulting in several widely circulated books on the subject of the social inequality of the times. Much of his subject matter in those volumes was illustrated by lives changed through the ministry of Booth's Army and the gospel he not only preached, but also *lived*.

These led Begbie to have ever-increasing interest in Booth and his Salvation Army, about which he originally had very negative feelings. As he had more contact with the Founder, his attitude was transformed. At the time of Booth's death, he wrote a tribute which included some of his earliest impressions of the Founder:

> "I remember very well my first impression of General Booth. I was young. I knew very little of the sorrow of existence, I was perfectly satisfied with the traditions I had inherited from my ancestors, I was disposed to regard originality as affectation, and great earnestness as a sign of fanaticism. In this mood I sat and talked with General Booth, measured him, judged him, and had the audacity to express in print my opinion about him—my opinion of this huge giant, this Moses of modern times. He offended me. The tone of his voice grated on my ears… I found it impossible to believe that his acquaintance with spirituality was either intimate or real. Saints ought to be gentlemen. He seemed to me a peculiar old man, a clumsy old humorist, intolerant and fanatical. Later in my life I met him on several occasions, and at each meeting I saw something fresh to admire, something new to love. I think that he himself altered as life advanced; but the main change, of course, was in myself—I was able to see him with truer vision, because I was less sure of my own value to the cosmos, and more interested to discover the value of other men. And I was learning to know the sorrows of the world."

As we know, Begbie came to know Booth very well, and saw something of his ministry at first hand. He went with him on one of his motorcades, and was even able to witness the Army's work with the criminal tribes in India. Shortly after the Founder's death he wrote, "For myself, I can do nothing but admire, revere, honor and love this extraordinary old realist, who saved so many thousands of human beings from utmost misery, who aroused all the churches of the Christian religion throughout the world, ... who was so tender and affectionate and cordial, and who felt for our suffering and sorrow and unhappiness wherever he found it with a heart entirely selfless and absolutely pure. When the dust has blown away, we shall see him as perhaps the greatest of our time."

Blowing Our Heads Off

When I was a cadet in 1949-50, when training sessions were still only nine months long, our brigade of eight or nine men always had field training at the same corps. We held open-air meetings regularly in front of a large billboard with an advertisement which was changed only infrequently. One night during the winter we faced a new ad for Kleenex tissues, featuring Little Lulu, a well-known comic strip character. Lulu was blowing her nose so hard that her head, along with her hands holding the tissue, had left her body and soared about three feet above it. Stressing this combination of the softness and strength of the tissues, the slogan was, "You can blow your head off." The billboard, with its little funny-paper friend, seemed both to amuse and taunt us as to how fruitless our musical efforts must have seemed on those cold winter nights when the streets were practically deserted. We could be pardoned if we sometimes wondered if it was an act of futility. But Salvationists witnessing in that manner never knew what might be in the minds and hearts of those who passed by.

Daryl Lach tells of an incident in 1953 in a small corps town in central Illinois. "The downtown streets were empty that Sunday night as then-Lieutenant Charlene Beach (now retired Major Charlene

Uptegrove) and Captain Violet Hasney faithfully marched out to their usual open-air spot. Lieutenant Beach played the accordion as Captain Hasney strummed on the guitar. While Lieutenant Beach spoke, one lone man passed by, stopped, listened for a few minutes, then turned around and walked back to an apartment building.

"After Christmas, Lt. Beach was on a Greyhound bus going home to visit her parents. A middle-aged man politely asked if he could sit next to her. While they were conversing he thanked her. She learned that he was the school superintendent for their township. One Sunday night, he had decided to kill himself. While on his way to the mailbox with a suicide note to his mother, the man stopped for a moment and listened to Lieutenant Beach testify to what the Lord had done for her. Then as the two women sang, he changed his mind, turned around and walked back to his apartment.

"And what eternal truth in song was proclaimed that Sunday night in the open-air, changing the direction of one man's life forever? 'There is power, power, wonder-working power in the precious blood of the Lamb.'"

It is a simple story, simply and clearly stated, which reminds us all that, whether it was an open-air meeting or some more contemporary effort at conveying the gospel message, the Lord can use our faithful efforts. The simple account also presents a message of encouragement as well as a challenge. There were, and are, many stories of lives changed which we'll never hear about. Our challenge: since we no longer "blow our heads off" or even sing in the open air, what are we doing to replace it?

Questions, Questions

The story of The Christian Mission in America seems to have no clearly satisfactory ending. When James Jermy returned to England with his family in 1875, he tried to leave his pioneering work in good hands, and the work continued for another two years, but then apparently languished for lack of the leadership he and his wife had provided.

Here we face some tantalizing "what ifs." What if William Booth had responded to Jermy's appeals from the U.S. for help? We must remember, however, that those appeals reached the Founder at a time when he was beset with problems of his own: He was recovering from a nervous breakdown which had laid him low for six months; his wife had a worrisome heart condition, and there must have been many small crises in the course of his Mission's growth.

There are other "what ifs" as well. What if Jermy had been able to find a stronger successor to take over, resulting perhaps in more cohesiveness, growth and cooperation among the five mission stations? What if they had continued to thrive until the coming of the Shirleys and the Railton group?

What if they had kept in closer touch with Jermy—or better yet—with the Christian Mission in England? Certainly, then, they would have known that this new Salvation Army and their Mission were one and the same. If they had known that the Shirleys in Philadelphia as well as Railton's "invasion" in New York were, in essence, an answer to Jermy's earlier plea for reinforcements, and if they had reached out and made contact with them, the new Salvationists' quasi-military distinctiveness might have provided a great impetus for their work, just as it was doing in England.

This does not mean that Jermy's work was in vain. He left behind five congregations of believers, and certainly many of them must have been of sufficient spiritual maturity to grow and thrive with the guidance of the Bible and the Holy Spirit. Perhaps some of the five stations later took on new names, thus obscuring their beginnings. Or perhaps the members gravitated to other established churches nearby. There is no reason to assume that Jermy's efforts came to naught.

Another question is seemingly more puzzling. Why didn't Railton try to make contact with the work in Cleveland? He must have Known of Jermy's efforts and of his successes; after all, both Jermy and Railton were closely associated with William Booth, who had been fully informed about the Cleveland enterprise and had enthusiastically written to Jermy at the time, as well as reporting the Cleveland successes in the *Christian Mission Magazine*. How could Railton *not* have known? The answer may lie in an understanding of Railton's unique mindset. He seems to have seen himself as a pioneer, enduring hardship for Christ, reaching out to virgin territory, leaving the "plowed and planted fields" to others. As for Jermy's Cleveland ministry, we can only trust in the words of Isaiah 55:11: that the Lord would not allow His Word to return to Him void.

"Invasion Ii" — A Second Wave

It was true that Annie Shirley, with her daughter, Eliza, came to America, first and foremost, to join Amos, Annie's husband, who had already found employment in a silk mill near Philadelphia. They wanted the little family to be complete, but as devoted Salvationists who perforce had left the Army in England, they sorely missed the soul-saving work they had known at home. As Annie later recalled, they started the Army work in America because "we could not live without it." When William Booth received word that the Army was indeed "up and running" in America, his remarkably prompt reaction to their request might have been partly because he didn't want to see a parallel group, perhaps even bearing the same name, without a tie to the parent organization. Furthermore, enthusiastic Salvationists were beginning to emigrate elsewhere from England. In his love for the Army, he probably feared the possibility of "his" Army being divided, with no central coordinating leader, and scattered around the globe. No wonder Railton and his group were dispatched only two weeks after receipt of the Shirleys' initial enthusiastic report!

Note the timetable of events. On March 10 Railton and his "splendid seven" marched down the gangplank to "claim America for Christ." New York's Mayor Edward Cooper registered strong disapproval of their methods and, in very tangible ways, made his displeasure known. For the moment at least, New York was seen as stony ground. Railton decided that Philadelphia showed prospects as being a more logical place for his new headquarters. The commissioner arrived there on

March 24, two weeks after his New York arrival. A special public meeting was held for the ceremonial presentation of Catherine Booth's Salvation Army flag. Let Edward McKinley tell it: "When he arrived at the hall, Railton was stunned; it seemed to him to be 'the biggest meeting of my life.' There were over two hundred cheering soldiers on the platform, each with a Salvation Army hat band. Fifteen hundred people crowded into Athletic Hall, hired for the festivities. For the rest of his life Railton retained a vivid memory of the three Shirleys singing to the crowd the notable black American spiritual, 'My Lord, What a Mourning, When the Stars Begin to Fall!'"

Philadelphia became the official headquarters of the movement in the U.S., and remained so for another year. When Railton reported to the General that there were eight corps in America, six of the eight were in Philadelphia. In McKinley's words, "The two Shirley corps were mined to provide leadership for four more." But New York was not entirely abandoned. Railton's first news sheet, The Salvation News, told of the valiant fight being waged by "brave Captain Westbrook," who had been left in command of New York No. 1 on Seventh Avenue, where she preached the gospel and collared roughnecks. Railton took long train trips to find likely places to "open fire." By autumn there were 12 corps in the U.S., and 1,500 souls had been saved. Franklin, PA, was opened as the "7th Pennsylvania," and in October two converts traveled to "open fire" in Baltimore, just a year after the Shirleys had begun.

A Kindly Kettle Worker

Dr. Norman Vincent Peale, with his skill at bringing the commonplace to life, wrote of Ursula, a girl in her teens who had come from Switzerland and spent some time as a live-in guest in his home for the purpose of perfecting her use of the English language. In return she acted as secretary, baby-sitter and in short, became a member of the household.

One of her tasks in the days preceding Christmas was to keep track of the gifts as they arrived. There were many and all would require an acknowledgment. She kept a faithful record, but the mere volume of gifts filled her with a growing sense of inadequacy. With her limited allowance how could she buy gifts for the family that wouldn't seem pathetically paltry? It seemed they already had everything.

Finally she had an idea. Although it was true that many people in the great city of New York had far more than she did, there had to be many who had far less. Her next day off was the day before Christmas. She would have to carry out her plan, from beginning to end, in that single day.

Wandering through a large department store, she finally selected a lovely outfit for a tiny baby—a very poor baby—and had it gaily wrapped. But where to find a baby belonging to a very poor family? Surrounded by the uptown aura of prosperity, how could she even begin to find a neighborhood such as she sought? Her inquiries to passersby about finding a "very poor street" drew mostly puzzled stares or mumbled responses. A uniformed doorman said she might try Harlem or the Lower East Side, but when she asked a policeman for directions to Harlem he said, "Harlem's no place for you, Miss."

She began fear she was on a fool's errand when, at a busy intersection she heard the cheerful tinkling of a Christmas kettle bell. At once, she felt better. The Salvation Army was a part of Switzerland, too. She crossed over to the bell ringer and said, "Can you help me? I have here a present for the poorest baby I can find."

"What sort of present?" He asked.

"A little dress for a small, poor baby. Do you know of one?"

"Of more than one, I'm afraid," he replied. "Is it far away? I could take a taxi maybe."

The Salvation Army man said, "It's almost six o'clock. My relief will show up then. If you want to wait, and you can afford the ride, I'll take you to a family in my own neighborhood who needs just about everything."

"And they have a small baby?"

"A very small baby."

"Then," said Ursula joyfully, "I wait."

The substitute came. Once in the welcome warmth of a taxi, Ursula told her new friend what she was trying to do. He listened in silence, and the driver listened, too.

When they arrived before a dark tenement, the driver said, "Take your time, Miss. I'll wait for you."

The Salvation Army worker said, "They live on the third floor. Shall we go up?"

But Ursula shook her head. "They would try to thank me. Take it up, please. Say it's from… from someone who has everything."

Back at the Fifth Avenue apartment she fumbled at her purse, but the driver flicked the flag up.

"No charge, Miss"

"No charge?" Echoed Ursula.

"Don't worry," the driver said, "I've been paid." He smiled at her and drove away.

Christmas morning, Ursula thanked everyone for the gifts she received, then hesitantly tried to explain why there seemed to be none from her. When she finished, there was a long silence. "So you see," said Ursula, "I try to do a kindness in your name. And this is my present to you."

THE ORDER
FOUNDER
of the

OUR AMERICAN HONOR ROLL

A Representative Hero

In World War I, some German immigrants were torn in their loyalties between their old homeland and the new. In short, we had a few spies and saboteurs in our midst. (It need hardly be said that, by World War II, virtually all German-Americans were loyal to the United States. Hitler did not seem to arouse their sympathies!)

The account in the next paragraph is given credence by something that happened soon afterward: three "women" tried to get into Commander Evangeline Booth's office while she worked late in the evening. They had a gift, they said, which could not wait until morning. Their insistence upon visiting her that night aroused suspicion, and they were asked to come back the next day. The police, when notified, picked them up nearby, penetrated their disguise, and found them to be not only men rather than women, but heavily armed as well.

Not long before, the New York Training College had burned down. The building was no firetrap; it had been a mansion, later leased by the Metropolitan Museum of Art for notable exhibits, then sold to The Salvation Army for use as a school. Yet the fire spread almost in a flash. Firemen said it must have been "smeared" with fuel and set ablaze by an arsonist.

Significantly, sleeping directly over the place where the fire started were several lassies waiting to sail for France in a day or two as war workers. The morale-boosting effect of the Salvationists was becoming a concern to the enemy.

A few days later, a detective eating lunch in a small German restaurant on a side street overheard a conversation: "Well, if we can't burn them out, we'll blow up the building and get that (expletive) Commander anyhow!" (The Headquarters was next door to the Training College, but it had been saved by a heavy fireproof wall.) The Commander was offered a bodyguard by authorities, but she declined.

The cadets, who had had frequent fire drills, reacted to the disaster with remarkable courage and coolness, a fact noted by the firemen. Without a doubt, their discipline under stress saved many lives. Some were truly heroic. One man died when he went back in to find a cadet unaccounted for. (Ironically, the cadet for whom he was searching got out.) Many acted in a way that "would have specially commended itself to our Beloved Founder"—to quote from the 1917 announcement of the award. In a sense, one person was chosen to represent all: Cadet George Benack, the cadet-watchman who discovered the fire. A cripple, he climbed to the top story, woke the men cadets on every floor, and ran into the street to the fire alarm box. Perhaps others did as much or more, but he was chosen because of the responsibilities he had so faithfully discharged. He did what was expected of him in a time of danger and difficulty. We can all do likewise.

A "Death Sentence" — A Divine Reprieve

The story of Henry F. Milans is one that every Salvationist should know for at least two good reasons.

First, it was chronicled by Clarence W. Hall in his memorable book, *Out of the Depths.* Grippingly told, it is available to anyone with the interest to seek it out.

Secondly, the account is much more than yet another story of God's grace applied to a hopeless alcoholic's condition. Henry Milans was not a ne'er-do-well who drank too much; he was a man of character and great ability who fell from the heights to the gutter.

Having started drinking as a very young man, he struggled to keep alcohol "in its place" for many years. But drink gradually gained the upper hand, and his life took on the character of a roller-coaster ride. In the "highs" he was editor of the *Southport Chronicle,* suburban editor of the *New York Tribune,* night editor of the *New York Recorder,* and managing editor of the *Daily Mercury*—but not in that order.

Finally, he spent three terrible years as a helpless skid row bum. In the alcoholic ward of Bellevue Hospital, a university medical professor used him as a "specimen" to show the end results of prolonged excessive drinking, the last stage before the grave. He was declared totally incurable and beyond the point where his life could be saved—all of this in his hearing. To the doctor-teacher it hardly mattered if Milans heard his words; he was beyond medical help, and if he wasn't beyond human feeling, he soon would be.

Soon afterwards, when a Salvation Army lassie found him huddled under a warehouse loading platform, nearly frozen to death on a Thanksgiving morning, events were set in motion which kindled his faith and led within a week to his glorious conversion. When he surrendered to Jesus Christ, all appetite for alcohol was taken away. He was new; clean; changed!

In his new life, he found new prosperity, reunion with his mother, and reconciliation with his wife. In his wife's case, it was more than mere reconciliation. Not too long after their reunion, she began to show signs of grave illness. Apparently it was cancer, although the biographer never names that dread word. Milans was a great comfort and a tower of strength to her in those final months—but not only that. Though his wife had been a church-goer herself, she had never been shown the way to true salvation. It was her husband, so tardy himself in coming to the Lord, but such a remarkable a trophy of grace when he finally did find the way, who led her gently into the experience of salvation.

His strong personal influence extended far beyond his own family, as well. He counseled hundreds of alcoholics, man-to-man when possible, and maintained a remarkable follow-up by correspondence. He donned Salvation Army uniform, spoke to countless thousands, and for years wrote a weekly column for *The War Cry*. His was a life of great influence and inspiration for over thirty-five years after that doctor's gloomy and seemingly certain prognosis!

So rich in drama, so full of hope for the alcoholic was the life of Milans that Dr. J. Wilbur Chapman, famous evangelist, undertook to write his biography, but died before finishing it. He once said, "I know all the famous converts of America, but Milans is the greatest of them all."

She Found the Prison Key

Ida Mae Jessop, born in Indiana in 1862, was orphaned early in life. Her foster parents instilled in her Christian values which she never forsook. When she married Marcus A. Lewis, they moved to Bennet, Nebraska. Friends in Bennet often visited an uncle who was the warden of the state penitentiary in Lincoln. Through these friends, Mrs. Lewis came to know the warden and visited his "pen" when she was 27 years of age. What she saw moved her profoundly. She began to visit the prison every Sunday, making the forty-mile trip by horse and buggy to teach God's Word to her "boys." At first, she was viewed with curiosity and amusement by inmates, and some prison officials tolerated her persistence simply because she was a friend of the warden.

Mr. Lewis, concerned for his wife's welfare during those long Sunday trips, moved the family into Lincoln to be near the prison. Soon she approached The Salvation Army. She had noted their unchallenged entree into the prison and feared that she, without organizational backing, might be barred when a new warden took over. After all, it was only a family friendship that had unlocked the prison doors for her until then.

Already a strong Christian, she gladly enrolled as a Salvation Army soldier, wore the uniform, taught an afternoon Sunday school class at the Red Shield Center, and was active in the Home League. But Sunday mornings she was at the penitentiary, where her large Sunday school class (now thought to have been the only one of its kind at the time) had a profound effect on many of the men. Out of one class, five later became ministers.

A young Irishman, left an orphan as a small boy, had ended up in prison. Mrs. Lewis became a spiritual mother to him, and his conversion brought a great change. On leaving prison, James P. Sullivan became an evangelist and never forsook that calling. The joy that had come into his life was reflected in the choruses he wrote: "Oh, say but I'm glad" and "It's bubbling," to name only two of many. The "key" to continued and unhindered prison visitation through the changing policies of fifteen different wardens may have been her Salvation Army uniform, but the key to the men's hearts was Mrs. Lewis's caring spirit. She radiated love; in short, she had those qualities of a real mother that many of the men had missed in their own childhoods. No wonder everyone within the walls called her "Mother"!

Mother Lewis fought for the removal of the ball and chain, which every inmate still wore, and she gave authorities no peace until a hospital and a chapel were built for the prisoners. She also pressed for the hiring of a prison chaplain, which did indeed take place. For a time, when there was an interval between chaplains, the state appointed Mrs. Lewis the official chaplain, the only time she ever received money for her labors.

For over sixty years, she visited one Thursday a month as well as every Sunday. Not only did she lead many to Christ, but her close follow-up gave men the hope and self-respect needed to "make good" after release. They could not let her down!

Mrs. Lewis was admitted to the Order of the Founder in 1944. Her work went on until she was injured by a fall six weeks before her death in 1951.

One Great Heart to Another

There were great contrasts in the backgrounds of Henry F. Milans and Mrs. Ida M. Lewis, but one incident linked them together with a common bond.

Milans was a man of great ability. In his early forties, he seemed to be a man destined for the top. Already he was managing editor of a major New York newspaper, anticipating more than twenty years of productive working life ahead of him. Ten years later, he was diagnosed as being in so advanced a stage of alcoholism that nothing was left for him but the grave—likely within weeks or months.

After he allowed the Lord to come into his life, there was a dramatic turnaround. The abilities which had been squandered and dissipated through heavy drinking were still retrievable, and this "trophy of grace" made a new career for himself. But this was not why he received the Order of the Founder. It was his caring, loving ministry to fellow alcoholics, his after-work hours given unstintingly to others, his effective application of the gospel message to fellow victims in far-flung places through his fellowship-by-mail.

One could hardly find a sharper contrast than that presented by a onetime bustling New York editor and a small-town Nebraska housewife rearing seven children and traveling long hours to be with her "boys" in prison. Her gifts did not seem to be those of executive ability, eloquence or brilliance in any field, but rather a Christlike love for others and a perseverance that would not let go. Here, she and Milans were on common ground.

During World War II, when Mrs. Lewis's Order of the Founder medal was delayed mid-Atlantic aboard a ship in submarine-infested waters and the time for its presentation neared, Milans was asked to lend his for the actual pinning-on ceremony. In his accompanying letter, he said, "I have been in jail myself, and I can easily understand how glad the men are when they see your dear face before them and hear your kindly words of sympathy and direction. Seems to me that they would just have to be better men for your visit."

He mentioned that he had by then spent thirty-four years in his ministry to "drunkards and outcasts," and he pointed out a coincidence. "I, too, am eighty-four years old. My days may end suddenly any time now; but I'm going to keep at it until I drop." And again, "I will now pray daily for your work and your health."

And so the same medal was used twice, pinned on two great hearts who did not know the meaning of the word "self."

There is a footnote to this story. Mrs. Lewis's medal eventually found its way across the submarine-infested Atlantic, though not in time for the presentation. Milans, of course, received his back soon after the simple ceremony, and Mrs. Lewis treasured hers until her death, when it was passed on to her granddaughter, Clara (Mrs. Stanley) Scoby, a faithful Salvationist.

Samuel Logan Brengle

Perhaps of all American Salvationists, the one who would be voted "most likely" to receive the Order of the Founder is Commissioner Samuel Logan Brengle. So it is no surprise to learn that he did indeed receive it. But the very reasons which elevate him in the regard of Christians are the very reasons which tend to make him and his doctrine of holiness seem beyond the reach of the man in the street. First, his saintly life is acknowledged by one and all—even by many who have read nothing by or about him! Second, he is legendary for the ability he had to make the doctrine of holiness come alive for the most untutored of listeners. Unfortunately, the word "legendary" has come to surround almost everything about the man.

The subtitle of Clarence W. Hall's excellent biography of Brengle, *Portrait of a Prophet*, is an accurate description—if we take the trouble to learn what "prophet" means in the Bible. Too many people unthinkingly consign prophets to a dusty shelf mislabeled "little plaster saints" and these days rarely take time to pick them up and dust them off.

Sam Brengle grew up in rural Indiana and Illinois. His father died in the Civil War when Sam was very young; his mother died a few years later, so he knew the deep loneliness of a teenager without living parents.

In college, he distinguished himself as an orator and debater. A fraternity brother, perhaps his closest friend at the time, shared a similar ambition: to go into law and to gain fame. The friend became a prominent U.S. Senator as well as a Pulitzer Prize-winning author. Another "frat brother" served later as an ambassador to three countries, so the young men's dreams were not unrealistic. These were sharp young men—Brengle no less than the others.

But God's working in his life eventually led Brengle to renounce such ambitions, although he said later that his greatest temptation was the realization, in times of trial, that he had given up a great deal of recognition to become a Salvation Army officer.

We would be foolish to neglect Brengle's books because we mistakenly assume he wrote his material in some rarified atmosphere, or because we think that a man with a doctorate and the rank of Commissioner could not possibly have shared our experiences and temptations.

The following little story, trivial though it be, does show something of Brengle's true humanity, his sense of humor, and the fact that he was not so sensitive that he'd be horrified or would fall to pieces if someone swore in his presence. A carpenter who was making a repair in the Brengle home mislaid his hammer. Looking around and not seeing it, he muttered, "Where in hell's that hammer?" Brengle, who was standing nearby, could see it on a step of the ladder. So he picked it up and, handing it to the workman, said with a bit of a smile, "You won't have to go that far; it's right here."

Brengle Speaks for Himself

Commissioner Samuel Logan Brengle still looms large on The Salvation Army's spiritual landscape. He is often quoted in holiness meetings and officers' councils.

During his lifetime, some of his listeners almost feared to talk to him one-to-one. They imagined he must be austere and that behind those alert eyes was a spiritual discernment that could see right through them! Yet he possessed humility, a great sense of humor, a gift for putting people at ease, and a readiness to kneel in prayer at any moment in any place to share his Savior and Sanctifier with a prominent businessman or a humble servant or laborer. Perhaps some felt uncomfortable with a man who might at any moment have them on their knees!

We cannot encapsulate Brengle's message, his ministry, and the essence of the man himself within the limits of a couple of pages. Instead, let's give him a chance to speak for himself. In a letter, he said:

> "Why are so many people afraid of me before they see me?
> They think that holiness makes my eyes flames of fire, that
> I will have no mercy on their infirmities, that they will be

searched and showed up as on the Judgment Day. And when they find out what a human creature I am, that I can laugh and be happy, it is such a surprise and a relief to them.

"There is nothing about holiness to make people hard and unsympathetic and difficult to approach. It is an experience that makes a man preeminently human; it liberates his sympathies, it fills him with love to all mankind, with compassion and pity for them that are out of the way. And while it makes him stern with himself, it makes him gentle with others. It is sin, selfishness, pride, self-conceit, and bad tempers that make one hard to approach. The spirit of Jesus in the heart, which is the spirit of holiness, makes all men brothers and brotherly."

And in an interview with a newspaper reporter:

"I am a constant student in God's school, the University of Hard Knocks. I have forgotten much that I learned in two universities, much of the Latin, the Greek and the Hebrew. But I will never forget the lessons I have learned in God's school. It is there that moral fiber is developed. When I get to heaven I'm not going to ask Daniel how many feather-beds he slept on in Babylon, but I am anxious to ask him about the night he spent in the lions' den. And the first thing I am going to ask Paul is about the shipwreck, and the times he spent in prison. It takes these things to make a man." Brengle was right on target!

Youth Has a Part to Play

Jeanetta Hodgen's early life was a series of disasters. Her parents were newly arrived Russian immigrants, and no record remains of what Christian name they gave her. Her father was a habitual drunkard. Before she was old enough to walk, he kicked her down a flight of stairs, resulting in serious back injuries, life-long physical deformity, and later attempts at surgery which ultimately led to her premature death. The father was never to realize the enormity of his brutal treatment, because he died soon afterwards in a drunken brawl. The mother died before the little girl reached the age of two. There were no other relatives.

She was taken in as a foster child by a couple who gave her the name she was to keep. Nevertheless, her childhood was difficult and unhappy. For reasons now unknown, she had left them by age twelve and, quite alone in the world, hired herself out to a family with a farm near Greeley, Colorado. Interviewed later, the corps officer who had served nearby at that time said of Jeanetta, "She was used almost as a slave. Being large and strong, she worked in the fields."

At the Greeley Corps a contest had been launched to bring in new young people. Some enterprising youngster found Jeanetta and brought her in. A hulking, ungainly fifteen year old with a bent back and plain features, she was dressed in men's work shoes and rough overalls.

She could have been shunned by the other young people; after all, she was unattractive, a school dropout, not at all "tuned in" to the ways of her contemporaries. But they treated her "like family." In fact, the corps really became her home. But because of her traumatic childhood, it took time for Jeanetta to learn to trust implicitly and to accept love unquestioningly. Thus it was two full years before she accepted Christ into her life, but in all that time she was kept in close fellowship by caring new friends—young friends who could so easily have displayed adolescent cliquishness.

How could these youngsters in their wildest dreams have imagined that, of them all, Jeanetta would be the one to receive the Army's highest award, the Order of the Founder? They simply accepted her as she was, with no inkling of the work of grace that would be wrought in her. It would never have happened if the kids in Greeley had "frozen her out."

She Did What She Could

The first really good thing that ever happened to Jeanetta Hodgen was being taken to a Salvation Army Sunday school as a fifteen year old. After Salvationists arranged for her to leave the farm where she had hired on as laborer at age twelve, she went to live with YPSM Mrs. Ahrend of the Greeley Corps, who found her something to wear besides men's work shoes and bib overalls so she would look more like the other teenagers.

It can take more than kindness to win a person to Christ. The Salvationists offered love and security with no strings attached, but evidently Jeanetta's "hidden wounds" were deep, and it took time for her to respond to love with a love of her own. Two years elapsed before she knelt in surrender to the Lord.

Meanwhile, one of the Salvationists had taught her cookery, discovering a natural aptitude, and at age sixteen Jeanetta went to work as a hospital diet cook. Before she was eighteen she had entered Training College, seemingly with little to offer but her cooking skill and a capacity for hard work. But as she grew as a Christian, the desire grew in her heart that she might work with disadvantaged young girls. If only she could do for them what the Greeley Salvationists had done for her!

Lieutenant Hodgen was appointed to Hawaii and placed in charge of a dormitory of forty-six young girls by night and a large laundry with ten girl-helpers by day. The laundry helped support the Salvation Army home for unwanted and abused girls. It was hard work, but she never tired of it. Many of the girls responded to her influence and accepted Christ.

After six years Jeanetta was sent to help an officer-couple in a new ministry among sugar-cane workers. Here she found many people suffering the ravages of beriberi because they ate little but rice. The former diet cook became a teacher as she showed mothers how to cook low-cost cuts of meat and to prepare balanced meals.

But Jeanetta's greatest work lay waiting for her in Damon Tract, a large piece of land given by a wealthy woman in an attempt to solve Honolulu's homeless problem. About 600 families had put up primitive shacks of corrugated iron, planks of wood, sheets of cardboard—any available material. Thanks to Hawaii's perpetually mild climate, the crude housing was not the serious problem it would have been on the U.S. continent, but this jumble of nationalities and races: Hawaiians,

Japanese, Chinese and Filipinos, with every mixture conceivable, was not a community. There were no recreational facilities, no wholesome activities for children or young people, very little attention paid by anyone to their spiritual welfare, and a long list of other lacks. Jeanetta gave up her town flat and moved into Damon Tract to be nearer "her people," as she called them. A small meetinghouse was erected, along with a little house for Jeanetta, but the premises had to be moved or enlarged four times to provide space for all who wanted to attend. The "Mother of Damon Tract" had her hands full from morning to evening. Youth work, classes for adults and, of course, cooking classes were packed into the weekdays, with meetings on Sundays.

Public schooling was provided nearby for the children, but until then, the building had stood empty all summer, while at the same time the Tract children were bored and often got into mischief. Jeanetta asked for the loan of the empty school building. The result was well-planned daily vacation Bible school for a couple of hours daily. Eight teachers were employed to take the children through an interesting curriculum. This went on for the next 10 years, with 300 children filling the classrooms daily, summer after summer.

During the regular school year there were many toddlers and small children not yet in school, some with no supervision during the day. Jeanetta started a nursery school with thirty of these children. The idea snowballed to another center which took in 100 preschoolers. Nine years later it was reported that 260 preschoolers were attending nursery schools led by Major Hodgen and her staff of nine helpers.

Through the nearest corps the major started a Home League, which can serve so effectively as a means of education and uplift. She made the most of the Home League's potential for those purposes, and soon she was running no less than seven separate leagues! She welcomed the opportunity to teach good homemaking, nutritious cooking and the many things which make for healthy, happy families.

There is no space to tell of her almost crushing schedule after Pearl Harbor and all during World War II. In 1946, Honolulu's Rotary Club presented Jeanetta with a gift inscribed "For the year's most significant achievement in promoting the ideal of service."

Five years later, she was suddenly promoted to Glory at the age of fifty-one. She was laid to rest in Damon Tract, where she had given so much of her life for the people she loved, and who dearly loved her.

A Different Kind of Courage

Captain George Benack was the first American to receive the Order of the Founder. He was the "night watch" cadet on duty at the time of a disastrous fire in the Training College in New York during the latter part of World War I. It was he who discovered the fire. In those days (before one could dial 911!), he had to run into the street to a public fire alarm box, then run back into the building and alert as many as possible to the danger. Within minutes, there were others pitching in to help, of course, and at least two other cadets were cited by name in *The War Cry* at the time for their heroism.

But Benack was the one officially on duty. Furthermore, he was somewhat crippled but had overridden his handicap to carry out his duties successfully in the emergency. Not surprisingly, he was the one selected for recognition, it being tacitly understood that in a sense he represented the others, since all had shown remarkable discipline and cool-headedness during the crisis.

One of the others declared a hero by *The War Cry* was Ernest ("Dutch") Higgins. For him there was no decoration, no Order of the Founder. But Higgins did not see in this a reason to feel slighted. He was too cheerful by nature, always too busy looking forward to the next challenge, to think about not having received such an honor. In fact, the possibility of his being considered for such recognition probably never occurred to him. So perhaps it is an odd twist that, thirty-six years after his heroism on that fateful night, the award came to him. It came to him for great courage, but courage of a sort quite different from that required for those few desperate minutes in his cadet days.

A review of his career reveals a capable officer who commanded three corps, served in the territorial finance department, and was director of three adult rehabilitation centers. He also had three appointments as a divisional commander.

But what is not revealed by mere facts and figures is that this work was carried out against a background of increasing pain and debilitation. From the time he was relatively young, arthritis had been slowly, inexorably taking its toll. Eventually he was confined to a wheelchair. He became so immobilized that, when his wheelchair was carefully eased into a van or panel truck to take him from one engagement to another, he could not even duck his head to avoid hitting the top of the doorway of the vehicle. It was up to those moving him to take whatever measures were necessary to be sure his head was not injured in these maneuvers. Friends found it painful to see him in this condition, knowing the agony he must be enduring.

But he found administrative work he could do; for seventeen years he was secretary of the Evangeline Residence Department. Subsequent reports said, "Much progress was made under his direction," and "Many were counseled and won for the Kingdom of God." He triumphed over personal difficulties and concentrated on helping others. Without self-pity he went far beyond the call of duty, always with a cheerful, buoyant spirit. It was for this patient, persevering courage that he received the Order of the Founder.

A Spiritual Father

This is the story of a seemingly "failed" mission. It took place in the "bad old days" in Alaska. After the huge tract of land (more than twice the size of Texas) was purchased by the United States from Russia in 1867, the treaty of cession stated that people living in the ceded territory could, if they chose, remain and be "admitted to the enjoyment of all the rights and immunities of citizens of the United States." These words, however, were really meant only for white men who had chosen to live in Alaska, because the guaranty of "rights and immunities" added: "…with the exception of the uncivilized tribes." The treaty went on to say that "the uncivilized tribes will be subject to such laws and regulations as the United States may from time to time adopt in regard to the aboriginal tribes of that country."

Today we would probably say that the life of the people who made up those "aboriginal tribes," as the treaty called them, was necessarily simple and frugal, since they drew their livelihood from the inhospitable and precarious ecosystem of the arctic and subarctic. But they had learned to cope admirably, and they had a complex culture which only an insensitive outsider would brand as "uncivilized." The promised laws took a long time in coming about. For seventeen years no action was taken regarding the newly purchased territory except to "protect financial interests," and a competent historian tells us that virtually nothing was done for these people for thirty years.

But while politicians sat on their hands, itinerant adventurers were not so slow to move. "Murder, rapine and lawlessness moved in," wrote Major-General Grielery in his Handbook of Alaska, and white men brought whisky (sic), prostitution and other vices. The condition of the Indians deteriorated alarmingly, and in some areas the death toll among them was devastating as their bodies tried in vain to cope with white men's diseases.

One who tried to counter these effects of "civilization" was the Rev. Charles Edwards, a Quaker who first took the gospel to the town of Kake. He lived with the Indian people in a community house, one of the great multiple-family winter dwellings. A small boy, whose parents, upon conversion, gave him the Christian name of Charles, was allowed to ring a small silver bell with which Edwards called the people to his services.

When a schooner laden with liquor put into Kake, the missionary, fearing the effect of the liquor upon his little group of converts, went from house to house in the village, warning them not to touch the fiery drink. Edwards went out to the ship and faced the schooner's captain who, in a rage, brutally shot down the gentle Quaker on the deck of his ship. Mortally wounded, the missionary was thrown on the beach, where he died. A tragedy? Yes. But as always, the Lord had the last word!

A Dream Fulfilled

When Quaker missionary Charles Edwards was killed while trying to keep liquor out of the Alaskan village of Kake, little Charles Newton, the Thlinget Indian boy who had rung the silver bell for services, grieved over the death of his friend and hero. As Commissioner A. J. Gilliard says in his book, *Gentle Eagle,* "The blood of a martyr was taken up as it ran on the beach ... and poured into the waiting heart of another disciple-to-be."

No missionary replacement was sent to the village; in fact, it may have been some time before the homeland Quakers even knew of the murder. The boy's parents, Timothy and Lucy Newton, had been truly converted, even though Edwards did not live to give them much instruction. Since their little son was by heredity a chief, they saw to it that he successfully underwent the rites demanded at puberty so that, one day, the tribe would have a Christian leader.

Circumstances forced them to leave their hometown for a time, and during that sojourn they met William Benson, another Indian who had become a Christian, and subsequently an evangelist. At first, he was used by the Presbyterians, but after a break with them he drifted for a time, hardly knowing how to use his great powers of oratory. He found work as a laborer for prospectors in the Klondike during the Gold Rush and was there when Evangeline Booth made her famous visit. The two met. She sensed his great ability, and he implored her to let him preach for The Salvation Army. She counseled with Benson, gave him a cap and a guernsey, a song book, and her blessing.

He crossed over into Alaska and there encountered the displaced Newtons. The seed planted by the martyred Quaker now sprang to life, and they returned to Kake to begin a Salvationist ministry. Later, brief training with Major Robert Smith, the Army's first officer in Alaska, resulted in Charles's being made a "sergeant" and his parents becoming more grounded in Army doctrine and methods. Soon afterwards, Timothy and Lucy sent Charles to an Indian school in Oregon to equip him for a more effective life of service. Upon his return from school,

Charles was made sergeant-major of the Kake corps. Without going to Training College, he received a direct commission to the rank of field-captain, an unsalaried position. Thus, he had to go into business to support his family. Repeatedly, he was elected mayor of the town. In his four-fold role of corps officer, tribal chief, mayor, and successful businessman, he brought about much good for Kake.

And true to the dream of Quaker missionary Edwards, he led in keeping Kake "dry" during his forty years of leadership. Charles Newton was admitted to the Order of the Founder in 1946.

He Touched the Lives of Thousands

Brigadier Julius Mack Satterfield was a corps officer in the Southern Territory, commanding only eight corps in fifty-two years.

He stayed in two of them for ten years apiece, and finished in Winston-Salem, N.C., where he stayed for twenty-five. It would be great if we could extract those qualities which led to his receiving the Order of the Founder in 1954 and implant them in others. But of course we can't, and no one else seems ever to have been quite like "Mack" Satterfield, as he was known.

"Mack" had great empathy for troubled youth—not necessarily bad, but aimless or unhappy with home life, or feeling the power of undesirable peer pressure. He started a club for eighteen boys in a basement, gathering the loneliest, the toughest he could find. At the same time he told of the need to help such youngsters and of the resources it would take. He pounded away at this theme from his corps platform, at service clubs, before citizens' groups, in the press, on the radio, and later on television.

Soon his boys' club was greatly upgraded and became a part of the Boys' Clubs of America. But Mack was never hesitant about adding his Salvationism to his formula. The eighteen boys became hundreds, then thousands, as he organized clubs in one corps and then another. In a day when the needs of girls were not yet being fully recognized, he founded a girls' club. Through his simple, honest and direct way of outlining need and approaching people to help, he raised hundreds of thousands of dollars.

Perhaps his first truly outstanding accomplishment was the summer camp he started in Lakeland, Florida, and operated for six or seven years during the Depression for boys and girls of Polk County, with two-week sessions all summer long, with plenty of good food, a good staff, and all on a shoestring. And it wasn't subsidized; he just kept it going.

His other great accomplishment was surely the work he did in his twenty-five years in Winston-Salem. But even though his work there might seem to eclipse his earlier commands, one who followed his progress said, "In every city Satterfield was remembered with affection, admiration and sometimes awe for fifteen or twenty years afterward. It has been over fifty years since he left, and people still measure the Army by his ministry." It was not fund raising that made him great, but his simple faith in Christ, and his ability to see into the hearts of individuals and help meet the needs and the hunger he found hidden there.

View from a Wheelchair

Tragedy struck twice in a Barberton, Ohio, home—and then struck twice again. Or perhaps we should think long and carefully before using that word. For what is tragedy? It is partly what we make of it.

Two little girls in the Dunlap family contracted the dread disease of polio which, before the Salk vaccine, used to leave hundreds dead, deformed or paralyzed each year in this country. Eva and Helen Dunlap survived, but their paralyzed limbs did not develop, since they could not use their muscles. As if polio were not enough, it was followed by crippling arthritis, which deformed Eva's hands so badly that she could not pick up anything with her fingers. Both sisters were confined to wheelchairs for life.

In 1970 Brigadier Raymond Baines wrote, "Eva continued her education and rapidly learned to paint and print. With painful effort she learned to pick up a brush, pen or pencil in her lips and then to hold it between the 'heels' of both hands. In this way she began to express her love for God by painting and printing texts. She loved animals, and some of her best paintings are of dogs and cats.

"Both sisters were enrolled as soldiers of the Barberton Corps in 1918 and were determined to make their lives count for God's service. Both were avid Bible students. Eva was for many years Corps Cadet counselor and Young People's Legion secretary, and Helen was the young people's sergeant-major. Their voices were in perfect harmony and their duets are remembered to this day.

"Eva was especially gifted with a seemingly unending supply of energy, wit and zest for life and living. This made her most attractive to young people to whom she became confidant, advisor, counselor, teacher, guide and example. Many of Eva's young people, now men and women active in church and Army circles all over the country, owe much of what their lives have become to the influence of these two women.

"Eva produced, directed, cast and coached plays, cantatas and entertainments as well as designing sets and costumes. The sisters accompanied young people on hikes in their wheelchairs, pushed by willing hands, to picnics, ball games and all sorts of outings. They listened, comforted and helped, but never themselves were heard to complain…. Somehow, it never dawned on us that the Dunlap sisters were handicapped. We never thought about them having problems of their own as we took our problems to them."

Eva received the Order of the Founder in March 1946.

The Man Who Lived Two Lives

No, this is not about a "double life," nor about reincarnation. Yet the title fits the life of Henry Rostett. Born in Sweden, he came to the United States at age 18, became a Christian and a Salvationist, and soon entered Training College to become an officer. He felt a call to missionary service, but his reporting of this call to his superiors did not result in an overseas appointment. Nevertheless he served faithfully and wholeheartedly wherever he was sent. His life showed charac-teristics usually ascribed to missionaries: a great kindness and love, a true concern both for people's spiritual lives and their material needs.

Late in his career, as a divisional commander, he was more than an administrator and advisor; he was a shepherd to his officers. Assigned to a division with a number of chronically struggling corps, he was notably solicitous about the hardships facing some of his officers, and he was able to offer some practical remedies.

Rostett the leader never forgot his calling as an evangelist. While a divisional commander, during the summers, he would bring together a number of kindred spirits to form a small evangelistic team. They "hit the road," traversing the division, giving a lift to small corps and visiting remote places to bring music and the message of salvation.

Rostett was a skilled craftsman. Had it not been for the demands of officership, he would have loved spending long hours creating objects of beauty and utility in wood. In the little time he could spare for relax-ation and diversion, he demonstrated this skill in a few practical and (let it be said) impressive projects, but his beloved hobby never over-shadowed his calling. Someday, he thought, when public life was over he could become an artisan; there would be time enough in retirement.

But hopes for an active retirement faded when he was stricken with painful, crippling arthritis. The bitter irony was that the retirement he had once looked forward to as a time of fulfillment was thrust upon him prematurely, bringing with it nothing but enforced inactivity. Lt. Colonel and Mrs. Rostett moved to Florida, where it was hoped that the hours he spent baking in the sun would ease the pain and slow the progress of the affliction.

But the Lord had better plans for this would-be missionary who had missed the boat, this craftsman who had put away his tools. His destiny yet lay ahead! Rostett's condition improved greatly, so much so that he and his wife celebrated by taking a Caribbean cruise with friends, stopping in four island countries and visiting Salvationists in each. The last stop was Haiti, and the Rostetts were moved by the hunger and poverty, and the wretched conditions in which the

Salvationists were obliged to work. Before he left, the colonel promised the island commander, Captain Egger, that he would return to help.

Let it be said that such promises, often sincere enough, are easily made in the emotion of the moment, perhaps especially so when the one making the promise has been transported there by a cruise ship, with all travel arrangements taken care of!

But such was not the case with Rostett. For the next twenty years he fulfilled that promise, long after Captain Egger had moved on to other appointments and greater responsibilities. Rostett, who was now wonderfully restored to health, returned for at least a part of each year, setting up shop and making furnishings for the schools operated by The Salvation Army, as well as for the officers' quarters.

Later a theretofore unsuspected talent for architectural design manifested itself as he drew plans for a whole set of buildings— corps, schools, quarters. Then while back in the U.S. he would tell his story with words and slide projector. Through his stateside presentations over the years he raised hundreds of thousands of dollars for his building projects. Then, returning again to Haiti, he took an active part in building many of Haiti's present corps, quarters, and primary and secondary schools.

This "bonus" life in retirement was packed with accomplishment, climaxed by his being admitted to the Order of the Founder on June 11, 1976.

God's Messenger on Horseback

Daisy C. Brown, a young mountain woman fresh from the hills, hesitated to attend a city church for fear that her plain cotton dress would cause raised eyebrows. Her brother, whom she was visiting in town, suggested The Salvation Army. She'd never heard of it, but she attended and was made to feel welcome. One day, years later, this shy stranger would be awarded the Order of the Founder! Her case should make us all ponder: does our corps make everyone feel welcome?

Daisy came to prefer her middle name, Cecil, and it was as Major Cecil Brown that she wrote the following: "Lifting her head from her task, a busy mountain mother paused to give voice to a prayer that had been burdening her heart for long, but more especially since the increasing clamor of little voices about her feet had awakened her anew to the need. 'O God, send someone who cares back to these isolated homes where children are growing up without God, and without help!'

"Some years later," Major Brown continued, "a young Salvation Army captain, home on furlough, said, 'Mother, the next time I come back to these mountains, I'm coming to stay, for my next appointment is right here.' With the revealing intensity of a lightning flash came again the half-forgotten prayer of long ago, 'O God, send someone!' And the mother's heart leaped in response to this unexpected answer.

"I was that young Salvation Army captain, and truly I have been made to wonder at the mysterious ways God used to bring me up to that hour. By way of a visit to my married brother in Asheville, and the discovery of The Salvation Army in my search for a place where my simple dress would not arouse comment; then came a sudden gap in the ranks of the fighting force there, and I found myself filling the gap as temporary helper. The inevitable followed—Training College days, and then came a year as sergeant at the Training College, followed by several on the field as a corps officer. But all the while, in my heart was a burning for the people who were still as I had been, and finally came the day when I left the office of my divisional commander with my heart lighter than it had been in months—the door was open at last.

"And now, in somewhat the manner of the old Methodist circuit rider, I am making the rounds of five mountain centers, finding in each one testimony of God's past and present blessings. And not only that, but there comes almost daily the call of outstretched hands in new fields, and thus the future stretching out into an ever-widening horizon. I thank God that He 'works in mysterious ways His wonders to perform.'"

Perhaps one can be pardoned for wishing that Cecil Brown's humility had not prevented her, in her statement, from really doing justice to the scope and effectiveness of her work. How she managed to influence and help so many, in so many different ways, in so many places, is a mystery not fully explained in her own account. Incidentally, the five centers of which she wrote in her testimony were later increased to eight.

It is easy to overlook one resemblance between William Booth's early mission work in the teeming London slums and the situation Cecil Brown faced. In London the church had failed to bring about for most denizens of those crowded areas any meaningful religious life, though it was not through a lack of trying. Booth was dealing with a vast, virtually pagan population. Cecil Brown, in a sparsely settled mountain region, was trying to reach areas, some of which had once been visited fairly regularly by circuit riders, but where those preachers visited no more, and the influence of the Christian message was fading alarmingly. She realized that in some areas something akin to paganism was taking hold of the countryside. The causes were different, but the result was the same: populations almost entirely devoid of religious influence.

As a beginning, the headquarters for this mountain work was the hayloft of a barn belonging to Cecil's father, and one of her early meeting places was also a hayloft, swept and tidied, with the animals put outside for the duration of the meeting.

Many of the homes were far from a road, so that Cecil spent much time in walking, following winding trails for miles through areas where intruders were not welcome, and the sound of gunshots reminded her of a danger that was very real. Many of the homes were in areas so remote and out of touch with the outside world that the children never went to school. Indeed, there simply was no school within reach. And consistent with the remoteness of the region, large areas had no electricity, and water had to be carried in buckets from a spring.

Although Captain Brown had to walk as far as ten or twelve miles to reach some of those who needed her, she did have the use of a horse, and it was the image of the captain on horseback with which she was identified. This was in the early years of her work there, which opened in 1934. Her original area of responsibility in upper North Carolina was 105 square miles, so it would have been impossible to cover the territory from one center, even on horseback.

Some of the eight centers were tiny and, in some cases, similar to the cabins nearby, of rough-hewn logs with the chinks plastered to keep out the wind and weather. Three of the eight buildings tell a story indicative of the waning Christian testimony in the area. One was a frame church building of a major denomination which could no longer support a pastor there, or could not find one willing to serve in such a remote area. So it had sat for years, abandoned and forlorn, until Captain Brown came along. Another was even smaller, its story much the same. The third little church had been kept going by a woman who held on heroically as long as she could. But age was taking its toll, and she feared she could not go on much longer. She rejoiced when she was able to turn it over to Captain Brown with the assurance that the ministry would continue, even after her own life ended.

In the twenty-two years that Cecil Brown served the area, many paths and trails in the mountains were widened, and she was able to drive a jeep or car on many of her rounds. She sometimes had to serve as nurse, even as doctor in desperate situations, and more than once the jeep served as an ambulance to get someone to a hospital many miles away.

When a headquarters was built, it was designed to serve several purposes, one of which was to provide a boarding home for a number of promising girls who lived too far from any school to get even a minimum of education. Thus they lived at the Army and attended school in the little town, while Cecil saw to it that their education continued informally during their "off" hours with Christian teaching and practical training as future homemakers.

Salvation Army administrators did not leave Cecil without help. Other officers were later appointed to assist in the growing work, and she in a sense reciprocated by sending young people to Training College. She also received a title: District Officer of Mountain Missions. But this did not keep her from her hands-on work with the people she loved. Regrettably, not every aspect of her remarkable work can be included in these few paragraphs.

Her twenty-two years in the mountain work were all too short, but as was commonplace at the time of her promotion to Glory, nothing was said in print regarding health problems. At any rate, it is enough to know that she retired at the age of forty-nine and died two years later. Her story was told several times in print and is now available on video.

Let's end the story of Daisy Cecil Brown by repeating some of the sobriquets bestowed upon her: Maid of the Mountains, First Citizen of the Smokies, Shepherdess of the Hills, God's Messenger on Horseback, and to all of this The Salvation Army added its highest honor, the Order of the Founder.

The Young Doctor Noble

Colonel (Dr.) William A. Noble was awarded his M.D. at age twenty through a most unusual set of circumstances. In this, surely we see the hand of the Lord, who had a lot of work for him to do in the mission field. Not only did he commence young, but he continued his ministry of healing well past the age set for retirement.

Dr. Noble's story is so intertwined with that of other great hearts, as well as with a great hospital, that any effort to isolate his story from the rest is to miss much of its significance. Perhaps it should be mentioned here and now that any reader who is interested in learning more about the subject is urged to buy or borrow the book *The Double Yoke*, by Mrs. Colonel Lillian Noble.

Was officership and a long ministry as a medical missionary in the Lord's plans from the first for William Noble? Read the facts and decide for yourself. The Noble family belonged to the Free Church of Scotland. (There was no Salvation Army in their small Scottish town.) Not long after William was born they moved to Aberdeen, where Mrs. Noble was attracted to the Army and took her children to all the activities. At age four William gave his heart to Jesus. When the family moved to South Africa, and later back to Aberdeen, and later still to Sorrento, Florida, they remained active Salvationists. But in the town of Eustis, where the boy spent his formative years, there was no Army. So they joined the Christian Church.

The Lord, having a lot for young William to do in His vineyard, caused things to happen in a hurry. Without finishing high school, at the age of fourteen-and-a-half, William went to work full-time in a drugstore. Eager to learn, he took a "practical home course" by correspondence, receiving his diploma in the "Art of Pharmacy."

Two doctors who regularly visited the drugstore took an interest in Noble and encouraged him to apply for "medical college," as it was then called. William applied to a school in Atlanta and managed to be accepted—a sixteen-year-old high school dropout! He had to talk fast and convincingly, however, to gain admission, using his pharmacy diploma to demonstrate his initiative and commitment. That admission came none too soon! The whole status of medical colleges was about to be elevated to the graduate level, thus requiring not only a high school diploma but college work as well.

In his sophomore year, the school amalgamated with the other medical college in Atlanta, and in his senior year the combined schools were taken over by Emory University. At age twenty he had his M.D. degree from a respected institution.

But we're ahead of our story. When sixteen-year-old William first arrived in Atlanta, alone and friendless, he determined to go to church his very first Sunday. Looking for a corps (such as he had known in his childhood), he walked toward downtown, where he encountered an open-air meeting in progress. He had planned to find the Army, but the Army found him! From that day forward he was again a Salvationist, and when at age twenty he became Doctor Noble, his course was already set—a head start on a long and fruitful career of service.

Never Give Up

No sooner had young Captain (Dr.) William Noble and his bride, Etna, landed in India in 1920 to begin work as Salvation Army medical missionaries, than they began to get a foretaste of the difficult situations which awaited them. Did I say difficult? Impossible would be closer to the truth! Only a lengthy (and absolutely devastating) description could show what the young couple faced. That description does exist in the aforementioned book, *The Double Yoke.*

Often the discouragements were crushing, but this brave and spirited husband-wife team refused to be crushed. Hopefully, the mere bits and pieces given here will not so much satisfy the seeker-after-truth as to arouse interest and serve as an appetizer for the whole story.

After they arrived in India, it took time for them to get used to the heat, the pervasiveness of insects, rats and snakes, and the lack of recognizable sanitary facilities. The people's outlook on life, the utterly different social organization—these and many more things were totally foreign to them. But that was only a prelude to their assignment. Often they faced situations where the only rational diagnosis was, "It can't be done." But impossible or not, there were things that *had* to be done, and Dr. Noble did them.

We use words relating to heroes such as insurmountable or insuperable difficulties, forgetting in our careless use of language that these two adjectives are just other ways of saying, "Impossible! There's no way over this obstacle." But heroes refuse to believe it; they never give up, and the thing is finally done.

Lord, give us the grit, the guts and the grace to do Your will and Your work, even when the natural man within us says it's impossible.

A Noble Vision Realized

The story of Dr. Noble is naturally included in this series because he was admitted to the Order of the Founder. But we cannot consider this man apart from the context of the Catherine Booth Hospital. Nor can we be realistic in our understanding of the hospital without acknowledging the great contributions of the people who preceded Dr. Noble, the doctors and their wives who made the hospital what it was before he arrived. It must be added that a whole roster of missionary nurses contributed significantly to the "CBH". The line had to be drawn somewhere however, so the account which follows deals only with doctors and, in some cases, with their wives.

Thus, the "conclusion" of the Dr. Noble story which follows is, in two distinct senses, much more than a mere a conclusion. First, it serves as an introduction to the men who preceded him, to the men who made it all possible. Their stories appear on the following pages.

In the second place, there were men who followed Dr. Noble who enhanced and extended the services of the hospital and, perhaps more importantly, greatly improved the teaching of doctors and nurses who could go on to serve their own people in the years which were to follow. This became crucial when India's growing nationalism and desire for self-determination had a marked effect on the welcome sign which formerly greeted "foreign" missionary doctors to the subcontinent. We have had to accept the fact that we are now foreigners! It is also true that qualified Indian doctors are no longer scarce.

What can we say about Colonel Noble in a paragraph? Volumes could be written about his skills, his boundless energy, his compassion for the hurting masses, his ingenuity and his genius for finding ways to extend the services of the CBH in South India. Not only did he find ways to extend the services to meet great needs in the area, he found ways to get the equipment to do so, and ways to bring in more income so as to make such improvements possible.

Is it possible that some Salvationists still have a mental image of the CBH at the southern tip of India as something rather small and primitive, with corrugated iron roofs and mud bricks? If by chance there is anyone like that left, wipe that idea from your mind right now! True, this hospital had no electricity when Dr. Noble arrived in 1921. There was none anywhere in the area, as a matter of fact. The hospital "went electric" quite a while before the adjacent city of Nagercoil (not a small city, by any means) had any generators at all, and the "Army folks" have been in the vanguard of progress ever since.

What Dr. Noble left behind in 1960 was a hospital consisting of 64 permanent buildings, some of granite blocks, most of concrete.

In 1960 more than 13,000 inpatients were admitted to the hospital, plus 72,934 outpatients. In the eight branch hospitals there were an additional 1,235 inpatients admitted, plus 27,477 outpatients. That's a total of about 100,000 outpatients treated per year!

Then there were (and are) the leprosy hospitals, one set up and staffed with his own people but funded by the government, caring for 600, and the Evangeline Booth Leprosy Hospital at Puthencruz, with 190 patients at the time Dr. Noble retired. He gave the first radium treatments for cancer in South India, and continually updated the hospital's cancer treatment as new techniques were developed. There is a fine training school for nurses. The list goes on and on, but space does not!

Let this brief enumeration stand as a tribute to the life and ministry of Colonel and Mrs. Noble, while at the same time providing an indication of the kind and scope of work The Salvation Army is striving to do around the world.

The Divine Problem-Solver

The story of Harry Andrews is certainly instructive. In Harry's case, would it not seem suitable to consider the words given to Jeremiah the prophet by the Lord? "Before I formed thee in the belly I knew thee; and before thou camest forth out of the womb I sanctified thee, and I ordained thee a prophet unto the nations" (Jeremiah 1:5 KJV). Harry Andrews was not a prophet, but one wonders if the Lord had mapped out a plan for him even before he was born.

Look at the situation. Here was a tiny baby in whom He had undoubtedly placed a keen mind and a high energy level. By the time the baby was barely a teenager, he would display a remarkable love for the disadvantaged around him, and a great sympathy for those who were suffering. Naturally, the qualities of which I speak were not yet fully formed in the infant, but they would manifest themselves as he grew older.

The problem was in the environment. From all appearances, Harry would be locked into the enslaving effects of the industrial revolution, and by a 19th century English class system more binding and rigid than most of us today can comprehend. That's what Harry had to look forward to; just like the hundreds of thousands around him; hapless babies born to live on mean streets and to miss the chance for a decent education. He would likely go to work in a mill or a factory by the time he was ten years old and grind away at it for the rest of his life. His father worked fourteen hours a day and took home such paltry pay, even as a foreman, that the family could barely survive.

How could a baby in such a home be somehow transplanted so as to get him off those mean streets, to give him a chance to get the education which would allow him to leave a legacy of great service? How could such a baby be enabled to establish a trio of hospitals whose healing ministry would be undiminished a century later?

There was another item of business for the Lord to handle. This baby's destiny lay in India, yet William Booth had no thought at that time of starting any work outside of England. How to deal with this problem?

A copy of *The War Cry* found its way into the hands of a judge appointed to the British court system in India, an English gentleman halfway around the world. Not only would this judge take the unprecedented step of going back to England to meet this Salvation Army, but he would marry the very woman who, for a decade and a half, had acted as Harry's "mother"!

There is a postscript relevant to our country as well, since this man—this former judge in the British Empire—would one day become national commander for the United States.

Having given this long parenthetical statement, I ask you to sit back and watch how the Lord works out His plans!

Noble Predecessors – I
A Promise Fulfilled

It is an old saying that each generation stands upon the shoulders of the previous one. Colonel William Noble accomplished great things at the Catherine Booth Hospital in Nagercoil, South India, and the Order of the Founder bestowed upon him was well-deserved. But we can profit by remembering those who began the work he enlarged and extended. Although we have no room for more than a mention of those who have followed in our day, the hospital, in its century of existence, has seen an unbroken line of leadership, service and accomplishment.

To understand how the Catherine Booth Hospital came into existence in the first place, we have to go back to about the year 1870. Bramwell Booth, at the time a youth of seventeen, was doing house-to-house visitation in a poor section of London. He prayed with a Mrs. Andrews who, not long before, had given birth to a baby boy, named Henry (a.k.a. Harry) by the parents. The mother was certain that her death was imminent. Her husband, a foreman in a paper box factory, would be left with their other children to care for after his fourteen-hour days at work. Who could possibly care for the infant during the long hours of his absence? The other children were not old enough for such a responsibility.

Knowing Bramwell's parents and all they stood for, Mrs. Andrews implored the young visitor to promise that, if she died, he would take her new baby home to be brought up in the Booth family. The kindliness, concern and impulsiveness so typical not only of Bramwell but, incidentally, of his father were exhibited in his response to this request concerning the whole future life of a newborn baby. Without consulting his parents, he simply said "yes" to the woman's plea.

We can only imagine the reaction in the Booth home during the discussion which followed the death of Mrs. Andrews. Bramwell was obliged to tell of the promise he had made. The Founder may well have exploded, "You *what?*" He already had a large family to care for on a very modest income. Furthermore, both he and Catherine were away from home much of the time, caught up in the demands of the Christian Mission.

It says a great deal about the Booths that they made good on Bramwell's promise. The baby kept his own family name but grew up from that day forward in the Booth family. Since both William and

Catherine were so busy with other affairs, little Harry was mothered by Bramwell's younger sister Emma who, at age fourteen, was not very strong, and who had to stay home much of the time.

Later, when she became stronger, she was made principal of the Officers' Training Home at Clapton. Although she was no longer at home to care for Harry, this did not sever their relationship; she placed him in the Salvation Army nursery at Clapton, right close at hand.

As he received schooling and grew into his teen years, Harry's ties to the family remained close, so much so that later, when Emma married Frederick Tucker and they readied themselves to set sail and plant the Army's Blood and Fire flag on Indian soil, fifteen-year-old Harry Andrews begged to accompany his beloved "mother" overseas. He was allowed to go along, and the stage was set for a whole new phase of Army work.

Soon after his arrival some dental instruments, sent to him in India by Bramwell, set Harry on a course of practical helpfulness to the needy. Moved by the misery of India's poor, and appalled by the disease rampant on every hand, the teenager resolved to help as best he could. At least he could relieve the pain! Soon he became adept at wielding the dental forceps and the few other instruments at hand. His efforts began in Bombay, where he continued until he became an officer at age seventeen.

He was appointed to assist Major William Stevens at the headquarters in Nagercoil. Mrs. Stevens, becoming aware of the youth's practical sympathies and his keen desire to relieve suffering, observed, "The boy wants to heal bodies, and I'm going to make it easier for him. He shall have that little bathroom at the end of the verandah for a dispensary." Using his bathroom as a makeshift dispensary, he began to see long lines of sufferers each morning, working wonders with simple medicines and occasionally with dental forceps.

Later, on a furlough in England, Harry took steps to prepare himself for better service. He took an intensive course as a dresser, which by definition was a medical attendant higher in status than a nurse, but not as qualified as a doctor. Returning to India, he carried with him not only new skills and certification which gave formal recognition to his healing ministry, but a generous financial contribution to establish a truly adequate dispensary, the real beginning of Catherine Booth Hospital.

And what of the little bathroom where it all began? If you know any Army history at all, you probably know that the door leading to it has been preserved, being carefully kept in place. The simple bathroom upon which it once opened was removed long ago to make way for a much larger modern wing which incorporates up-to-date facilities. You can still swing that old door open and walk through, but what you enter is nothing like the original nineteenth century bathroom!

Perhaps Harry Andrews, if he could step through that doorway today, would feel a bit like Dorothy in the Wizard of Oz who, when she caught her first glimpse of Munchkinland, said to Toto, "I have a feeling we're not in Kansas anymore."

In like manner Harry might feel a bit disoriented by all that has changed, but doubtless he would be thoroughly delighted, perhaps bedazzled, by the enormous accomplishments of those who followed him.

Noble Predecessors – II
A "Macedonian Call"

When Harry Andrews, the founder of the Catherine Booth Hospital in Nagercoil, South India, went back to England to train as a dresser, he was able to return to India with three extremely important things. The first, of course, was his diploma as a dresser, a document carrying enough weight to enable him to do a good many things in the area of medical practice. It was a real step toward becoming a doctor.

The second was not something he actually carried with him, but it was to be of the greatest importance in the years to follow. During Harry's time of study in England, he met a young corps officer, Captain Percy Turner who, after encountering the Army and accepting Christ as Savior, had become a medical student. Halfway through his studies he committed himself to Salvation Army soldiership and would gladly have become an officer at once.

But after much thought and prayer, he heeded his father's counsel to finish his medical studies before taking such a step. Only then did he go to Training College. Thus he had his formal medical training but none of the experience he would have gained from private practice. In today's terms he was like a young M.D. who had finished school but had never had his internship. He loved his profession, but because he loved his Savior more, and greatly desired to preach the gospel, he set aside his skills, believing in simple faith that God, in some as yet unforeseen manner, would open a way for him to use his hard-earned qualifications.

Harry Andrews was thrilled to find such a man, and he was quick to tell of the great medical needs in India. Years later Turner said, "He was insistent with the 'Come over and help us' plea. We sat by the fire and talked for long hours. He made me feel willing to go." This was followed by an official consultation and a consequent agreement which gave Harry virtual assurance that in three years or less there would arrive in India a qualified doctor, with experience in private practice and a specialist's training, to meet the most pressing needs of patients who looked to Harry for help. Furthermore this doctor could then firmly establish and consolidate the work which Harry had launched.

Thus it was that in 1897 Harry Andrews returned to India, not only with his certification as a dresser and with the assurance that Captain Turner would follow later, but with a grant of money for the construction of the "Catherine Booth Dispensary." By the time Dr. Turner arrived, the new dispensary was a going concern, and with the presence of a full-fledged doctor, the stage was set for transition to a real hospital.

Andrews was then farewelled to do evangelistic work in another part of the subcontinent. But that also became a two-pronged ministry. It seems to have been almost inevitable that Harry, with his great heart of sympathy for suffering people and his boundless energy, would start another Army hospital in his new area.

There is a footnote to all of this which will interest Centralites. When things were finally in the hands of other capable people, Harry

Andrews took time to become a fully qualified medical doctor. He earned his doctorate at the medical school connected to the University of Illinois, located in Chicago.

In 1919 Andrews, by then long having been a doctor as well as Salvation Army officer, and having established a third hospital in India, was conscripted by the British government during an Indian uprising to care for wounded troops. He was non-combatant, of course, but was sent into some of the hottest combat. When a British unit was pinned down in an ambush, Andrews risked his life to treat the wounded on the field, fully exposed to rebel gunfire. Then he dragged or carried them to safety. While loading the last man into a van, Andrews was killed by a sniper's bullet. Thus he lost his life but won the Empire's highest award for bravery and gallantry in action, the Victoria Cross. No doctor since that time has ever been thus decorated.

Dayanasen: "Man of Loving Kindness"

There can be nothing more disheartening to a pioneer in any field than, upon his retirement or his transfer to another area of service, to see the work he commenced dwindle and wither away in the absence of his strong leadership. Harry Andrews, when he'd been trained as a dresser but not yet as a doctor, had two concerns. Not only was there no one to carry on his work when he eventually would be farewelled to pursue evangelism elsewhere in India, but his vision for a real institution of healing in Nagercoil was nowhere near fulfillment.

When the meeting of Harry Andrews and Captain Percy Turner is considered in the light of these facts, it is clear why that meeting has been termed "historic" by one Army writer. It is also clear why, when Captain Turner requested an interview with the Chief-of-the-Staff, Bramwell Booth was already prepared to outline the great opportunities awaiting him in India; Harry had made sure that Bramwell was thoroughly briefed for this interview. He had, during his study-furlough in London, spent time talking to the Chief-of-the-Staff about progress in Nagercoil. After all, Mrs. Booth-Tucker was Bramwell Booth's own sister Emma, and the Chief couldn't help but be vitally interested in this medical phase of the first Salvationist missionary endeavor.

Add to this the fact that Bramwell and little Harry had lived in the same household for a time and it is clear why Harry found a sympathetic listener in the Chief, who not only knew him well, but realized he could trust his judgment. It also explains why Bramwell, who was by now convinced of the great need for Harry's new endeavor, saw in the person of Captain Turner the solution for turning a dispensary into a hospital.

Bramwell would gladly have sent him right away, but the young doctor pointed out that such a hasty move would be unwise in the long run. Later he wrote, "By becoming an officer I had had no practice except a clinical assistant's post at an eye hospital while in the training college. I said that I must have practice." He saw that if the Army were to open up medical work officially, they would need people of higher qualifications than he yet possessed to give the work status. He proposed that he be given two years' working furlough, to obtain medical practice and to gain the higher qualifications he felt would be in the Army's interests. He saw William Booth himself who said, "If you think that is the best way, go and do it!"

After earning two more degrees, he took the D.P.H. at Oxford. But Captain Turner still felt he must know more about the treatment of eye disorders and diseases, so prevalent were these in India. His request for a further extension of furlough was granted and he became Resident Surgeon at the eye hospital in Kent. Here he met a nurse— "an amazing person"—who would later become his wife. But that was some time in the future. After she had become an officer, she would follow him to India, where, in 1902, they were married in a remarkable outdoor ceremony watched by thousands.

Some clue as to his wholehearted acceptance by the Indian people can be gained from the name they gave him: Dayanasen, "Man of Loving Kindness." The building of new wards for men and for women was soon undertaken, and funds were granted which made it possible to add an operating theater and laboratory. A real hospital was in the making!

More on Dr. Turner

It would be a disservice to stop with a mere word on Captain (Dr.) Turner's acceptance by the Indian people without providing some description of what he accomplished. In addition to his surgery and the usual duties of a physician, he began training Indians as pharmacists while his wife began the training of nurses.

Visiting the Maharajah of Travancore, Turner sought financial help for his project of a four-year medical school, with laboratory work and dissections within the hospital. With the help of another doctor the courses were launched. Among those who trained under Turner, three of the Salvation Army officers recognized by the government as Registered Medical Practitioners gave valuable service over many years.

As the first students neared the end of their four-year course, Turner set about finding sites for branch hospitals. Two were built and another started before the Turners left for their first homeland furlough in 1908. Two of the qualified men were put in charge of the completed branch hospitals and the third was left at the Catherine Booth Hospital. It could not have been a very restful furlough, because Turner earned another medical degree at Durham. Later, in 1917, he wrote of four branch hospitals by then established.

One could write several chapters about all the improvements and expansion, the high standards set by both the doctor and his wife, and the many nurses trained. At the time of his farewell in 1922 for International Headquarters, where he became Chief Medical Officer, someone wrote the following: "A quiet man of marked professional integrity and enterprise, Dr. Turner (by 1922) successfully trained twenty-five doctors in his medical school, which operated under the approval of the state government of Travancore. In his twenty-one years of command he and his associates had ministered to 487,519 outpatients and 14,114 inpatients. From 1908 to 1921 he had performed 15,205 operations."

In 1922 an account of the development of the hospital was published. In part it said, "And now Dr. Turner is leaving India. For twenty-one years he has given of his best to the Catherine Booth Hospital of Nagercoil. The hospital stands now a monument to God's loving-kindness and power. Spreading from the first small amateur dispensary, it has grown till it covers a vast expanse of land, on which have been erected no less than some score of separate buildings. Said a recent visitor: 'I came to see a hospital; I never expected to find a garden city!' It is indeed a wonderful place, wonderful in its surgical and healing work, and wonderful also in its human and missionary element."

Let us allow Dr. Turner himself to have the last word. He wrote, "To bring men and women to this Saviour is the supreme end and object of all the work; to heal the sick is indeed in itself a true work of mercy, and one which all the world, Christian and non-Christian, recognizes as worthy of commendation and help; but that which differentiates a missionary hospital from others is the foundation recognition of the fact that the needs of the spirit, wounded by sin and sorrow, are even more important than those of the sick body."

Noble Predecessors – III

Jewish convert, Christian missionary, military hero

Charles Steibel was born into a wealthy Jewish family in London's West End. His education began at home under both French and German governesses. His further education followed the typical route of wealthy, intelligent young men: excellent schools and, in his case, qualification as a medical doctor.

After this he had taken an assistantship with a general practitioner in Scarborough, followed by another in a small village. These first encounters with the burden of responsibility which falls upon a doctor quickened his sense of inadequacy, and he returned to London to take up an appointment as a house surgeon at the West London Hospital, where he spent two years.

His recreational reading had given him the desire to visit Africa, which resulted in his signing on for a one-year term assisting a doctor in the Orange Free State. But a vacation at the end of the year ended up with his contracting typhoid fever, causing a six-month delay in getting back to England.

Once back in his homeland, he served for a time in one hospital then at a second, where he met Agatha Cook, who had been a Florence Nightingale probationer and now was nurse-in-charge of the male wards. Miss Cook was highly amused when an orderly approached her and requested "a piece of flannelette for Dr. Steibel to clean his rifle." This rather inauspicious first encounter marked the beginning of their romance, which resulted in marriage two years later.

It was during this time that Dr. Steibel, at his sister's urging, attended a week-night meeting at The Salvation Army's Regent Hall. At the end of the meeting he knelt at the mercy seat "in great agony of soul" and found Christ not only as Messiah but as his personal Savior.

His conversion and his subsequent introduction to the many facets of the Army's work opened his eyes to the many opportunities to serve the poor as a Salvationist. We can be sure that his fiancée was totally in accord with his feelings because, when they married early in 1912, they sailed the same day for India to work with Captain Turner at the CBH.

In his term there Dr. Steibel shared many of the duties Turner had been carrying alone. The two men both taught in the new medical school, and both performed surgery. You will remember that Steibel was by this time highly qualified in that field. He was of inestimable help when a cholera epidemic struck in the area surrounding the hospital. All through his time there he spent so little time sleeping at night that one wonders how he could have done it.

His shy nature and gentle manner won over the populace very quickly. He would take village calls whenever possible, and was known for invariably praying before each surgery. The richer patients were amazed at his devotion to destitute patients.

At the outbreak of World War I, Dr. Steibel, whose term of service with The Salvation Army was nearly up, felt he must volunteer for the

Indian Medical Service. Mrs. Steibel returned to England to await the war's end, meanwhile doing her part as a nurse. It was in England that their second daughter was born.

But Charles was never to return. He had looked forward to serving again in Nagercoil when the war was over, but saw his military service as a solemn duty. He wrote to a friend in Nagercoil that no matter where and how he served, "I do so want to be a soldier of God's." While serving in Mesopotamia, he gave his life while picking up wounded Indian troops who had been struck down between the Indian frontline trenches and the enemy lines. It was February 2, 1917, ten days short of the Steibels' fifth wedding anniversary.

Two-and-a-half years later, Lt. Colonel (Dr.) Harry Andrews was killed under similar conditions, both men having been in line of fire, caring for the wounded. As we have noted, Andrews received the Victoria Cross, a decoration that is generally considered even more prestigious than America's top military honor, the Congressional Medal of Honor, because the V.C. is so rarely awarded, and under such stringent conditions. As for Dr. Steibel, his widow simply received a letter from his colonel.

Medical Missionaries Par Excellence

Ruth Nichols (now Mrs. Major Alloway) did not always live in Burwell, population 1,425. Her parents were ranchers, and the nearest town was Bartlett, population 125. She and her parents did not even have a church nearby. Some of the ranchers met on Sundays in the local schoolhouse for a meeting. The pastor from Bartlett came out once a month for a service; otherwise the ranchers were on their own. But the Holy Spirit does not need clergymen to bring down revival. And revival is what happened spontaneously on one of those Sundays with no pastor present. Ruth, about ten at the time, was impressed, but only an observer on that day. Soon afterward she accepted Jesus into her heart and consecrated her life to Him at her bedside, all by herself.

Years later, when the Nichols family moved into Burwell, Ruth did not plan to move with them. But the Lord's plans prevailed, and she ended up teaching school near Burwell.

Lyle was nearly out of high school before he was converted. The two of them were casual friends at church, but they had never dated when both of them left for the college run by their mainline Protestant denomination. They soon found that the college did not have the same strongly evangelical character which they had known in their home church, and thus both of them decided to go to a Nazarene college in Nampa, Idaho. Meanwhile love and marriage had intervened.

While still looking around in Nampa for a church to attend regularly, they encountered The Salvation Army. They learned that the Army's doctrines were in accord with what they had known at home, and they really liked the corps officer. But it was characteristic of them that the precipitating factor in their choosing the Army was that they were needed, not so much to serve someday in some faraway place, but to help out then and there in the corps.

While motivated by the desire to be medical missionaries, the Alloways still had no clear idea of how or where that desire might be fulfilled. One of the people they encountered after joining the Army was Colonel William Noble, who was looking for someone to succeed him at the Catherine Booth Hospital in Nagercoil, South India. Not surprisingly, Dr. Noble saw the Alloways as an answer to prayer. Lyle wanted to be an internist, but Dr. Noble urged him to fill the need as a surgeon.

After medical school at Northwestern University and Training College, Captain (Dr.) and Mrs. Alloway went to Nagercoil, Ruth (with her bachelor's and master's degrees) as a nurse and instructor, Lyle as a surgeon, with a major emphasis on eye-surgery. He made a bit of history by performing the first successful cornea transplant ever done in South India, not to mention the countless other surgeries he performed day after day.

Eventually Lyle, on an extended stateside furlough given over to long months of intensive study, earned a diploma from the American

Board of Ophthalmologists, giving him official status as an eye specialist. As for Ruth, she wrote a portion of a textbook on nursing which was adopted by the Indian government and used all across South India. They served for nineteen years on Indian soil.

Later they served, at the Army's request, for four years in Africa and for three at the Army's hospital in Flushing, New York. Upon retirement they were welcomed back to their tiny town, where Lyle's skill as a doctor was put to good use. They may be back where they started, but their wonderful life has been anything but a mere merry-go-round!

Cap'n Tom

The life of Captain Tom Crocker, Order of the Founder, was not unique in his "hitting the bottom" as an alcoholic, nor in his remarkable conversion. Thousands have experienced this miraculous gift of divine grace. Before we look at events which led to Tom's being inducted into this select group of Salvationists, let us review briefly what we might call his "wilderness years."

The earlier part of his life followed a pattern not unlike that of many others who have wound up on skid row. He learned to drink in the Navy during World War I. Later, in Detroit, he would hold a job for a while and excel in his work, only to lose everything through another binge, often ending up in court. Recognizing the seriousness of his plight, he went to a clinic which claimed to have an effective cure, the key to which was the administering of morphine. For a time it would drive away the desire for liquor, but Tom developed a craving for the drug. So he went back for more "treatments." The book *Cap'n Tom*, by Mrs. Brigadier Margaret Troutt, gives details of this time in Tom's life, when he forged checks and stole and lied to get morphine.

When he could not pay the price of morphine, he would resort to cheap liquor. A long period of living in flophouses, in parks and in alleys, coupled with disregard for nutrition as long as he could meet his body's insistent demands for alcohol and drugs, ruined his health and brought him near death. Even the hospitals would no longer accept him for treatment. The last word of the courts was to commit him to the state mental hospital as "hopeless, incurable and a menace to society."

At this point, a desperate visit to the Army led to his dramatic conversion. At age forty-five Tom became a new creature in Christ. From that moment he never took a drink nor used dope again. Perceptive officers saw great leadership potential in Tom, and when he became a soldier in the Detroit Harbor Light Corps, they began grooming him to take on increasing responsibilities. He was made corps sergeant-major, then an envoy, and later, when placed in charge of the corps and its ministries, a captain. He fulfilled their expectations at every step.

A fruitful and innovative ministry in Detroit came to an end when territorial leaders saw an urgent need for his ability on Chicago's skid row. Once there, he steered efforts for the construction of a new Harbor Light building, right in the midst of skid row, where nothing new had been built for decades.

He also began a concerted effort to meet a new problem. Great numbers of soldiers and sailors had learned to drink during World War II, and many of them discovered too late that they had taken on a habit they couldn't handle. In other words, they had become alcoholics. Going out on the streets to talk to these young men as well as seeing those who came into his center, Tom interviewed about a thousand of them. A conviction grew in his mind that, if possible, they should not be allowed to congregate in flophouses with longtime derelicts, who would inevitably contaminate them with an attitude of hopelessness.

So Tom launched what he called "Operation Salvation," specifically designed to reach young men who had failed to readjust to civilian life and who, in their restlessness and discouragement, had been drawn to Chicago's skid row. This operation was far more than a catchword; so much so that The Salvation Army authorized Tom to rent an entire hotel building across the street from the Harbor Light Corps, to be used exclusively for the housing of returned veterans.

A feature of the program was having a Salvation Army representative—usually Tom himself—at the nearby police court every day when cases were being heard. The judge was only too happy to turn men over to the Army, since sentencing them to jail was admittedly a fruitless procedure. Every effort was made to evaluate those who might profit from the Army's program, and about twenty a day were assigned to Harbor Light rather than being sentenced to jail.

Captain Crocker's ministry went beyond his responsibilities in Chicago, as he was called upon to help in creating and improving Harbor Light programs in other major cities, all the while continuing his work on West Madison Street.

Tom was tireless in presenting the message of Christ's power to break the chains of habit, and to give men new life—a message made more effective by his charisma and unique personal touch. As the results of his ministry became more widely recognized, the city honored him and his work by naming him "Chicagoan of the Year," an award presented by the mayor himself.

Captain Tom Crocker, O.F., showed what God can do with a fully surrendered will.

A Second Career, a Whole New Life

The story of Envoy Walter McClintock, who went from client to convert to director of Harbor Light work, is not quite the usual "battle with the bottle" saga. He was the only child of a well-to-do railroad lawyer whose roots were firmly established in railroading. The father and mother were often gone for a month at a time, traveling in his private railway car, while young Walter was left in the care of a housekeeper.

After graduating from high school at age fifteen, Walter went to the state university, majoring in math and engineering, which he also taught in the evening at a local vocational school. Upon graduation he became a designer and builder of homes, one of which earned the American Institute of Architects award and was featured in *Better Homes and Gardens*. He says now that he prospered, but was a cold, callous, uncaring person.

During World War II he served four years in the Marines in the South Pacific. Death was often very near; more than half of his company were lost in combat. After the war, for eighteen years, Walter found success and prosperity in an internationally known architectural and construction firm. Finding life unsatisfying, he began to drink more and more, but his work did not seem to suffer. He often complained of his discontent to a doctor friend, who finally suggested he turn to The Salvation Army.

It was not a down-and-out Walter who came to the Army. His story left the territorial headquarters receptionist puzzled; such desperation seemed incongruous, coming from such a well-dressed man. After being referred first to one institution, then to a second, Walter ended up at the Harbor Light on Skid Row. He humbled himself and went "on the program," working up through various levels beginning with cleaning the bathrooms. It was a long time, however, until his tough shell was penetrated and he surrendered to Christ.

His old business connection was held open for a long time, but he finally turned his back on his past, which had brought money but no satisfaction.

Eventually Walter was given full responsibility for the Harbor Light Corps in Chicago. Moving the whole operation from West Madison Street to the Freedom Center brought greatly expanded opportunities, and Walter (by then an envoy), with his great abilities and God-given sensitivity to men's needs, found scope for his gifts, some of which he had never suspected before the Lord took over his life.

Envoy McClintock, Order of the Founder, retired in June 1989 after twenty-seven years of distinguished and fruitful service through the instrumentality of The Salvation Army.

The Child Who Sang on Skid Row

Not long after Evangeline Booth became the Commander of The Salvation Army in the United States, she preached in a rally attended by a very small girl, Helen Justus. The Commander turned the prayer meeting over to Colonel Samuel L. Brengle with the words, "Tell the children to come." Helen came forward and was led into a genuine Christian experience.

Not only did little Helen thus get an early start in the Christian faith, but she had opportunity to witness for Jesus at a tender age. Her parents were active soldiers of the New York Bowery Corps. Her own work for God and man began at the age of seven when she stood on a box and sang to the social outcasts of the notorious skid row surrounding the corps. Tears came into the men's eyes as they thought of their own children. The desperate plight of these victims of alcohol, men and women alike, left a deep imprint on Helen's mind.

Attending grade school near the Bowery, Helen was often teased by children who could not understand the work of the Army. "The teasing made me stronger," said Helen in later years. "I'm grateful for it. I might not be able to carry on my work now if I hadn't learned to forgive at a very early age." Until she was a teenager her family continued to "soldier" at the Bowery Corps. When at last they moved, they carried on the same work at corps in four major cities across the country.

Helen met her husband-to-be when his Salvationist family emigrated from Norway. The young couple had one daughter, Esther. Without neglecting her family, Helen spent many years working in Salvation Army social work in the New York metropolitan area. When she was in her mid-forties, she became director of the Army's welfare program in Hartford, Connecticut, where she served tirelessly for twenty-eight years. All the social services came under her direction, and the quality of her work was recognized by her being elected president of the Greater Hartford Social Worker's Organization.

But she always had a special place in her heart for those fighting a battle with alcoholism. She organized an Alcoholics Anonymous group at the Army. The aura of warmth and love surrounding Helen gave the program a special effectiveness. She also played a vital part in Hartford's "Honor Court" counseling program, inaugurated by a city judge especially for alcoholics who ran afoul of the law. Two of the most committed aides in her work were her daughter, Esther, and her son-in-law.

Civic recognition was heaped on Helen because of her lifetime of service, climaxed by her receiving the Army's Order of the Founder.

A California Saga

Captain Harry Stillwell, was one-half of the team which officially opened the Army's work on the West Coast. What he faced when he stepped off the train in 1883 was, to use the mildest term possible, a challenge. The Gold Rush of 1849 left an ugly influence for decades. San Francisco, the metropolis of the West, was still deeply affected 30 years later, and its Barbary Coast was a moral cesspool. The word "hoodlum" originated there.

A small group of Christians living in the Bay area were trying desperately to do something about the deplorable conditions. Some thirty of them banded together as the Pacific Coast Holiness Association and strove valiantly, though without great effect.

When one of them received a copy of *The War Cry* from England, all agreed that the methods of William Booth might work in their case. But they were told in reply to a letter to the General that the Army could not spare any leaders for the time being. So they collected uniforms, gave themselves titles, and organized processions. Renaming their three missions as "corps," they took the name Salvation Army without waiting to make it official.

In the summer of 1883 Major Alfred Wells, age twenty-four, arrived from England by way of New York as General Booth's answer to their letter. On October 6, Captain Harry Stillwell, age twenty-two, joined the Major in San Francisco. About half the Holiness Association men found the Army's methods or discipline not to their liking, so the group quickly dwindled to about fifteen men who stood by Wells and Stillwell. Opposition to the Army's preaching was ferocious at first, but souls were saved here and there.

Four years later the California work had expanded to corps in twenty-five cities, and there were sixty-three officers and cadets. A year later, in April 1888, there were five districts, thirty-two corps, thirteen outposts, and over 100 officers in the West. In addition a rescue home and training garrison were in operation. The grim prospects of 1883 had already turned out to be a "field white unto harvest."

Our Weakness, God's Strength

Brigadier Josef Korbel (R), a Salvation Army officer imprisoned in Czechoslovakia after the communist takeover in the 1950s. His "crime," that of proclaiming the gospel, cost him ten years in prison and complete separation from his family.

Before becoming a Christian, young Josef had been an artist, by nature sensitive, and with what one might call an artistic temperament. He would never have dreamed he could face up to one-tenth of the brutality, suffering, ridicule and risk of sudden death that was to be his lot for those ten terrible years.

As officers and faithful witnesses for Christ, the Korbels were willing to take risks for the sake of the gospel. So much so that, when Josef was arrested, he and his family were awaiting passage on a ship bound for overseas missionary work.

The Brigadier hastens to tell anyone who hears his story that he is not a courageous person. Yet, because he depended entirely upon his Lord for the courage as well as the wisdom to say the right thing at the right time in those most difficult of circumstances, the Lord gave him the strength to pass every test.

A Very Dangerous Man

Josef Korbel had been a Salvation Army officer for eleven years when the Nazis first set foot in Czechoslovakia in 1938. Though not yet defined as "war" by neighboring nations, for the Czechs the invasion had already begun. Things were difficult during World War II, and the young officer had some worrisome encounters with the Gestapo. But these were nothing compared with the disastrous events following "liberation" by the Allies. As a "liberation" it was a mockery, since it placed Czechoslovakia behind the Iron Curtain and under the domination of the communists.

Because of his Christian ministry and continuing efforts at evangelism during the atheistic communist regime, Korbel was arrested in 1948. He was a prisoner for nearly two years before his case was brought to a hearing in court. Not unexpectedly, the so-called trial was a travesty, and his imprisonment continued for another eight years. When he was finally released, a communist guard was considerate enough to read from his files, suggesting it might help Korbel to avoid being arrested again. The file said: "Josef Korbel, a very dangerous man for his strong religious influence, especially on young people and children. His return (to freedom) is undesirable."

If *In My Enemy's Camp* were simply a book about persecution by the communists and the perfidy of turncoats who would go along with any ruling party; if it were simply a book about cowardice and courage in the midst of suffering and injustice, it would have its merits. But it would be distasteful reading, something like taking bitter medicine in order to learn some footnotes and sidelights of history. No, it is far more than that, and the reader is propelled along thorough some wonderful reading, because all the grim and unpleasant things that are said are there to provide a setting for an array of answered prayers and remarkable evidences of the Lord's continued caring for His own children.

There is nothing of the Pollyanna about Korbel's experiences. His sufferings were at times excruciating and protracted. To be separated from wife and children for 10 years was in itself a terrible blow. At times he was bitter and suffered hopelessness. But although the Lord allowed suffering, He always stood by to comfort, to provide deliverance in times of great danger, and to give Korbel a ministry to desperate men. Souls were saved in spite of the vigilance of the guards. In ways which were at times miraculous (a word not lightly used), God continued to work in the midst of the "enemy's camp"!

How Long, O Lord?

We are most fortunate that Brigadier Korbel was at last persuaded to write a book on his experiences. The observations you are now reading are all based on the aforementioned *In My Enemy's Camp*, but later he wrote a second volume, whose title says it all: *When the Prison Gates Were Opened*. The first of these books contains instances of God's absolutely remarkable care for him in the direst of circumstances. We can only marvel at how, through God's grace, bitterness and hate failed to find lodging in his heart.

One question whose answer is woven into the entire book is: How long must a Christian be expected to wait for an answer to prayer? Korbel's undeserved imprisonment by the communists on trumped-up charges, and the subsequent suffering experienced by him as well as by his family, would have been bad enough if it had dragged on for several months. But ten years! So, what kind of timetable may we expect from the Lord?

A partial answer (inadequate, but at least indicative of his ordeal) is to make a list of where Josef spent those years. 1. Orli police station, 2. Znojimo prison, 3. Cejl, the state penitentiary, 4. a forced-labor camp commonly called "The Camp of Death," 5. Jachymov prison, 6. the prison at Brno in Moravia, 7. in solitary confinement for two months in an underground cell where, day and night, there was complete darkness, and 8. Pangrac prison in Prague. Each of these places holds for him its own memories of horror, suffering, and even imminent danger of death.

Yet even in the darkest hours, when he humbly and irrevocably left everything in God's hands, he was able to see some good coming out of his imprisonment and privation, and his being kept from the work he saw as his real calling. But ten years without the freedom he longed for! What about his prayers? Yet the Lord knew exactly what He was doing.

A Gift Like No Other

During Brigadier Josef Korbel's long imprisonment in communist Czechoslovakia for "high treason" (translation: proclaiming the gospel of Jesus Christ), he experienced in many ways the repression of an atheist regime which was trying desperately to stamp out all acknowledgment of God. We now know how it failed, but it was a terrible time for Christians.

Christmas was an especially bad time for the prisoners, since they could not help but think of happy Christmases in the past. Even unbelievers, Josef found, had that same feeling, since Christmas is so widely celebrated, even by those who think nothing of the true events which give meaning to the season.

One year, just shortly before Christmas, one of the prisoners received word of a family tragedy which left him without any hope for the future. In despair he told Korbel he was going to end it all. When words of encouragement seemed to be of no avail, the Salvationist tore a piece of paper from a cement sack and wrote Psalm 46:1 on it. Apparently it was of such comfort to the man that, without thinking of the consequences, he fastened it to the wall over his cot. A guard saw it with the result that Korbel was handcuffed for many hours to a barbed-wire fence, his hands high above him so he was almost hanging.

Out of this terrible incident when he nearly froze to death, there came to him an experience that can only be described as one of the most sacred of his life. He had already learned that, when he was in the most excruciating and hopeless of circumstances, seemingly abandoned even by God, the Lord would somehow break into his life, or would somehow intervene, giving him absolute assurance that he was not alone, and that, for reasons that Josef himself could not fathom, he was nevertheless exactly where the Lord wanted him.

After hours of exposure in the bitter wind, when his hands were blue from the cold as well as from being elevated above his body, he looked up and saw ever so clearly a white, nail-pierced hand clasping his. At first he thought it was a hallucination, but he looked again very carefully, and it was plainly there. He later said, "Through my own hands a stream of warmth ran right into my heart!" Slowly it began to disappear, but Josef knew; he knew it was the hand of the Lord. He could actually feel it.

Ambassador to the Man on the Street

Lt. Colonel Lyell Rader, O.F., combined energy, drive and enthusiasm with a zeal for souls. But he was more than a zealot. His father was a scientist of whom his contemporary, Evangelist Billy Sunday wrote, "I know of no man who is recognized as an authority on scientific subjects who can present the truths of the gospel more vividly." In fact, this scientist produced inventions of value and great utility, and he helped to confirm the faith of many by demonstrating that biblical miracles were not "impossible" and unreasonable, as many of his day asserted.

Like his father, Lyell was well-versed in scientific matters, and he employed an impressive array of scientific demonstrations, complete with high voltage sparks, whirring wheels, and a great deal more to illustrate spiritual truths and to present a compelling statement of the gospel's validity for today.

But his pulpit was not restricted to the indoors, where scientific apparatus could conveniently be set up and operated. He managed to make many of his approaches highly portable, taking them to the crowds on the street. His faith in the continuing value of The Salvation Army's open-air meeting was so great that he became a most eloquent advocate of outdoor evangelism. Not content with preaching from the curbstone, he designed and used an array of conveyances from which to proclaim his message: a Roman chariot, a lifeboat on wheels, a mobile platform canopied with a beach umbrella, and many more.

He was also wise enough to realize that fellow Christians anxious to share Christ on the street and in the marketplace are all our friends and allies; his methods were not trade secrets, but something to be shared with all who would use them for the glory of God. Thus he became a mentor to a noteworthy para-church group which has gained recognition for its aggressive and innovative outdoor evangelism. Probably few Salvationists realize the extent of Lt. Colonel Rader's influence on that dedicated group. Among them he is known as a great and good friend and advisor.

Two tangible evidences of his efforts to promote open-air evangelism in the Army were his book, and the portable public address system he designed, which would operate on any car battery, and which could thus be powered nearly anywhere. In their younger years his sons helped to produce the P.A. units, which were sold without profit across the nation to Training Colleges and other units which would find them valuable. His book *Rediscovering the Open-Air* has long been the standard work on that subject. Lt. Colonel Rader: a man after the Founder's heart!

She Loved the "Front Lines"

It is probably typical for a Salvationist who is admitted to the Order of the Founder to be taken completely by surprise when the award is announced. In fact, many of these people would have told you, midway through their lives, that it could never happen to them. Had they even thought about such a thing (which they probably wouldn't), they would have been convinced that it was beyond the realm of possibility.

One whose life story illustrates this is Brigadier Mary Nisiewicz (R). For her, the ideal of a life dedicated to "service beyond self" seemed to come to a screeching halt in early middle age—after she had sacrificed so much to become a Salvation Army officer. Taking this step in her teens had meant a complete break with her Polish Catholic family, who could not understand her decision.

Officership brought some great opportunities, including the command of the Marion, Ohio, Corps. When she went there, she had not yet turned 30, but to put it in football parlance, this young woman "took the ball and ran." While there she initiated one of the first summer day camp programs in the Eastern Territory. Her golden age program was one of the first of its kind. Her highly successful capital campaign (reflecting the community's faith in her highly effective spiritual ministry) resulted in the city's first Army-owned building. Under the circumstances, it is not surprising to learn that her stay in Marion lasted fifteen years! And probably the townspeople would have been glad to have her stay on forever.

But discouragement lay ahead. Because of poor health she was appointed to the divisional finance department in Metropolitan New York for four years, followed by a year in the Women's Correctional Service. There are those who give unstintingly of themselves through what we might characterize as "office work." As a matter of fact, Mary was no less a selfless servant of the Lord when enclosed by four walls. But such work, necessary as it is, was hardly the choice of a person who yearned to serve in the front lines!

Although those five "desk-bound" years were doubtless a source of frustration to her, the time away from the stress and exertion of corps officership led to the recovery of her health. With health restored Mary, by then in her late forties, made it clear that she wanted corps work again—a corps with great challenges, with unlimited opportunities to serve the needy and the desperate, and the opportunity to present the life-changing gospel to those who needed it so badly.

She was given command of the Manhattan Citadel Corps, located in New York City's East Harlem, then the drug capital of the world. Besides using every means possible to meet the needs of "her" people, she did what she could for the drug addicts she encountered.

She realized, however, that far more was needed. After four years she was able to open a Corps Outreach Program staffed with former addicts, four of whom had become strong witnessing Christians. But the fact that Brigadier Nisiewicz now had an outreach program to multiply and amplify the effect of her own efforts did not mean that her work in East Harlem was done. Far from it! She continued for another dozen years before retirement caught up with her.

Because of what she accomplished in those sixteen remarkable years at Manhattan Citadel, there is no question that her "memorable service… would have specially commended itself to our Beloved Founder." Those words, quoted from the special 1917 Minute of the General which defined the conditions governing the admission of a Salvationist to the Order of the Founder, certainly applied to Mary. And thus it was that Brigadier Mary Nisiewicz, O.F., joined that select group.

The Mayor Wore Uniform

Frank Staiger who, with his wife, resigned after about a decade of officership in the 1920s, went back to Port Huron, Michigan, and continued to serve the Lord, "not somehow, but triumphantly," to quote an old motto. It is this wonderful upbeat spirit which should inspire others. Mr. and Mrs. Staiger directed the Army's North End Sunday school for thirty-five years. In the corps itself he served as a youth leader, bandmaster, and then as corps sergeant-major for twenty-five years after that.

During that time he was asked, because of his obvious ability and integrity, to fill out the unexpired term of the city's mayor, who had resigned with two years yet to go. After the term ended, Frank wanted to return to private life, but the people would not let him go! He was elected by an overwhelming majority for a full four years, even though he did not run a single ad, give one campaign speech, or spend a dime. People grew used to seeing the mayor in his Salvation Army uniform, in his role as corps sergeant-major leading an open-air meeting on the street corner.

He was deeply committed to the community, as seen by his service as school board president, library board president, Salvation Army Advisory Board member, chairman of the city charter revision committee, and president of the YMCA board of directors.

In Kiwanis, which he served professionally as state secretary for many years, he was also elected district governor for Michigan, editor of the state magazine, and director of music for Kiwanis International. Known by all for his Christian stand, he served his fellow man ably on many fronts.

Kiwanis honored him by bestowing upon him their coveted Distinguished Kiwanian Award, an honor given to very few members in the organization's history. Commissioner Richard E. Holz called him to the stage at the Central Music Congress in 1981 to admit him to the Order of the Founder.

When he went to be with the Lord the following year, Port Huron's newspaper headlined a lengthy obituary, "He left his imprint." One can only draw the conclusion that, not only did he leave his imprint upon civic affairs—indeed, upon Port Huron itself—but that, in his sharing of the gospel in the marketplace as well as from the speaker's rostrum, Frank Staiger left an imprint on the hearts of many people as well.

Exponent of Holiness and Prayer

When Lt. Colonel Mina Russell was admitted to the Order of the Founder at the Eastern Territorial Congress in June 1992, the recognition obviously came about partly because of her involvement with Brengle Memorial Institutes around the world. In 1947 she was on the planning commission for the very first one, and she conducted a seminar on prayer in each and every Brengle Institute in this country from the '40s well into the '80s.

As one of the Army's foremost exponents of holiness and prayer, Lt. Colonel Russell has been a participant in Brengle Institutes and in prayer seminars in all four U.S.A. territories and in Canada, Kenya, Zimbabwe, Nigeria, Ghana, India, Sri Lanka, Singapore, Indonesia, The Philippines, Hong Kong, Japan and Korea.

One might assume that a person who had made personal prayer such a matter of study and practice, and who had learned to communicate vital truths about this aspect of the spiritual life to people of all nationalities and cultures, would live in a rarified spiritual atmosphere a bit beyond the reach of most of us. This is not true, however. Consider the colonel's sense of humor. It may be quiet and low-key, in keeping with her personality, but that in no way subtracts from her ability to see the funny side of events and of life in general, and to share with others this humorous view of things that might otherwise seem cloaked in solemnity and not-to-be-questioned protocol.

Her off-the-record telling of the events surrounding the first National Brengle Institute contains comedic elements which should be enshrined in Salvation Army archives somewhere, somehow, so that we never forget that the Lord can work through fallible people like ourselves, and that even the General and a National Commander can be tripped up by a communications gap of their own making! That 1947 institute came very near to not happening, and in a six-week mad scramble, virtual miracles of organization were worked, and gallons of "midnight oil" were burned in order to prepare a curriculum which would merit the summoning of officers from their appointments all across the nation.

Someday perhaps the whole story can be told in a history book. Perhaps! But there is no denying that what emerged from a shaky beginning and from frantic efforts to meet an unexpected timetable has become a solid, superbly organized, and highly effective annual institute which has brought spiritual strength and encouragement to a host of officers for at least two generations.

The significance of all this is that people like Lt. Colonel Russell, with their spiritual maturity, can, upon looking back, see God's working and His sovereign overruling in happenings which at the time, perhaps, caused considerable head-shaking among those who are always quick to criticize.

It should be noted, too, that this woman who came to be known as an authority on prayer did not spend her officer-career in a cloistered setting. During the Depression she supervised a women's canteen in New York City. Subsequently she was a corps officer, then served at the School for Officers' Training, and later as Territorial Social Welfare Secretary. All of this had its part in preparing her for her longtime role as trusted counselor and confidant to a host of cadets and officers.

Miss Billie

As you read this, think about two questions: (1) When is a missionary not a "missionary"? and (2) How can a missionary with less-than-robust health come home and yet serve as meaningfully as ever? Major Billie Jean DeArman of the Southern Territory has provided the answers through her full and useful life.

Billie Jean was born in Dallas, Texas, but as a young child moved with her parents to Oklahoma, where her father became a peace officer. Her mother, a devoted Christian, died when Billie Jean was only six years old. When she was twelve, a young Salvation Army officer visiting the neighborhood attracted Billie Jean to the Army, where she first became a Girl Guard, then a soldier. Her father, who had hopes of seeing her become a nurse, accepted her decision to become an officer. She never forgot his admonition: "Remember, when it gets hard, don't turn back. Give it your very best."

After being commissioned in 1946 Billie Jean had a number of appointments in Oklahoma, but her great desire was to serve in Mexico in the new ministry which The Salvation Army had undertaken there. She learned to speak Spanish in preparation for such work. In

1956 she received the appointment she was looking for. Sent to the Army's Mexico City children's home, she served twenty-two years as its superintendent.

Those who knew her best said it was only a short time before she ceased to be a "missionary." She became native in the truest sense of the word, with a command of the language and complete adaptation to Mexican customs and culture. The only thing not indigenous about her was her birth certificate. Not only did she accept those around her, they completely accepted her.

She was sacrificial in her lifestyle, faithful in her calling and successful in carrying out her mission. More than 100 children each year regarded her as mother, mentor, teacher, disciplinarian, counselor, spiritual leader, and bandmaster, plus a host of unknown titles only a special children's home director could carry. With meager funds, inadequate facilities, and insufficient water supply, Major DeArman somehow found resources to house, clothe and feed her children.

In her day, Mexican national statistics showed that only thirty percent of those who started school finished even the primary grades. Few went on to secondary school; only the rich to preparatory. She was determined that her children should have not only a rich educational experience, but that they would stay until graduation. She personally made sure that each child, as long as they were in the Home, continued his or her education. She saw them through primary and secondary school; then she contended with officialdom, lack of funds and other obstacles to see them through preparatory school and university. So Billie Jean has an ample cadre of her "children" who are lawyers, doctors, engineers, and clergy, including Salvation Army officers.

In 1979 health concerns forced her return to the U.S., but in Dallas's Little Mexico Village she began immediately a ministry which has spread throughout the Texas Division. Soon, when Major DeArman would drive into Little Mexico, children and adults would come from everywhere calling "Miss Billie, Miss Billie!" They knew she brought food and clothes, but most of all they knew she brought them love and kind words, and often hugs. For most of them, these were scarcer than money. As truly a "missionary" in Texas as in Mexico, she had given forty-six years of outstanding service when the General admitted her to the Order of the Founder in 1992.

The Boy in the Soup Line

Consider a family living in a junkyard, the mother and children unable to speak English even though the children, having been born in the U.S., were American citizens. The father, who had turned to crime, was in jail leaving his wife and four children in dire poverty. One of the children, a son, later said, "I will always remember standing in a Salvation Army soup line when I was seven. The Army folks came and took care of our family. Then they ministered to my father who was in jail."

It would be easy to assume that a family which spoke no English lived in an urban ghetto, perhaps in New York City when the great influx of immigrants was pouring ashore. Actually the picture was quite different. At least some of the children were born in a little French settlement outside Green Bay, Wisconsin. Milton, the little boy who stood in the soup line, is our informant. In retrospect he saw the results of the Salvationists' caring ministry, especially the jail visitation, as a miracle. The father's life was transformed from one of crime to a life of serving Christ. Much later Milton recalled, with obvious emotion, "I saw it with my own eyes, this change." His parents became Salvation Army officers and served faithfully the rest of their lives.

As for that memorable year during the Great Depression when he was seven, Milt says, "The Army fed us, and taught me the basics of English so I could go to an English-speaking school. I became a junior soldier that year, too." Not long afterwards he experienced something else that was for him a near-miracle. When he contracted polio, the Army again came to his rescue. They arranged for medical help. He credits that help, along with the spiritual encouragement given to him, for his recovery. He had beaten polio—no small feat in the 1930s.

As he grew up, having seen the wonderful changes that took place in his own family, Milton Servais decided the Army's programs offered the best place for him to serve. His first post was in a St. Louis community center. While playing in a youth band he met the girl who has been his wife for fifty years. A few years later he moved to similar work in Richmond, Indiana. By 1952 Milt's first boss from Richmond days was city coordinator in Nashville, Tennessee. Needing a good community center director for the Magness Center in East Nashville, he made a special trip to offer Milt the job. He took it. During his 32 years at the Magness Center, Servais came to be known as "Uncle" Milt, but to thousands of children, so many of them from one-parent households, he was like a true father, the father they had never known. Mere statistics cannot reveal the lives he helped change. The honors, awards and recognition he received in Tennessee and beyond are too numerous to list here.

The Green Bay Salvationists who went out of their way to help a very needy family had no way of foreseeing the results of their caring ministry. Not only did the parents become officers, but Milt, the boy in the soup line, was ultimately admitted to the Order of the Founder, the highest honor which can be bestowed upon a Salvationist.

It's a reminder that no family or individual in need, no matter how unpromising at first glance, can be written off as lacking in great potential. Besides, great potential is not a prerequisite for becoming one of the Lord's children.

Evangelist, Counselor, Trusted Friend

A few years ago a Salvation Army officer became state president of a large and influential women's organization. It didn't happen overnight, of course; she had been elected to a succession of local, district and state offices. Always she wore her uniform, which constantly bore witness to the fact that a Salvationist was speaking and working on behalf of these several thousand professional women.

At length the state presidency took her to Washington, D.C., where she met the national president, who found the opportunity to take her aside. She too, she confided, had been a Salvation Army officer.

She and her husband had become discouraged and had left the work. But that feeling of kinship with the Army was still there.

One significant reason for that sense of kinship was that The Salvation Army had never lost touch with them; not the Army as an organization, since an organization has no reality outside of the people of which it is comprised. But the "Army" contact was real, warm and caring; it was Brigadier Clifton Sipley, who had long made it a personal concern to keep in touch with those who had left the ranks.

There were others besides former officers who were on his visitation list—and of course on his prayer list. Naturally they were widely scattered, so he could not make his rounds like a country parson. In addition to personal correspondence, his extensive itinerary took him to many places where one or more of these people lived and, because he had maintained contact with them, he could incorporate visits with them into his travels. For fifty-five years the life of Brigadier Sipley has been a life of unceasing ministry.

He served as a corps officer in six corps, followed by two appointments as divisional evangelist. Finally he became territorial evangelist, serving a total of twelve years in this phase of the Army's work. After retirement, he and Mrs. Sipley continued their evangelistic work unabated. As a matter of fact, the brigadier and his wife have conducted more evangelistic campaigns in the Eastern Territory than anyone else.

Along with this ministry they have served at retreats, and the brigadier taught at officer refresher institutes for thirty years, twenty-five continuously while a corps officer. For many years he served on the faculty of the Preaching Seminar for Salvation Army Officers at Asbury Theological Seminary and taught classes at the College for Officer Training. When he conducted the Southern Territory's Bible Conference, there was "a great outpouring of the Holy Spirit." He also taught at the National Seminar on Evangelism at Glen Eyrie.

For years he served as counselor on the staff of the National Brengle Institutes held annually in Chicago. As Brengle Institutes proliferated beyond America's boundaries, he was called upon to serve in those held in Third World countries and the Caribbean Territory.

So it should have been no great surprise when, at the Eastern Territory Congress in 1996, Brigadier Clifton Sipley (R) was called to the platform to be admitted to the Order of the Founder. The presentation was made by General Paul A. Rader while the 7,000-plus delegates rose en masse in a standing ovation.

Mrs. Brigadier Gertrude Purdue

It is no coincidence that there exists in Memphis, Tennessee, a 41,000 square foot, state-of-the-art Salvation Army center named the Purdue Center of Hope, while just a few miles away lived Mrs. Brigadier Gertrude Purdue, retired. When in 1997 the Army began a capital campaign to build the institution, Mertie Buckman, a co-founder of the international chemical company, Buckman Labs (and a founding member of the Army's Memphis Women's Auxiliary), was asked if she would make a substantial pledge to the campaign. She replied that if the building could be named in memory of Brigadier Bramwell Purdue and in honor of his widow, Gertrude, she would give a million dollars and challenge the Auxiliary to raise another million.

Of her childhood she says, "When I was seven years old, I knelt at the altar with my mother's arms around my shoulders and gave my life to Jesus. I grew up in the beautiful environment of service (my father and mother were always field officers) and at fifteen I decided to become an officer." But even before that, when fourteen, she had conducted services for neighborhood children at The Salvation Army's local outpost.

She was commissioned as a Salvation Army officer in 1930 and in 1934 married fellow officer William Bramwell Purdue. (His very name leaves no doubt as to his Army background!) They both began their officership in the Central Territory but spent most of their years of service in the South. During World War II they gave much time and effort to The Salvation Army's part in the USO, and in all the years since then Mrs. Purdue has labored to help servicemen in every way possible. She had four brothers who served in WW II, and one of them took part in the Normandy landing. No wonder it has been said that "she has a strong heart for service personnel."

The Purdues retired in 1973, but as one writer said, "Retirement seemed to energize her." Mrs. Purdue has a special way of lifting the spirits of all to whom she ministers. During her retirement she served as Quota's president in 1975-76 and was named Outstanding Quotarian in 1988, 1992 and 1994. She received the Memphis Volunteer of the Year award in 1989 and the J. C. Penney Golden Rule Award in 1990, plus being made a lifetime member of the White Station Optimist Club in 1998. In 1999 she received the Mertie Buckman Empowerment Award, and in 2001 was honored as the National VA Hospital Volunteer of the Year for her forty years and over 4,000 hours of service to the patients. In 2003 she was honored by the *Commercial Appeal* as one of ten Jefferson Award winners.

Some people, perhaps due to heredity, live very long lives, and are able to remain vital and useful for all that time. However, many of us who won't live so long can nevertheless choose to be useful throughout all our years, whether few or many. But long or short, each of our lives can be productive and beneficial. It is up to us.

A Life Crowned by Honors

When Delores Rivitt was commissioned in 1950 from the Training College in San Francisco and appointed to assist at The Salvation Army's corps in Sitka, Alaska, she had no inkling that nearly all of her life, from that point onward, would be dedicated to the people of that vast land. The explanation may lie largely in her ability to identify with the Indians of the various tribes which comprise an important part of Alaska's population, and who make up a significant portion of the soldiership in some of the corps. Her faith and personal qualities doubtless contributed to her effectiveness. In a letter she wrote, "How great our God is!" Then added, regarding her experiences in Alaska, "Not always easy, but great! And filled with many blessings."

151

There is no question that, even in retirement, she still loves to share the gospel message. All of this is enhanced by her spirit of adventure and her vitality.

These qualities have led to some interesting assignments along the way. In 1954 she led the Western Territory's contingent to the Concordia Girl Guard Encampment in Norway. In 1963 she was a delegate to the Brengle Memorial Institute in Chicago. (That was when she met again the former Probationary Lieutenant who had stood by helplessly when the officer in charge told Delores to leave, and not to come back. Imagine this officer's thrill to look up from her desk, years later at THQ, to see Delores standing in her doorway, a uniformed Army officer!)

Without taking events chronologically, let me mention that Delores was appointed corps officer in Kalinspell, Montana, in 1955. However, she must have made her preference clear; in just two years she was back in Alaska as corps officer in Kake. Financially, Kake was not an easy appointment. So in order to pay the bills, she followed the example of the Apostle Paul, who sometimes worked as a tentmaker. In her case she worked as Postmaster, landed seaplanes for Alaska Airlines, ran a short-wave radio, and (as she added in a note) "etc. etc." But the bills were paid!

From 1972 to 1978 she was divisional youth secretary in Anchorage. During this time she was privileged to attend the International College for Officers in London, England. The following year she received additional administrative training in Portland, OR, then became assistant administrator in Anchorage, followed by a stint as coordinator for the Army's Redwood Glen Camp in CA. Then it was back to Alaska, where she served for a decade as divisional secretary in Alaska. During this time she was also privileged to travel with an Army group for an educational tour of Israel.

Her work among the Alaskan tribesmen was recognized in 1991 when she received an Award for Exceptional Service from Commissioner Paul Rader. After retirement in 1992, her life was just as busy, as she pitched in willingly to fulfill one need after another.

But the climactic point was her being admitted to the Order of the Founder "in recognition of outstanding service to the people of Alaska." This is the highest recognition which can be awarded to any Salvationist.

The
TWO WORLD
WARS

Tumulty and the Lawyer

Someone once invented the phrase "hinges of destiny" and illustrated from mankind's saga how, time and again, some seemingly trivial thing turned out to be a pivot-point upon which turned a major event in history. There was such a point in The Salvation Army's history in America which, though all but forgotten, was indeed of crucial importance to all that followed. The "pin" in that hinge was the timely testimony of a certain alcoholic who was saved and restored.

For The Salvation Army, there was a sharply-defined turning-point in the public's attitude which literally transformed our standing in this country. It was our remarkable work in France during World War I, sometimes carried on right behind the front-line trenches, and even in those trenches during the darkest hours of a long night.

When Evangeline Booth committed Salvationists to that terribly risky work, it can also be said that the extent to which she strained the Army's resources to provide money for our Salvationist war workers was risky. The furnishing of those funds, however, was extremely important. Because of her vision, those workers were able to distribute supplies freely to soldiers without charging for every item or having to balance the books for a picky auditor. There was an endearing air of generosity and openhandedness about the whole operation which became legendary.

As for the risk-taking, the Commander (as she was affectionately known) had great faith that the public, once it learned what we were really doing, would rally 'round and help make up the deficit. Yet even the Commander's optimism fell far short of the result. She dared to hope that a 1918 fundraising campaign would bring in the then-unheard-of sum of a million dollars. The public gave $2,370,000! This outpouring reflected a wave of gratitude generated by glowing reports in the letters the soldiers sent home. America's attitude toward The Salvation Army was dramatically and permanently changed by our work in that war.

It is all very well to remind ourselves of these things, but the hard fact is that Salvationists could never have served with the troops without authorization from the office of the President of the United States. But was The Salvation Army needed? Already the Red Cross and the YMCA, both far better known, had been granted official status. Evangeline Booth wired Washington, offering the services of her people for overseas work. Her offer was refused. So that was that... or was it?

The Commander was not yet through. She sent her property secretary, Lt. Col. William Barker, for an interview with Joseph Tumulty, Secretary to the President. Tumulty was talking to a man at the far end of the room when Barker entered. After Barker made his request, they were interrupted by the other man. "Joe, give the colonel what he wants and make it good. The boys over there will need help, and when I think what Major Winchell has done for me..." Barker then recognized a prominent Jersey City lawyer, now a volunteer on the Attorney General's staff. His conversion through the Army's ministry had caused a sensation in New York society circles. He told his story to Tumulty, then said, "You know what The Salvation Army has done for me. Now, do what you can for The Salvation Army."

A letter to the American Ambassador in France was speedily written, and the door to our overseas service swung open. But the "hinge" was the testimony, in that crucial moment, of a lawyer who had found the Lord through our work with alcoholics!

A Kindness Repaid

We have just seen the "ripple effect" of one Salvation Army officer's patient ministering to alcoholics, specifically to a lawyer who had fallen from high places into desperate straits. One totally unforeseen effect of that lawyer's remarkable conversion and restoration was the writing of a general letter of introduction from President Woodrow Wilson's secretary to the American ambassador in France.

Armed with that letter and sent to France by Evangeline Booth, Lt. Col. William Barker was able to deal directly with American military officers. In truth, they were the leaders of a fighting force which as yet hardly existed. The conscription and training of an American army was still in its early stages. The French, British and Italians were not looking for an American army as an entity; they wanted a manpower pool, insisting that we turn over the American soldiers to them as replacements to use in their own severely depleted fighting forces. But Major General John J. Pershing was determined to carry out his directive from Washington, D.C., which stipulated that the American Expeditionary Force was to retain its own identity as a "separate and distinct component of the combined forces."

Into this tense situation, with Pershing beleaguered by the representatives of three Allied nations, came this Salvationist, offering to place young civilian men and women side-by-side with American troops, possibly even in combat zones. Perhaps it is hard to grasp the situation after all these years, but what we are looking at must have seemed to some of those who stood by like a scene from a comic opera. Consider: the YMCA and the Red Cross, both large and well-known organizations, had already been granted authorization to work among the troops. Now, in the midst of a tense dispute involving four nations, came this man from a smallish and little-understood religious group, bearing nothing but a letter to an ambassador.

The letter did not grant The Salvation Army authority to put any plan into motion; only to carry to U.S. military leaders the offer of placing Salvationists at their disposal. As a matter of fact, some of the military officers whom Barker had approached had brushed off the idea as ill-advised and, in thus dismissing his offer, had brushed him off as well. But now he faced the top man, a man described by one historian as "cold-eyed" and "granite-faced" — not surprising after what he had suffered in 1915. In that year, after a tour of duty in the Philippines, he was living in San Francisco with his wife and four children when he was hurriedly called by President Wilson to halt the depredations of the Mexican bandit, Poncho Villa.

In his absence his house burned down, killing his wife and three small daughters. Only his son, Warren, survived. The Salvation Army's provincial officer, Colonel Henry Lee, had shown great personal interest and sympathy, as had many Salvationists, while the respectable Bay Area churches had somehow ignored the incident, failing to offer even perfunctory condolences to one who was essentially an outsider. Ofttimes in those days, American military personnel and their "Army wives" and "Army brats" were not highly thought of in the settled communities where they temporarily resided. They would move in, stay for a time, then suddenly move out again, at the behest of military leadership. Pershing never forgot the Army's kindness, which touched him deeply.

And so it was that when Barker's proposal came to Pershing's attention, he readily approved. Out of an act of caring—one of many such acts directed to people who can so easily be overlooked, and perhaps in most cases can do nothing to repay that act—came the opportunity for overseas service which forever changed the public's perception of The Salvation Army.

August 13, 1917

On August 13, 1917, the first contingent of Salvationist workers embarked for France to do what they could for the American troops. The U.S. had entered the first World War shortly before, and Commander Evangeline Booth wanted our Christian workers to move with the soldiers, providing spiritual counsel, emotional support when needed, wholesome leisure activities, whatever creature comforts were feasible in a given situation, and accessible role models of womanhood at its best. The mere presence of a substitute for mother, sister or girl-friend gave many a man the inward strength to say "no" in moments of great temptation.

Volunteering for service with combat forces meant the prospect of being placed very near the front lines. Indeed, some of our people set up "huts" between the American heavy artillery (with gun barrels aimed over their heads) and the front-line trenches, sometimes no more than 200 yards away. A worker could find himself, at one time or another, on that dreaded turf known as "no man's land." More than one Salvation Army officer voluntarily entered such an area, at tremendous risk of life, to carry out a mission of mercy.

This was not a call to fame or glory but a challenge to accept the most difficult, most dangerous assignment that could be offered a Salvationist in 1917. It expressed a willingness to sacrifice life itself, if needs be. No one yet knew just where the American troops would be called to go—only that, when the troops moved, the Salvationists meant to move with them. This "opportunity to serve" looked more like a death sentence!

Yet they offered themselves—single male officers who, as clergy, were exempt from the draft but could thus offer their lives both to God and country; single women (now the most celebrated, as we hear of the "lassies"); and married couples, whose joint service was often singularly effective.

Was the blessing of the Lord on this work? Certainly the stories of returning veterans would affirm this. More important, there are doubt-less rank upon rank of former servicemen in Heaven today because of that witness of practical Christianity seen in life's darkest moments.

And what of those Salvationists who dared lay their lives on the line? There were well over 200 of them. Of those, one died in the great influenza epidemic (as did many thousands of civilians). But that was the extent of the casualties. The rest came back, sound and whole, in spite of some very close calls and a few relatively minor wounds caused by nearby exploding shells—wounds which were not reported or even shown to medics for fear that the military authorities would forbid further movement of women officers with the troops. Dare we see that as a miracle of preservation? It does not seem presumptuous to say that God's blessing did indeed rest upon this work.

Our "Doughnut Girls"

The people who made the incomparable wartime reputation The Salvation Army has enjoyed in America, were not a part of the military establishment. They were what we might call 200-plus "irregulars" — American Salvationists who went to France and into Germany, often right along with our American fighting units.

These people who, by that day's military protocol, should not even have been there, gave so unstintingly of themselves, regardless of risk, that the same Salvationists who had so recently been ridiculed or ignored in their Stateside open-air ministry were now admired and—how shall we say it?—regarded with something approaching reverence. Often their arrival near the leading edge of battle was entirely unexpected by all but a very few of the "brass" who had to be informed, causing the troops to react with something akin to bewilderment.

And no wonder! Absolutely no female U.S. Army nurses were sent into such areas. First aid and front-line medical attention were given by the "medics" —enlisted men trained to render whatever binding, bandaging or relief could be done under such adverse conditions, in order to prepare the victims for transport to a first aid tent or field hospital somewhere behind the lines. That transporting, if and when it could be done, was often an ordeal in itself as men were carried on litters or loaded into rough-riding ambulances (1917 style) for their trip. In such cases haste, not gentleness, was necessarily the governing factor.

But suddenly, unexpectedly, into this man's world of blood, broken bodies and shattered limbs appeared these women! Not angels (though some at the time might have suspected that they were); not hallucinations (though some at first feared that, like hallucinations, they might soon disappear); but real women. American women!

There was at the beginning no set formula for the Salvationists to follow except to alleviate suffering and loneliness in any way possible. Consider one incident at the beginning of the Argonne offensive, as recalled by Mrs. Major Louise Holbrook. She and Violet McAllister (later Mrs. Major Harry Booth) were asked to help comfort young American troops who had just experienced the horrors of their first real battle, with some wounded and quite a number just as effectively incapacitated by what was then called shell shock. They were lying in tents hastily pitched on soggy ground; no cots, no floors, no stove, with winter's first cold spell just setting in. The "mattresses" were bed ticks, not even filled with straw, and there were so many wounded that there were not even enough of these ticks. The two women put the ticks together in pairs, with three men lying crosswise. In that way two blankets would cover three men.

During the night there was intense shelling nearby, and many of the men would start up, often into a sitting position, and commence to shake. The women tried their best to allay their fears. Because the Salvationists were in their third such battle and were unharmed thus far, their words had a calming effect. All during the long night they served cocoa, heated over candles burning inside a perforated tin box, and listened as the men talked and talked. There was something so surrealistic about the experience, following as it did on the heels of their first terrifying battle, that some of the boys felt almost as if their own mothers had been allowed to come and visit them in hell.

The next day brought no rest as the two women hung on for dear life to a telephone-reel cart towed by a truck as it bounced along a miry road which the Signal Corps ahead was trying to make passable. Thus they were transported to a makeshift hospital in a large cave which, Mrs. Holbrook later recounted, "the Germans had fixed for us very nicely" before they had retreated. She was assigned to do first aid in the shock and fracture ward. In all, there were four Salvationists in that military cave hospital, but no other women—never at any time any female nurses.

Our Salvationists did more than smile and hand out coffee and the soon-to-be-famous doughnuts. Theirs was a hands-on ministry, often in the very worst of circumstances.

The First "Army" Doughnuts

When the first American Salvation Army workers went overseas in 1917, there was no plan at all to provide doughnuts. Commander Evangeline Booth could envision the male officers serving some of the functions of unofficial chaplains, coupled with a broader role: providers of rest, respite and recreation for weary troops under whatever roof could be found or erected on short notice. They would furnish reading material, possibly a phonograph, games, and spiritual counsel when sought. As one would expect of Salvation Army officers, a feature of their Sundays, plus other times as well when feasible, would be song services, with pungent, practical, and by all means brief messages rather than full-length sermons which might scare off those soldiers leery of anything stuffy or too "religious." In a word, the Salvationist workers were not being sent to supplant or compete with chaplains but, to whatever extent possible, to bring a bit of home to the troops.

Women in combat zones were something new and different. Up to that point, the only women who might have met that description were camp-followers or, in plain language, prostitutes. There was certainly no question about their presence near the camps—even within an encampment's borders when it could be managed by devious dough-boys. The prostitutes concerned the Commander greatly. She knew the mothers, wives and girlfriends at home would never want soldiers consorting with such women. Yet the temptation was all too real.

The Salvationist women, she hoped, could to some extent fill the void created by the absence of the women and girls who had formerly been a part of soldiers' lives, and who were waiting at home to resume their rightful place after the war.

These women, soon to be nicknamed "lassies," would endure all the dangers and hardships confronting male officers. Like them, they would offer similar rest centers which, it turned out, were often no more than tents, huts or basements of bombed-out houses. Perhaps the words "no more than" are misleading. It was the very nature of those rough, makeshift and sometimes dangerous "digs" which brought great respect toward the Salvationists. They were voluntarily risking their lives and sharing many of the privations facing the troops, yet doing it for a higher purpose.

There was the question of how, in some practical manner, to bring a touch of home to those huts and tents. The lassies soon sensed that something more was needed than sympathy, counsel and manufactured treats—if indeed such treats could be transported by some means to the Red Shield huts.

Many years later Lt. Colonel Helen Purviance recalled how the doughnut first came to be made in France. She was teamed with Ensign Margaret Sheldon, a nurse who had been in the Army's slum work in Chicago. They had a tent behind the battle lines in Montiers, France.

"There must be something we can do, Margaret, besides give these boys stuff to read and feed them fudge. Fudge is all to the good, but after all…" Sheldon agreed. Cakes were out of the question. Their little wood-burning stove, 18 inches wide, had no oven, just a flat top. And as for pies, even with an oven, they were impossible. No way to get filling at that time, although that came later.

No inspirations came all through autumn until they went for a Sunday stroll toward a village near where they were encamped.

"Pancakes?"

"Messy—and no good without syrup."

"Doughnuts?" They looked at one another. "Doughnuts sound like a good idea," Purviance responded. "But how do we cook 'em?"

Sheldon knew how. Along with their little wood-burner they had a pan in which, conceivably, they might fry seven doughnuts at a time.

Helen checked with the commissary. There was flour, some sugar, baking powder, canned milk and lard. But Margaret was not satisfied. "No eggs, Helen? Doughnuts without eggs?"

If Sheldon knew how to make doughnuts, Purviance would do her part. She knew very little French, but she knew how to say eggs—*des oeufs*. Donning her steel helmet she went into a nearby French village and, after some inquiring and dickering, accompanied by many

165

gestures, "was able to buy some; maybe two dozen of them," as she recalled. "And we were in the Salvation Army doughnut business."

The first batch of doughnuts cooked on the tiny stove were cut with a knife. But that was obviously too slow for large numbers. Next they cut the outer circle with a condensed milk can, the inner hole with a cylindrical metal tube used in those days for men's shaving sticks. This was a start. A village blacksmith was asked in fractured French and appropriate gestures to join the tube and condensed milk can into a one-piece cutter which could do the job in one movement.

Lt. Colonel Purviance recalled that he "rose nobly to the challenge," and his cutter served them well until they received a real cutter from the States.

To the Unknown Soldier

In a way it's strange. Veterans of World War II, Korea and Vietnam are honored by a day associated with the end of World War I— nothing more recent. Veterans Day used to be called Armistice Day and always fell on November 11, the day of peace in 1918. It is still observed in November.

Edward Carpenter, editor of *A House of Kings*, the official history of Westminster Abbey, noted the British viewpoint regarding the two world conflicts. "Everyone seems to have wished to remember the earlier one and everyone wished to forget the later one. In the years after 1918 memorials were erected in almost every parish; after 1945 the memorial was often only the addition of more names to those of 1914-18, or something useful to the parishioners, or possibly an improvement to the church."

Carpenter wonders if a Tomb of the Unknown Soldier would ever have became a reality if it had been suggested for the first time after 1945. Yet in 1920 it was an idea whose time had come. A chaplain who had served in Flanders proposed it to Dean Ryle of Westminster Abbey. The Dean talked to the right people, and within months, four unidentified bodies from battlefields in France were selected. The director of the War Graves Commission in Flanders chose one of them at midnight, November 8-9, 1920. It was encased in a coffin which was at once sealed, and the other bodies were then reburied in Flanders. In the morning a joint service was held with chaplains of several denominations, then the coffin was transported to a public gathering in France where Marshal Foch himself gave a speech. The solemn journey continued across the English Channel and to London, where King George V and many other dignitaries followed the coffin on foot to Westminster Abbey, the resting place of royalty. The body was placed beneath a slab of black marble bearing the words, "An Unknown British Warrior."

The idea was so meritorious and so logical that, historian Carpenter states, "It has been copied in many other countries and helps to make the nations feel a kindness for one another.

"A Head of State on an official visit to a foreign country invariably lays a wreath on the grave of an Unknown Soldier."

The man who started it all had his finger on the pulse of humanity. He was in touch with people's feelings. It is not surprising to learn, therefore, that he came from a people-oriented family—a Salvation-ist family. The Flanders chaplain was the Rev. David Railton, son of Commissioner George Scott Railton, that faithful comrade-in-arms of William Booth.

A Cup of Cold Water—or Hot Coffee

If you have wondered why Salvation Army workers were not sent overseas in the second World War as they were in the first, here is the explanation. With the threat of war looming over the United States, The Salvation Army had centers operating in or near many American military camps.

At this point President Franklin D. Roosevelt stepped in and said he did not want a multiplicity of organizations quarreling among themselves and scrambling to get the best locations for their clubs near military bases. Roosevelt, it must be remembered, had been

Assistant Secretary of the Navy during the first war, and evidently he thought there had been too much friction among the various service organizations.

In early 1941 the six service organizations which would soon join together under the banner of USO were basically the same organizations (some with revised names) which had served in the first World War. In the first war, however, there had been a seventh: the American Library Association.

Despite Roosevelt's opinion, by 1918, when their work was well underway, there been considerable cooperation among the organizations, as evidenced by their being nicknamed the "seven sisters." But Roosevelt was determined to prevent any of them from doing a similar work overseas in this second war. Nor was he enthusiastic about their being permitted to serve within our own boundaries. This, he believed, should be left exclusively to the American Red Cross.

Spearheaded by The Salvation Army, the six organizations set up a proposal whereby they would work together, coordinated under a single "umbrella," thus avoiding possible friction. John D. Rockefeller Jr., acting as their spokesman, approached Roosevelt with the new plan. The President approved, with the stipulation that their service clubs could only be located on American soil. Thus in February 1941, USO (United Service Organizations) was born. Later this was broadened so that many USO entertainment units (camp shows) were sent overseas. But except for Hawaii, the clubs never left our shores.

However, more than a year before the words "Pearl Harbor" were on everyone's lips, The Salvation Army was serving American troops outside the continental United States. By 1940 Major General William H. Wilson, the Commandant of Schofield Barracks in Hawaii, had specifically requested that a Salvation Army presence be established near his camp. (In what follows it must be borne in mind that there had been less than 21 years between the Armistice in 1918 and the German attack on Poland in 1939.)

Major and Mrs. Alva Holbrook, who had served with The Salvation Army in France in the first war, were sent to open a Red Shield club near Schofield Barracks as requested. (Mrs. Holbrook, who was in her twenties while in France, was now in her late forties, still looking much the same.) It was not long before the Holbrooks were invited to meet the Commandant. When they were introduced, General Wilson took one look at Mrs. Holbrook and exclaimed, "I remember you! You practically saved my life." He went on to tell the story of the very tired and hungry infantryman, the story of the solitary soldier on a forced march.

As the general spoke, he took pains to make it clear that his use of the word "you" did not refer to The Salvation Army as an organization, which had indeed helped him in his hour of need, but by a remarkable coincidence, he was speaking to the very woman who had treated him so kindly, the one who served him from that canteen in 1918!

The general then indicated the colonel at his side and said, "If there is anything you need, just tell him; and if he doesn't get it for you, you come and tell me, and I'll see that he does."

We as Christians give the "cup of cold water" of which Jesus spoke without thought of reward or repayment. But sometimes, whether it be a cup of cold water or of hot coffee, there can be an unexpected and wonderful aftermath to a simple act of kindness.

Harry Made It Happen

It is a hitherto unpublished story recorded by Mrs. Major Holbrook. She and her husband had served in France in World War I, and in 1940 were assigned to Hawaii at the request of the U.S. Army commandant of Schofield Barracks, near Pearl Harbor. There the Holbrooks set up a Salvation Army Red Shield Club. This was not strictly war work, since the U.S. was not at war.

But the Japanese attack catapulted the Holbrooks into genuine, round-the-clock war work the very night of December 7, probably the first by American Salvationists anywhere. Much of the credit for the speed with which it happened must go to a government employee who worked wonders in mere hours.

Mrs. Holbrook and her husband, as soon as the planes had wreaked their havoc, offered their services for first aid work or whatever else was necessary. But the wounded were being cared for at facilities which they could not reach, due to roads which were blocked. Mrs. Holbrook returned to the house only to find the power cut off. A Japanese plane, having been disabled and plunging earthward, had dived at a power plant. He missed the plant but got the wires providing electricity to the immediate area in which their home was located. She collected all the raw perishable foods, such as meat, from the refrigerator and cooked them up, then made every provision she could for a siege. Her husband came in with some people who had had no breakfast and she fed them. They told others, so her supply dwindled rapidly.

There was a knock at the door. The visitor was Harry of the Federal Security Administration. He was responsible for surplus commodities on the island. Someone had told him that Mrs. Holbrook was feeding people on duty. He asked her to set up a canteen to feed the locals who were on guard, as well as the police, nurses, Territorial Guard and others who, called into action so suddenly, had no provision for eating.

As she recalled later, the conversation went like this: MRS. H: "But I have no supplies."

HARRY : "I'll get you supplies."

MRS. H: "But I have no cooking utensils for such an undertaking."

HARRY : "We'll get some for you." MRS. H: "But I have no room." HARRY : "We'll get a building."

MRS. H: "But I am only one person."

HARRY : "Mrs. Holbrook, if you will do this for us, we will get you all the help you need. You cannot say 'no.' I don't know a soul this side of Honolulu who can do it but you."

What he didn't need to add was that all traffic to Honolulu was blocked off. It meant, in his eyes, that there was simply no one else with the organizing abilities to do the job.

What else could she say but "yes"? Later she wrote, 'No one expects a resident of Oahu to hurry. It's against all precedent. But I will vouch for the fact that in half an hour's time that man had secured the new, and hitherto unused, fire hall; had got an electrician to turn on the lights, and had connected up the electric stove. On Sunday, mind you! In an hour's time I was standing over a big table up to my elbows in doughnut batter, my mind fairly whirling as I tried to plan as I worked." She went on to list the people who came in to work alongside her, all recruited by Harry.

Harry was truly an American patriot, responding to the emergency in the best tradition. Oh. Did I mention his last name? Harry Okomura, a Japanese-American, just as loyal to our country as anyone could be.

On the Staff of the Chief of Chaplains

The fact is, even though The Salvation Army barely squeezed onto the roster of chaplains in World War I with its total of five, it came within an eyelash of having a brigadier general among it chaplains during World War II. A brigadier general in the Chaplains Corps was a rare distinction. Probably there were no more than three American chaplains in the world bearing that rank at that time. Today there is one. Exactly one.

Why, you may wonder, was this an "almost" thing? It wasn't because of any negative decision on the part of the military that it did not come to pass; it was because of the officer's personal decision, arrived at after considerable wrestling with the alternatives which confronted him.

You have read earlier about John J. Allan, the corps officer of the Bowery Corps in New York City who became one of our five chaplains during World War I. Because of his conspicuous bravery he was awarded the *Croix de Guerre* by the French government, a great honor indeed for an American.

He was quite a musician as well; in fact, his brilliant cornet playing resulted in a command performance before King George V of England. It was John Allan who organized and conducted The Salvation Army's very first music camp. That was in Long Branch, New Jersey, in 1921.

The following year he organized and led a larger version at Star Lake, the Eastern territorial camp.

The intervening years need not be detailed here, except to say that by 1940 Allan was a colonel in The Salvation Army. In November of that year he was asked by the Secretary of War to join the five-man staff of the Chief of Chaplains in Washington and was granted official permission to do so by The Salvation Army. He took up his duties with his old military rank of lieutenant colonel, and soon was promoted to full colonel—a colonel, you may note, in both armies.

Let me reiterate that, when the United States first entered World War I, Salvationists were not eligible to become chaplains, since The Salvation Army had never been officially recognized as a church by the U.S. government, or at least by that branch of government related to the military.

Inasmuch as only five officers became chaplains after the way was cleared, one would have to say it was a small beginning. So it was quite a contrast when, in 1940, one of those original five was added to the Chief of Chaplains staff.

Because the war was fought on several distant fronts, it was decided to have a representative of the Chief of Chaplains in each theater of operations—a "theater chaplain"—closer to the action. Colonel Allan was to be one of those overseeing the chaplaincy in a major sector of the world. Because each of these men would, in a sense, stand alone in his sector, he would need sufficient rank to be listened to and heeded. So each theater chaplain was to be a brigadier general. (A brigadier general is only one step up in rank from a colonel, but that one step would give him the "leverage" needed to get things done.)

By the time this reorganization of the chaplaincy was proposed, my father was The Salvation Army's USO regional supervisor in the Central Territory. Thus he was conversant with things military. Furthermore, in 1917-18 he had been in the Army's war work in France, often near the front, just as Colonel Allan had been in his work as a military chaplain. Because of this, as well through their contacts at Salvation

Army conferences over the years, they knew one another well. So it was to Brigadier Marshall that Colonel Allan confided.

He was, he said, suddenly confronted by a dilemma. The Chief of Chaplains wanted him as a theater chaplain, a job which would carry the rank of brigadier general. This would indeed be a great help to the standing of all Salvation Army chaplains—the fact that one of their own was a brigadier general in the Chaplains Corps!

The problem was that The Salvation Army was short of officers. So many had been pulled off their regular assignments for USO and Red Shield work that there were some very hard-to-fill gaps. One of those was territorial commander for the Central Territory. Colonel Allan was desperately needed for that job. He could, he knew, quite legitimately and honorably resign his military commission. He did not want to, but he felt his first duty was to The Salvation Army, and his leaders had made it clear that their need was genuine and urgent.

So with deep regret, the colonel left the military and became a commissioner in Chicago. The result? We missed having a brigadier general among our Salvationist chaplains.

The Red Shield at Normandy

A description of the Normandy invasion calls for more superlatives than any other military-naval event in history. Untold gallons of ink have been expended on the risk factors, on the conditions and on the events of those earliest days surrounding the Allied landings in France. Reports of the uncertain weather, the largest armada in history, the thousands of warplanes overhead, and so on seem to eclipse the work of The Salvation Army. In Britain, Red Shield centers served a very useful purpose while the troops were waiting and waiting…and waiting. But the troops have finally been galvanized into action and The Salvation Army has been left behind. Right? Well, not exactly.

On June 6, 1944, American troops had their own assigned landing areas on the Normandy coast, while the British and Canadians, who fought just as courageously, were responsible for separate sectors. Thus it never became an item of news in the U.S. when the first Salvation Army mobile canteen landed on the Normandy beach.

Considering that the specially-designed canteens were six-ton vehicles, with insulated bodies and facilities for serving 4,600 men before they had to be re-supplied, plus a small library, a radio, a record player and a sound film projector, one needn't be told that they weren't in the first assault wave! But neither were they far from the action for very long. They could be very useful when there were casualties nearby, since some of them carried, in addition to all the items mentioned above, folding racks for stretchers so they could double as aid stations or even as ambulances.

How long until they arrived on the beaches? The first Salvation Army Red Shield officer in Normandy landed with the Royal Canadian Air Force before dawn on June 9, 1944 to reconnoiter. The big canteens soon followed. This was hardly their debut, since these same vehicles had been with British and Canadian troops all through the hard fighting in North Africa and Italy.

Because The Salvation Army was prevented by the U.S. Government from sending any of its workers overseas with the American forces, it sometimes puzzles people who never left American soil to hear American veterans of World War II speak in glowing terms of their encounters in many combat areas with Salvation Army canteens and huts, and with Salvationist workers in remote and unexpected places. It should come as no surprise, however, since the Canadians, Australians and British did what the American Salvationists were not allowed to do; they made the Red Shield a familiar and welcome sight in places as far-flung as Singapore, Syria, New Guinea, North Africa, Greece, Crete, Palestine, Egypt, Iceland, Alaska, Hawaii, and many South Pacific islands, not to mention the many places throughout the British Isles where American troops had been concentrated and equipped for the liberation of the European mainland. Americans were made as welcome as any from the Commonwealth by the "Sallies" or "Salvos." Always international in practical help as well as in outlook, they fed and "coffeed" and made as comfortable as possible any

American who showed up. It's no wonder so many veterans returned to the States with glowing reports.

Red Shield units, 3,000 of them, were strategically placed throughout the world. They ranged from spacious hotels to "huts," clubs and mobile canteens. Of the latter there were a thousand, many in the thick of things, moving frequently to keep up with the tide of combat, to be near the embattled soldiers who so needed them.

And so it was that our veterans came home singing the praises of The Salvation Army, not because of what American Salvationists were allowed to do, but because of Salvationists from other countries. For this great reservoir of good will we can thank our Army's truly international spirit, which springs from the Spirit of Christ.

War and Peace

In 1945 the special Easter issue of *The War Cry* carried on its back cover a full-page painting which seems to have had special significance when we learn the story behind it.

In order to appreciate fully that significance, one has to realize how far in advance the artwork for the Christmas and Easter issues was prepared. Remember that, in those days of fifty-two weekly *War Crys* a year, only those two "specials" were printed in full color. And since they were the only two published for all four territories, literally millions came off the presses. Knowing that, we begin to see why lengthy preparation was necessary. Artists had to be commissioned to paint the covers as well as illustrations for the stories and articles. The process consumed several months.

In late 1944 and early 1945, the Allied march toward Berlin did not always go well. Need I mention the Battle of the Bulge, which led to the death of so many Allied soldiers? Even during that dark hour, artists were doing their work for the Easter *War Cry*. The back cover pictured an American chaplain tending to a wounded man on the battlefield. In the near background stood a German soldier, his hands at his sides, his head cocked a bit to one side, with a look on his face which conveyed mixed emotions. He withheld his fire, making no effort to reach for his gun. His inclusion in the painting silently conveyed a message of the basic decency of so many of the combatants, regardless of which side they were fighting on.

Months later, when Easter arrived and the picture was in the hands of millions of readers, the whole military situation had changed. Germany was just weeks from total surrender, and the process of reconciliation was already beginning. The painter had caught that spirit of reconciliation long in advance of its becoming a reality! Is it any wonder that the U.S. Chaplains Corps had that *War Cry* cover enlarged and hung in the office of the Chief of Chaplains in Washington?

Reconciliation, Divine and Human

When, in May 1945, Germany capitulated, the world could begin to see daylight at the end of the tunnel. But, it was assumed, getting to the end of that "tunnel" might be a long haul, and a most difficult and costly one in terms of loss of life. However, for a short time at least, people celebrated, sometimes wildly, because one giant hurdle to peace had been removed. For those of us in the Armed Forces already in the Pacific, that celebration was more subdued, tempered as it was by the grim prospect of what still lay ahead.

Salvationists, like nearly everyone else, shared a love of country and a great desire to see an end to Hitler and his increasingly insane leadership. To characterize him thus does not seem unjustified since, as his desperation increased, he became obsessed with hurting the Allied Forces as much as possible as they rolled on to victory. He would make them pay in blood, even though that payment was to be extracted by pathetically over-aged and underage German males, many of them mere boys. The last speeches of his spokesmen as well as his own messages to his generals showed that he believed any German male left alive at the end of the last battle was a coward, not fit to live. This was not at all what his dream and his promises had been, but if he was to go down, the nation would go down with him.

The extensive work carried on through The Salvation Army's Red Shield clubs and canteens, as well as our part in US0 was not, as some might imagine, the work of an ultra-patriotic, "my country right or wrong" sort of organization. Back in 1914, at the beginning of the first World War, there had been grave doubt among The Salvation Army's leaders as to whether we should involve ourselves with any warring nation. Bramwell Booth loved and was guided by the motto (referring to our Heavenly Father): "Every land is my fatherland, for all lands are my Father's." In 1912 he had declared: "The Salvation Army belongs to the whole world. It knows no nationality as such." The work among soldiers and sailors of various countries was to be done simply because they were young men with great needs, far from home, often sorely tried.

By the time American Salvationists went to France in 1917, the mood had changed considerably, however. It is probably accurate to say our work was suffused with patriotism. Certainly in the public eye, The Salvation Army was equated with patriotism as our workers did so much to improve the morale of the troops.

In World War II, great care was taken by Army leaders, especially at International Headquarters, to remind Salvationists that people in nations fighting against the Allies were also suffering hardship. In Britain, 556 Salvation Army properties were destroyed or damaged by the end of 1944, but General Carpenter would not allow use of the word "enemy" in any Army publication, nor did he ever use it in any public utterance. Salvationists strove to meet human need whenever they could reach the needy.

Thus in March 1945, while war still raged in Germany, Salvationists crossed the channel and had relief teams at work among the suffering, the starving, the homeless and displaced in vast areas which by then had been liberated. They moved on into Germany soon after the surrender. The Army's message of love and reconciliation went before it so that, when our General entered Germany in 1946, he was greeted warmly by large congregations in Hamburg, Dortmund, Mulheim, Wuppertaal-Barmen, and finally in Berlin, where the Burgomaster welcomed him as "a voice of love and fellowship." The Spirit of Christ had prevailed.

Against All Odds

In December 1941 Maurice was a small-town boy from downstate Illinois. His response to the Japanese attack on Pearl Harbor was to enlist in the Navy. Then came a letdown. The Navy suddenly found itself swamped with young patriots eager to avenge that "day of infamy." Thousands who were sworn in on the spot were sent home, with no uniform and no pay, until housing could be set up and staff provided to train them. For two months Maurice, now irrevocably committed to naval service, cooled his heels at home. Finally he was summoned to Great Lakes Naval Training Station to be outfitted and assigned.

During his eleven days there, he was granted one evening of liberty. Determined to make the best of that one evening, he boarded a train for Highland Park but got off at the wrong stop, namely Highwood. Trains were infrequent, so he decided to make the best of a bad thing. He asked what there was to do locally, and was told of The Salvation Army's USO club. What he didn't know until later was that the government (not the USO) had decreed that certain clubs were strictly for soldiers while others were for sailors, thus avoiding possible friction among men from the two services. No one at the USO told the seaman that he was "off limits"; that little *faux pas* was tactfully ignored.

Soon Maurice forgot all about being in the wrong town. A group of very nice co-eds from North Park College were serving as hostesses that evening. They had been scheduled for the following week: March 13, but there had been some breakdown. Consequently, at the last minute they were asked if they could possibly come March 6. The answer was yes.

During the evening Maurice was attracted to one co-ed. Realizing they would never again meet in this way, he overcame his natural shyness long enough to ask for her phone number. But she had no telephone. However Gladys, one of her classmates, volunteered her own phone number and offered to relay any messages or to summon her friend to the phone if at all possible.

That phone number? Maurice did call, but he and Gladys got so busy talking that she never called the other girl to the phone, nor did

Maurice ask her to! It was one of those things that "just happened." He and Gladys corresponded all during the war and were married six days after he was discharged in December 1945.

Shortly before their golden wedding anniversary they wrote to Highwood to see if they could visit the spot where they had first met. Of course the "spot" was still there, but the building which had stood on that spot had been torn down and turned into a parking lot for a very nice restaurant next door. They were a bit disappointed, but decided that, when the time came for them to pass through Highwood (as a part of a business trip involving Maurice), they would visit the spot anyway and have a nice dinner at the restaurant.

But there is more to the story. Someone who heard of their upcoming visit had an inspiration. Why not re-create the Salvation Army USO club, just for one night of nostalgia? There was a large community hall nearby which could be used, and certainly there were willing volunteers who would help to make a big thing of it!

In one month of whirlwind preparations, a committee arranged a highly successful fiftieth anniversary of the closing of that Salvation Army USO. In a remarkable re-creation of the old club, with Salvationists and former hostesses present, with photographs from The Salvation Army's archives, as well as exhibits provided by several World War II buffs, the place took in a wonderful '40s atmosphere.

The Two World Wars

But there was more! What would a USO have been without "eats"? So there were sideboards spread with a variety of refreshments, and enough small tables in the main hall for everyone to sit down together to reminisce and to enjoy the program. The committee had even arranged for a '40s-style orchestra to provide "big band" music, and for a little surprise feature which would cap the evening.

There was still more! Authorities at nearby Great Lakes Naval Training Station graciously sent their famous Bluejacket Choir to sing. The young sailors added a lot of zest to the festivities because, after their mini-concert, and at the end of the planned program, they went to the tables where former hostesses sat and, escorting them to the small dance floor, danced with them while the orchestra played in the style of Glenn Miller. They did it so gallantly that one could easily forget for the moment the contrast between their youth and the fact that their dance partners were sexagenarians and septuagenarians!

We who were there to represent The Salvation Army in this tribute to the USO it had once operated felt pleased and honored to have been a part of it all. Nor were we bothered by the slight historical inaccuracy of having dancing in the re-created "club." It's true that there never was any dancing in The Salvation Army's club in Highwood, but the whole celebration took on the general atmosphere of that long-ago wartime era as remembered today. Besides, the sight of those young sailors doing their part so gallantly was absolutely refreshing.

All in all, it was quite an evening as more than 200 people took a sentimental journey along with Maurice and Gladys, who mused upon their meeting long ago, against all odds, and their long and happy life together.

A Salvationist Survivor

Among the many sidelights to Salvation Army history deserving mention, I would include some of the experiences of Major Gordon Coles, a son of Army composer Colonel Bramwell Coles. Gordon was in the Canadian Army early in World War II, when Singapore was captured by the Japanese. The 50,000 British and Canadian forces were nearly out of ammunition, so to continue fighting would have been tantamount to committing mass suicide. Thus they were ordered to lay down their arms and surrender.

Gordon Coles had five remarkable escapes from death during his three-and-a-half years of captivity. Let me tell you about three of them.

The Japanese wanted to send a large supply of ammunition and high explosives to an island not far to the west of Singapore. Some of the captives were conscripted to load a barge with those supplies, then were to remain on board to unload them when the barge reached the island. However, the Japanese officer-in-charge deemed it unnecessary to have so many men to unload them on the island, so some of them, including Gordon, were ordered off before the barge left for the island. On the way out, something caused a tremendous explosion killing all of the men on board. Gordon could only marvel at being spared.

Later, the Japanese had to face the immense problem of how to feed 50,000 prisoners, far more than they knew how to find useful tasks for while trying to conduct a war. So they ordered them to line up in ranks. There seems to have been a double purpose: the Japanese would reduce the number of mouths to feed, and they would intimidate the Allied troops, showing what kind of a ruthless enemy they were facing. Officers went down the lines choosing some to step out of the formation. (They might have been those who were smaller or appeared less physically promising for slave labor.) Soon it became clear that these men would be shot, thus eliminating the "excess" men. Gordon was among those told to step out of the formation.

Suddenly a small group of British fighter planes roared overhead. They did not fire on the men below, probably because it was clear they were their own men. With the noise of the planes and the sudden confusion, everyone ran for cover, Japanese, Canadians and British alike. What was left was a scene of utter confusion. The Japanese did not even try to reorganize the huge formation; the whole plan was abandoned.

The third escape came when Gordon was a slave-laborer for the Japanese in a coal mine in southern Japan. One day his overseer shouted to him the equivalent of "Hey you, come over here right now." Gordon naturally responded immediately. Hardly had he gotten out of his cramped tunnel and reached the overseer when there was a rumbling roar behind him, and the whole portion of the tunnel where he had been collapsed. He would have been crushed to death.

After these close brushes with death, you can understand why Gordon was sure the Lord had a plan for him: *officership!*

Blessed are the String-Savers

When the Salvation Army's International Headquarters (IHQ) was destroyed in World War II, apparently it was not the result of explosives, which had previously damages "101" twice before. Rather, the death blow was caused by incendiary bombs. A fire officer at the time described how he saw the planes flying abreast against the moon and seeming to bomb "almost to orders." Steadily, and against little opposition, the row of bombers moved back and forth across London "like tractors plowing a field." The German intent had been to turn the entire area surrounding and including St. Paul's Cathedral into one blazing inferno. This time they succeeded, although the great stone church itself refused to capitulate. As for our IHQ (which had grown from an original row of old adjoining buildings, bought up as more and more space was needed), the brick and stone exterior of IHQ still remained, refusing to collapse. But it was a forlorn ghost of itself. Photos of the ruins show skeletal remains still standing, but nothing remained inside. And because of the intensity of the heat, some of the parts made of iron were twisted and deformed grotesquely. From this description it is not to be assumed that most of the other Army properties in the United Kingdom escaped destruction or grievous damage. In fact, by the end of 1944, no less than 536 Salvation Army properties in the United Kingdom had been totally destroyed or heavily damaged. For some reason, in his book Colonel Sandall did not give the final figure at war's end for England, although he did cite the continuing effect of the V-1 and V-2 bombs in 1945.

When the Colonel, who was to write the first volumes of the history of The Salvation Army, asked permission to borrow some of the historical source-materials from IHQ for research purposes at home it was to minimize the increasingly arduous trip from his suburban home through London's debris-filled streets. He was not necessarily thinking about "rescuing" those records from a danger zone. In fact the mere prospect of IHQ being so obliterated by a firestorm such as that of May 10-11, 1941, must have seemed almost beyond imagining. But it happened. Thus there is reason to be extremely grateful for Sandall's project, which led to saving of such a portion of our history. However, being grateful for what was saved was one thing, but the loss of all left in IHQ was something else.

But the story did not end there. There were many official sources such as carbon copies of vital correspondence, safely filed away in the Army's offices world wide, which were retrieved. As word was circulated regarding the loss, many long time Salvationists began to offer their stack of back issues of Army publications, some ranging back to the 19th century. Earlier, people might have smiled condescendingly at them as compulsive "savers". Why did they do it? Ah! *Now* they knew! They were needed, and delighted to have a part in saving our history. Ultimately the carefully kept publications, music, copies of photos, etc. filled the void beyond what anyone could have hoped for.

The old IHQ was gone, but the "savers" helped us survive!

How Things Have Changed!

In order to give the full impact of this story, I have to tell you first about Vidkun A. Quisling, a Norwegian whose name came to mean "traitor" in its very strongest terms during and after World War II. Quisling was trained in Norway's military academy, entered the army in 1911, and by 1931 reached the rank of major of field artillery. In 1931, he became Norway's minister of defense, but in 1934 resigned his post in order to found the National Unity Party, patterned after that of the German Nazis, with whom he had allied himself strongly.

In 1940 with his experience as minister of defense and the secrets entrusted to him, he helped the Germans to plan the invasion of Norway. After the Germans landed on April 9, he used his authority to hasten his country's collapse. In September 1940, the Nazis rewarded him with the appointment as sole political head of Norway, and on February 1, 1942 he was made premier.

Immediately after the German surrender in 1945, he was brought to trial for high treason and found guilty of betraying his country, causing the death of innumerable Norwegian patriots, and incitement to mutiny. When found guilty, he was shot by a firing squad.

Now we turn to a subject completely different, but related to the meaning of the term "quisling." A hundred years after the conversion of William Booth, the dean of Britain's St. Paul's Cathedral, the Very Rev. W. R. Matthews, felt that the anniversary was significant enough to be recognized by a Meeting of Thanksgiving, held Friday, June 2, 1944, at 6 p.m. in St. Paul's. Not only did the Dean give rather reserved praise to the Founder in his carefully chosen words, but he invited General George Carpenter to read the Scripture lesson for the day. This did not involve comment, only the reading of the assigned Scripture portion. In the next issue of the *Church Times,* the official or quasi-official publication of the Church of England, there appeared a page one editorial branding the Dean as an "ecclesiastical quisling," for his recognition of the Founder, and The Army as a schismatic body. Bearing in mind that World War II was far from over, that D-Day had not yet taken place, and that Quisling was still in office as premier of captive Norway, we can begin to see what a damning term this was for the *Church Times* to use against one of its leading churchmen. The Dean of St. Paul's a traitor to his own church! As General Frederick Coutts observes in volume six of *The History of The Salvation Army,* "Providentially the Dean had secured in advance the approval of both the Bishop of London and the Archbishop of Canterbury."

Why is this incident and its aftermath recalled after all these years? Simply to show (to use the words of General Coutts) "how much closer believers have drawn together" since that time. Who, at that time would have dreamed that, in the years to follow, a bronze bust memorial to that same William Booth would have been placed in Westminster Abbey? But there it is, for all to see!

TOUCHING LIVES
MANY *in* WAYS

Only the Names Have Been Changed

It was a small mishap, and the young people's sergeant-major tried to make the best of it. There weren't enough *Young Soldiers* to go around that week in Sunday school, due to an unexpectedly large attendance. In order that those who missed their usual paper would not go home empty-handed, the YPSM gave them each a *War Cry*. Granted, it wasn't a very good substitute for a child's Sunday school paper; it was the British edition, tabloid size, on newsprint, with small type—not the kind of thing a child would even try to read. To compensate for this very obvious shortcoming she said, "Now children, take this home to your mum and dad and get them to read it."

One of the children who had to take home a *War Cry* burst into the room and, with childish zeal, exclaimed, "Mum, you've just got to read this. Miss Langworthy at the corps said we should be sure you look at it. So, pleeeze." Janie, the girl in our story was, at age eight, the eldest child of Roger and Dorothy Underwood.

Dorothy (Dot to her friends) had been through troubled times before she met and married Roger. In her late teens she had gone with a Jack Moore, who did not meet with her mother's approval. After her mother, Mrs. Babcock, told Dot in no uncertain terms that Jack would never do as a husband, Dot had packed her things and stormed out of the house, vowing never to speak to her mother again. Later she regretted the harsh things she had said but assumed she had done irreparable damage to the relationship with her mother, whom she was sure would never want to see her again.

Mrs. Babcock, assuming Dot and Jack had married, gradually became reconciled to the idea, and hoped for the best. The truth was, she ached to see Dot again and to let her know she loved her, and that she would willingly accept her husband as well.

But things had taken an unexpected turn. When Jack's undesirable traits came to the fore, Dot became almost afraid of him. She gave up the "bedsitter" near his home and moved to another town so he could not find her. Thus Mrs. Babcock had no way of knowing where to look for her daughter, and none of Dot's old friends could be of any help. When all else had failed, the mother tried The Salvation Army's Missing Person's Bureau. Their efforts were equally futile. But what else could be expected? They were looking for a nonexistent Mrs. Dorothy Moore, when in fact the "missing person" was Mrs. Dorothy Underwood. When the Salvationists' efforts proved fruitless, they suggested that Dot's mother advertise in the Missing Persons column of *The War Cry*.

Meanwhile Dot allowed Janie to attend the Army's Sunday school nearby, although she herself was not involved in the corps. When Janie came home with *The War Cry* and insisted that Dot read it, she good-naturedly complied, perceiving what it meant to the child. Her eyes fell on the "We Miss You" column. Someone was searching for a Dorothy Moore. The age of the missing person tallied with hers, and she guessed that her mother (whose name did not appear) must have assumed that she'd married Jack. None of Dot's current friends knew anything about her former boyfriend, so even if they happened to see the notice, they could not possibly realize it was she who was being sought. Only she—she who had never read a *War Cry*—could have recognized the truth.

A whole gamut of feelings swept over her, but mostly feelings of joy and of love. Her mother, bless her heart, still loved her and wanted to see her, despite her defiance in marrying Jack! Now Dot could hardly wait to tell her mum that a reunion wouldn't mean forcing herself to make Jack feel welcome; wouldn't require saying, "I was wrong about him." As for Roger, Dot was sure her mum would be thrilled with the man she had actually married.

It was a joyous reunion: Mrs. Babcock, Dot, and her lovely family, all because of a shortage of *Young Soldiers* on that one crucial Sunday! Salvationists who seek the missing tend to believe the Lord sometimes steps in, in ways we don't imagine, to heal old wounds.

Back From the "Dead"

Inasmuch as The Salvation Army has successfully completed liter-ally hundreds of thousands of missing persons investigations since the inception of this service in 1885, the variety of case histories is practically limitless. If you are really interested, there are a couple of books documenting The Army's work in this field. For the greatest concentration of fascinating reading in one sitting, one can do no better than to open the book *Missing!* and turn to the chapter entitled "Coincidences." The experience will be truly rewarding. I'll not spoil your pleasure by trying to repeat any of those absolutely remarkable stories here, but leave it to you to find a copy of that book. Instead, allow me to recount two others, not so spectacular, but representative of loved ones reunited.

Consider the bartender in Switzerland who, it must be said, was affable toward the Salvationists who entered his establishment weekly to sell *The War Cry* and talk with his customers. Some bartenders might find such affability, or even toleration, a bit of a strain, knowing that real success on the part of the Salvationists could greatly reduce his clientele! This man often bought a copy himself, although no one knows how often he read its pages.

It is certain he read one edition, however, for the paper brought him the surprise of his life. In its Missing Persons section he found that his mother was seeking his whereabouts—his own mother! True, he had neglected to keep in touch, but he had thought little of the grief he might have been causing her. Stabbed with the realization of the anxiety he had caused, he immediately got in touch and renewed their relationship.

In 1972, when I was on the *War Cry* staff, we received from Europe a delightful picture of two very pleasant-looking people who had been reunited. The photo was a "natural" for our news pages. Attached was a fairly lengthy caption, but it was hardly complete enough to make a news story. At nearly the same time we received from England an account regarding the same people. It too was brief, containing additional facts but lacking some of those given in the photo caption. It was odd; facts missing in one were given in the other, so it was possible to fit them together like a jigsaw puzzle. The result? The story which follows.

In 1943 James Bath, a British soldier on leave, came home after an air raid to find his street cordoned off and his house practically flattened by a direct hit. His mother? He was told there had been no survivors. Not only was searching the rubble forbidden because of the danger of further collapse, it would have been futile. The next day his leave was over, and the grieving Jim had to return to his unit. Soon afterwards he was sent to North Africa.

Mrs. Ellen Bath had been shopping when the bomb destroyed her house. Unaware of what her son had been told, she failed to make contact with Jim before he was shipped out. (One must remember the chaotic conditions after such a raid.) He never wrote to his home address, since the postman cannot deliver a letter to a pile of rubble— nor to a dead mother. Later the same year a War Office telegram informed her that her son was missing, presumed dead.

After the war Jim settled in a small town in Buckinghamshire, still thinking his mother was dead. She, on the other hand, could not quite bring herself to believe that her son was really gone. For some years she went on annual pilgrimages to France to check military cemeteries, just in case he had died there. Unable to find his grave, she continued her inquiries over the years and, as a last resort, contacted The Salvation Army's Investigations Department in London.

The department's investigators traced Jim to his home in Buckinghamshire where he lived with his wife and two grown sons. One evening Mrs. Mason (for Jim's mother had remarried after the war, but was again widowed) heard a knock on her door. "Who is it? She asked. "Your son, James Bath," was the reply. In a moment the door was open and a separation which had lasted nearly 29 years was ended.

Soon afterwards, Mrs. Mason's flat in Stratford, London, was a festive place as she gave a party in honor of the son presumed dead for so long, and she got acquainted with the family she never knew she had. The Investigations Department closed the file on another case with a happy ending.

Yet Another Happy Ending

It must be understood that not every person who is located wants to communicate with relatives again, so not every case which is "successfully" concluded results in a reunion. But at least worried loved ones can know that the missing person is safe, and someone is in touch with them. However, many endings are very happy indeed. Twins separated at birth have been reunited; mothers who gave up their babies for adoption—and the following, which is a joy to read.

Brian and Sally (not their real names, of course) grew up in the same neighborhood. In 1953 they were 17 and 18, very much in love and planning to be married. They let their feelings run away with them, and Sally became pregnant. When they shared the news with their parents, their lives were torn apart. Sally's parents refused to permit the marriage and sent her off to have the baby and to place it up for adoption. Brian's parents forced him to join the Coast Guard to keep him away from Sally. As far as the parents were concerned, that was the end of the story.

Sally missed her baby desperately and wanted another one to take its place—not a good motive for marriage! In 1955 she met the man she would marry three weeks later. It was not long until she knew she had made a terrible mistake, but she was a good and faithful wife. She became the mother of five beautiful children. After 12 years her husband left her. All of her children, who were loving and supportive, knew of their mother's broken heart over Brian and encouraged her to search for him.

Sally contacted The Salvation Army, and Missing Persons was able to locate Brian. Happy but almost stunned to learn that Sally was searching for him, Brian expressed his longing for contact with her. He would have searched for her himself, he said, but was afraid of disrupting her life. He explained that he had always loved her, wanting nothing more than to marry her and raise their baby together. But because their parents had been so determined to keep them separate, he eventually married someone else. Their life together had been happy, but she had passed away four years previously.

Brian called Sally immediately and they talked at length. A meeting was arranged. When they met face to face it was as if they had seen one another only yesterday. At the time of the report, they had reacquainted themselves with family members and had met one another's children. Of the wife now deceased, Brian says he loved her very much, but Sally is the woman he should have married in the first place. At the time of writing, wedding plans were well underway.

As for the baby whom Sally had allowed to be adopted, they found that they would have to accept that as final; there was no way that person could be brought into the family circle. But they have each other and are surrounded by loving children.

God's Agents: Ordinary People

God's power to work miracles is unlimited, but He prefers to accomplish his miracles through ordinary people. Let's consider a case as it stood in the early 1950s. A South American Indian tribe, really a nation within a nation, spoke a language which had not yet been reduced to writing. They had no alphabet to reproduce the sounds, and of course no Bible. Missionaries had never broken the language barrier so as to tell them of God's love.

Two Salvationists played a part in the Lord's plan for that tribe without ever realizing it. Salvationist Number One was a young man who grew up in a boxcar, no longer on wheels but converted into a home. He had little education and was rather inarticulate, but perhaps because World War II had created a scarcity of male candidates, he was accepted for officership. Painfully aware of his shortcomings, he soon resigned to join the U.S. Army. He served in Europe as a chaplain's assistant in a unit which for a time was without a chaplain. Realizing his efforts to explain the plan of salvation were not very successful, he got a number of GI's to promise to attend at least one Salvation Army meeting when they got home after the war. "They'll make it really clear how you can be saved," he assured them.

Salvationist Number Two was an English woman who became an officer in the United States. She had a special talent for doing personal work in meetings. Although skilled in bringing people to a realization of their need of the Savior, she was sometimes criticized by her peers for being overly tenacious in dealing with seekers. The criticism hurt, but she felt compelled to continue her ministry.

The third person in this drama was John B. He and his sister were left alone in this world before age ten when their parents both died. The foster home in which they were placed was a disaster, and John and his sister finally ran away. John somehow managed to make his own way until old enough to enlist in the U.S. Army.

Shipped to Europe, he was assigned to the same unit as Salvationist Number One who, as I have said, did not feel capable of explaining the way of salvation clearly or convincingly. John was one of those who promised he would attend a Salvation Army meeting when he got home. We don't know about any of the others, but we do know that, to John, a promise was a serious matter. So once he was settled in Chicago, he sought out a Salvation Army corps. He must make that visit! Whether he would have visited more than once, no one can say for sure.

Salvationist Number Two was in that meeting and dealt personally with John during the prayer meeting. The encounter took all her skill and sensitivity, since his childhood church participation led him to assume that he was already a Christian. At length John was led to see his need, and he wholeheartedly accepted Christ as Savior before the meeting was over.

Through a remarkable series of encounters in the days that followed, John's life was completely changed and redirected. For one thing, he enrolled in a Christian college which he had never even heard of at the time of his conversion. After earning his degree and undergoing special training he became the missionary the Lord needed for that South American tribe.

In the two succeeding decades he, with his wife and children, settled in among those people. John painstakingly analyzed their speech, devised an alphabet which represented all the sounds needed to reduce the language to writing, wrote primers and textbooks, taught them to read, and completed a translation of the New Testament in their language. Of course, in addition to this, he and his wife were the evangelists.

The Salvationists who had a part in John's conversion never knew of all that he accomplished. But the time will come when all will be known.

This goes for you, too! That's a part of the excitement in faithfully witnessing to those around you. Perhaps when you get to Heaven, some who seemed to be hard cases in this life may, because of your witness and nurture, be there to say, "Surprise!"

Doing What We Can

Do you consider yourself a failure as a witness to the Christian faith? Probably most teenagers feel they can't put the essence of Christianity into words, much less enunciate their personal faith in terms which would be meaningful, relevant or compelling to an unsaved acquaintance or inquirer. Unfortunately, too many of us carry this feeling of inadequacy over into adulthood. We assume we could never lead a person to Christ and, crippled by that assumption, fail to do the tangible things we are able to do.

Perhaps we draw a parallel between our imagined inability and that old saying: "You can lead a horse to water, but you can't make him drink."

But there is another thought which could be important to you in helping you see your potential. That is the "flip side" of the old saying quoted above; namely that, even if you can't get a horse to drink, you can at least lead him to water. Someone else may be able to complete the job. Getting friends to come to meetings or join the Home League may not be soul-winning, but such a step may lead to the desired result.

Consider the sons of a corps officer in a fairly large Midwestern city who were faced with a high school bandmaster who was at first intimidating, but...well, read on.

At least one of the sons was of high school age when the father received that appointment, so the eldest immediately signed up for the school band. He, as well as his brothers, had played in a corps band from an early age, so they entered the school group with a fair degree of competency. The first son found it none too pleasant, because the bandmaster, when he wanted to describe the playing as unsatisfactory said the students "sounded like a Salvation Army band." (One has to remember that the Army held many open-air meetings in those days, and it was often difficult, if not impossible, to put together a good ensemble for the street corner. Consequently, what the public often heard was the worst sound Salvationists could generate! In the indoor meetings, the band would invariably be larger and, playing from the Band Journal under much better conditions, would sound greatly improved. But that sound never reached most of the public. Hence our reputation.)

For a while, this student was not able to do a great deal about his teacher's opinion, but he did attempt to tell him there was more—far more—to know about Army music. When, a year later, the second brother joined the band and immediately earned first chair in the trombone section, the bandmaster's unfavorable comparisons were less frequent. After all, derogatory remarks began to sound a bit hollow with two Salvationists holding top positions. By the time the third brother came in and earned second chair, solo cornet, right next to his brother, the teacher began to show real interest in this religious group which turned out such players.

It should be no surprise to learn that the school bandmaster later attended a Salvation Army music festival and eventually, Army meetings. In fact, he fell in love with Army music and, at his request, served for some years as an instructor at the divisional music camp.

Unfortunately, I don't know any more about the instructor because the corps officer-father, with his sons, was transferred. But the boys did what they could, through their patient, non-confrontational conversations with him about the Army, with their fine playing and exemplary deportment.

There are limits to what one can expect from a normal, active teenager. I would say that these boys let their light shine, wouldn't you?

A Drama in Two Acts

This story is not the brainchild of a playwright. It's true.

ACT ONE

Back in the days when *The War Cry* was a weekly publication, Mrs. Glenna Coulter was the longtime *War Cry* seller for the Wichita Citadel Corps. Wichita, Kansas, was a bustling, prosperous city, a commercial hub for trading in wheat, plus serving as home to three or four aircraft factories. It was also said to have had more Salvation Army per capita than any other city in the Central Territory.

Each week Mrs. Coulter would go through all the downtown office buildings with her *War Crys*, selling them to businessmen as well as their receptionists and clerks. Many were "regulars," buying a copy every week. One thing that made her so effective was her remarkable memory for the names of customers' children and spouses. In the brief conversations she had weekly with many of them, she inquired about their children by name and listened to many bits of family news. She had an encyclopedic knowledge regarding these people, and she really cared about them.

But not all her *War Cry* selling was done in the daytime. A couple of nights a week she made the rounds of taverns, selling the "white-winged messenger" and getting to know many of the habitués. One night she had to miss a special evangelistic meeting at the corps in order to do her route. As she left one of the taverns with a bundle of *War Crys* over her arm, a young man hurried out and stopped her. "Is that a Bible you're carrying?" He asked. She replied that it was The

Salvation Army's magazine, not a Bible, but that she hoped to get the gospel message into people's hands through its distribution.

That was good enough for him, so he poured out his story. He had come to Wichita to find work. Everything had gone wrong, and he was in despair over the mess he had made of his life, so much so that he had just bought a gun to kill himself. But he found he didn't have the nerve. That was why he had been in the tavern. "I'm not a drinking man," he said, "but I wanted to get enough liquor in me so I'd have the nerve to pull the trigger." Mrs. Coulter was a good listener but realized that the special evangelistic meetings taking place at the corps at that very moment might present a better opportunity for this young man to hear the gospel presented in its fullness. So she urged him to go to the corps, which was only a short walk from there.

When the altar call was given, he went forward and was soundly converted. Furthermore, he placed his gun on the altar and confessed why he was carrying it. A cynic might say that was a bit theatrical, but it was sincere.

Act Two

Many years later, three Salvation Army officers attending a large national ministerial conference, were having lunch at a table for four. The fourth place was vacant. A tall, impressive-looking man asked if he could join them. As they ate, he asked if he could tell them a story. It was the story of that young man in Wichita, whose life had been changed that night many years before.

Then he said, "I'm that man. I gave my life to the Lord and entered the ministry." He went on to mention the church of which he was pastor—the third-largest his denomination has in the country.

Sometimes such *War Cry* selling may seem discouraging, but if the seller is alert for opportunities to witness, there is no telling what the Lord may bring about through that witness.

Out of Harm's Way

Let me take you back to the earliest days of World War II. After some terrible events on the European Continent, there was a brief period when very little seemed to happen, or seemed to be in imminent danger of happening. Some shortsighted people began to appraise the situation as a "phony war." From our perspective that is hard to believe, isn't it? But it's true. In our country there was a long-running comic strip about the folks in Toonerville. (Did you ever hear of the Toonerville Trolley? That was a part of that comic strip.) One of the "regular" characters was the "terrible-tempered Mr. Bang." In the running narrative, he bought a big map so he could plot the course of the war on his own wall. Although it may sound bizarre now, when no action was reported day after day—no troop movements, no trenches—he became infuriated at having wasted his money on buying such a big map. With his face contorted in anger, he beat the map with his fists and perhaps even tore it down from the wall. For those days or weeks, that was considered to be funny!

Tragically, the seeming inactivity did not last long, and one of the ensuing events was the bombing of England. At about the same time, Colonel Robert Sandall (probably retired) had commenced a major project at The Salvation Army's International Headquarters: the publication of an authoritative history of the Army. When Colonel Sandall, who lived in an outlying suburb of London, found it difficult to get to IHQ for his research because of bombed-out buildings and debris choked streets, he asked if he could take home some of the resource materials which he was using for the history. At home, he could sit down and go to work right after breakfast, and not waste hours trying to navigate his way through the beleaguered city. This would speed up his work a great deal. Of course, asking to take those invaluable papers and photographs to his own home was admittedly a big and rather bold request. But those in authority decided to risk allowing him to take many irreplaceable photos and documents from the safety of the IHQ archives to his suburban home. Although the scope of his request, and the increasing number of papers and photos needed, might have worried some, Colonel Sandall knew what he was doing, and his good judgment was trusted. As he got deeper into the task, he found that "one thing led to another," resulting in his home becoming a virtual warehouse for precious papers.

Then came a particularly disastrous air raid on the heart of the city. Evidently St. Paul's, the mighty landmark dominating the area, was intended for destruction. Indeed, one incendiary bomb did penetrate the famous dome and burned fiercely upon a supporting timber. But brave men risked their lives to crawl out over the vast space within the dome and extinguish it.

The Army's IHQ, a block from St. Paul's was totally reduced to ashes. The loss of many Army treasures was devastating, but everything at the Sandall home was perfectly safe.

Out of the Depths

Clarence Hall, a former *War Cry* editor, wrote a book which became a classic: Out of the Depths, the true account of Henry F. Milans, a former New York newspaper editor. In the early 1900s Milans had lost everything due to a worsening alcoholism. Not that he didn't struggle valiantly with the habit. In his sober periods he had key positions on several of New York City's dailies, but then, after a time, he would "blow it all" with another catastrophic binge. For years, his widely recognized ability had enabled him to secure, after recovering from one of his prolonged drinking bouts, a responsible position with yet another of New York's newspapers. But after many failures it became general knowledge that, despite his great talent as an editor, he would eventually let the paper down with yet another of his disastrous binges. The result was that he ended up jobless and broke, a man whom no one would hire.

His patient and long-suffering wife finally had all she could stand, and although it broke her heart, she left him. Soon he was a shambling wreck who lived only for his next drink, ending up on the city's skid row.

After three years of this terrible existence, after doctors declared he was beyond help, Milans came under the influence of The Salvation

Army and found in the Lord the answer to his needs. His deliverance from drink was nothing short of a miracle. After some months, when Milans had regained his health, found a secure position in the very printing company in which he had once been partner, and was transformed in appearance, Milans wrote to his wife, at first cautiously. She was happy to hear he had changed, but she had no idea how great that change had been. After three months she finally accepted his invitation to meet him. Here is a part of Hall's description of that meeting.

"He dresses his best for the occasion ... His appearance stamps him as nothing less than a Wall Street banker on a holiday. They are to meet at the New York entrance to Brooklyn Bridge. Suddenly he sees her coming, a slight figure pushing her way through the crowds, her eager eyes searching for him.

"He knows for whom she is looking—an unkempt figure with bloated face and red nose, the only Henry she ever knew in those latter years of her misery. He wants to rush forward and take her in his arms. But he checks the desire. He allows her to hunt for a few minutes. Then suddenly, he stands before her. She looks up timidly as at a stranger, then her face is swept with surprised recognition of the vision of prosperity before her—her husband. For just a moment she stands off to survey the results of the wonderful change that has been wrought in him. A look of timid, eager pride supplants the stare of incredulity.... Smiling, Milans reaches out for her hand, tucks it in the crook of his arm, and leads her away from the Brooklyn Bridge and its confusion." The rest is a wonderful story of joy and love. Could there be any doubt of Henry's rock-solid stability? Well, the book was written 25 years after those events, even as Milans continued his decades-long ministry to struggling alcoholics as well as his *War Cry* writing.

Meeting Changing Needs

Let me tell something of the background of the Army's once highly publicized open-air meetings at the famous intersection of Hollywood and Vine. Bandsman Harry Sparks, after more than fifty years as a Salvationist bandsman, recorded it in his book, *With a Thousand Bands*, the title taken from a verse of an old Army favorite, "Joy in The Salvation Army." Partway through Bandsman Sparks's account, his corps became the Hollywood Tabernacle Corps, with its high-profile open-air meetings, led by its enterprising Corps Sergeant-Major whose name sounds almost as legendary as the famous intersection: Doctor Docter. But none of this was by pure chance. Dr. Robert Docter, known by his many friends simply as Bob, earned his doctorate and was highly influential in the education field as a department head at the University of California's Davis campus.

Bob is still active, influential, and a part of the editorial staff of the Western Territory's *New Frontier*, where he regularly writes a column with a name reflecting the exciting years of the Hollywood and Vine street ministry: "On the Corner."

If you think naming a corps "Hollywood Tabernacle" was a bit "Hollywoodish," you'll need to know it came about through a year-by year adjustment to changing—and sometimes seemingly unfavorable circumstances along the way, and a loyal, close-knit congregation willing to trust the Lord through it all.

We pick up the story with the Los Angeles Citadel Corps in a neighborhood which eventually found itself deteriorating to the extent it could only be described as the Skid Row area of Los Angeles. After a series of unpleasant incidents, soldiers no longer felt safe bringing their families to meetings there. So the building was converted into a Harbor Light Corps which better met the needs of the area's new inhabitants, and the congregation searched for something which would better meet their needs.

The only thing suitable at the time was a former tabernacle structure in a strictly residential area of the city, quite a departure in terms of tradition, since most corps were located in or near downtown areas, with at least one busy intersection suitable for open-air witness. The tabernacle was set in the center of an otherwise empty block, with a large parking lot on the south end, while the north end held a playground and a patio. The Army bought the entire block with its tabernacle, and used it for years, thus giving the corps its new name: Tabernacle Corps. But the strictly residential neighborhood was a limiting factor, since the truly excellent corps band limited opportunity for open-air witness.

Much later, when it was learned that a large movie theater on Hollywood Boulevard was up for sale, the Army bought it and moved the Tabernacle Corps there, thus adding the "Hollywood" to its official name. Much later, after an outstanding ministry, the famous Hollywood and Vine intersection, only a four-block march away from the corps, had changed so much that it was no longer suitable for those open-airs. But as needs have changed, the Army has again adapted and moved their ministry elsewhere to meet those changing needs.

SALVATION ARMY MUSIC

I Wish I Had Known

The incident told here has, until now, been confined to the realm of "oral tradition"—really true, with a verifiable source, but never published. It concerns John Philip Sousa and his encounter with Salvation Army bands in 1930. The man involved in conversation with Sousa was Hubert Burtenshaw, long a member of the Chicago Staff Band, for many years a cornettist, later a drummer known for his "drum solos," employing a skill from the British Isles rarely seen in our country. Burtenshaw was a veteran bandsman when I was one of the youngest; he was by then a brigadier, later to become a lieutenant colonel.

In 1930, as a member of the Chicago Staff Band, he had gone to the 50th anniversary celebration of the official opening of The Salvation Army's work in America. It was held in New York City, where Railton and his "hallelujah lassies" had landed in 1880.

In preparation for that great 1930 event, the representative Army bands had a lot of great new music to perform for the vast crowds attending. Two brilliant Salvationist composers had come to make America their home: Erik Leidzen, described in later years as Swedish-American, although his mother was Irish and he had spent part of his boyhood in Denmark; and Emil Soderstrom, who was Danish both by birth and by residence. Both were gaining a reputation in the secular music field. They were to become composers and arrangers of note in the burgeoning field of radio, and both were destined to be identified with that medium for many years.

But along with their work as professionals, these two Salvationists would, in the decades to follow, produce for the Army a seemingly endless flow of brilliant music, as well as beautiful and sensitive meditations and selections—in short, some of the finest music in The Salvation

Army's library of thousands of published pieces. And all of this because of their love for the Army.

Anyone familiar with Army music will know just what is meant when I point out that Erik Leidzen had written his brilliant "Pressing Onward" in 1925, and Emil Soderstrom had won first prize in a Salvation Army international music competition with his "Fighting for the Lord" in 1929. These and many other pieces were soon to be played by the outstanding Salvation Army bands of the country, including the New York and Chicago Staff Bands.

If this weren't enough, someone (probably Evangeline Booth herself) thought the "frosting on the cake" would be to have the famous John Philip Sousa, known as the "American March King," as a guest at the concerts, to lead the massed bands, and hopefully to compose a special march dedicated to The Salvation Army for the occasion.

Poor Sousa! Apparently no one bothered to give him any idea of the capability of Army bandsmen. It must be acknowledged, however, that any orientation accomplished by playing for him the phonograph records thus far produced by the New York and Chicago bands would have given no clue as to their capabilities. Their first records, all acoustically recorded (rather than electrically), were of the simplest marches and selections, perhaps because the pieces had to be short so as to fit the records of that day.

Thus it was that Sousa wrote a simple and (dare I say it?) lackluster march which he thought these amateur bandsmen could handle. He entitled it simply "The Salvation Army March." It was hardly what one would expect from the man who wrote "The Stars and Stripes Forever," the "Washington Post March," and so many others.

Sousa not only composed a march; he attended the concert and served as a guest-conductor. Obviously he was deeply stirred by the experience, as eyewitnesses later recalled. But because the march he contributed was so overshadowed by music of the Army composers, he was rather embarrassed. This embarrassment was apparent as he stood near the stage after the concert, graciously conversing with various bandsmen and listeners, and shaking hands with many who felt privileged to meet the Great Man. Looking for someone who might understand his chagrin, Sousa singled out a substantial-looking officer approaching middle age, a member of the Chicago Staff Band's cornet section: Burtenshaw.

As the colonel recounted it years later, Sousa said, "I wish I had known you Salvationists had players of such ability. I certainly would have written something more challenging, more suited to the occasion." It was true; he had obviously scaled down his work to produce a march of less than moderate difficulty, which meant sacrificing any of the musical pyrotechnics for which he was known. One might be tempted to suspect that Sousa, who was "getting on in years," no longer had the spark of inspiration he once had. But less than two years later he demonstrated that this certainly was not the case; he produced a Washington Bicentennial march with all his old flair.

By contrast, in writing for the Salvationists, Sousa had carefully avoided anything very difficult, incorporating "the Founder's Song" and keeping the rest simple for well-meaning musical dilettantes—about whom he had been told practically nothing! Of course, therein lay the problem, the problem of communication.

It's a rather sad little story, and it leaves a nagging question: could the "American March King" have written a great march for us which would still be a classic if he had been properly informed?

The key word is "informed," which transfers over into a subject far broader than music alone. You and I have a responsibility to inform people with whom we come into contact about vital matters; matters beyond music; yes, matters of life-and-death importance. Let us all take to heart the challenge of Romans 10:14. "How, then, can they call upon the one they have not believed in? And how can they believe in the one of whom they have not heard? And how can they hear without someone preaching to them?"

All Christians, whether soldiers, officers, or any other believer, can, in a hundred ways, in a hundred situations, be among those who, simply and in a practical way, inform their fellow men about the Christ they serve.

One Man's Family

Since their growth from the original Fry family brass quartet, Salvation Army bands have been considered a weapon in the "Great Salvation War." Perhaps bands were at their most meaningful at the height of our open-air evangelism, when a corps band was a central factor in that outreach. Such bands were organized and maintained strictly for the purpose of soul winning, and bandsmen were expected to be ready with a testimony on a moment's notice, and consecrated to the ministry of music.

But there were some who saw another way to use a band for soul winning. Admittedly it was unconventional; it even utilized government-paid workers in the midst of a corps program! In St. Louis, Missouri, one corps building had been an automobile-repair garage in a lower-income section of town. When the business closed during the Great Depression, The Salvation Army bought the large, barn-like structure, which looked like an airplane hangar that had gotten into the wrong neighborhood. But it was exactly the *right* neighborhood for a corps, located just across the street from a public school. The government, with its WPA program which paid the unemployed who were able and willing to work, was trying hard to "invent" jobs for all the recipients, many of whom were skilled in fields of endeavor which were the first to fall victim to the depression. An enterprising officer took on seven or eight unemployed professional musicians, paid by the WPA, to build a youth band at the Tower Grove Corps.

Thus it was that the invitation went out to the school; any student, with the consent of a parent, could learn to play a horn, regardless of church affiliation or lack thereof. In response, thirty-five to forty students crossed the schoolyard to the corps regularly to take music lessons. The music classes were small: six to eight in a class taught by a professional; and the kids practiced twice a day on weekdays: during their lunch hour and again after school. Not surprisingly, many progressed rapidly. As soon as they could play some tunes, they were invited to play as a band if they would come to Sunday school. One unchurched family had three in the band, ages fourteen, twelve and nine.

The mother soon started attending, and all four found Christ as their Savior. The father, a laborer for Swift Packing Company, did not respond so quickly. But eventually he began to attend and was converted. Both he and his wife became soldiers. As years passed, WPA was disbanded because of wartime prosperity, but the corps program continued with lay leadership. A younger son who had been two years of age in 1938, when the family first attended Tower Grove, and another who was not yet even born at the time, later followed the same path.

As time passed it became clear that these working-class parents and their five children not only had great musical ability, but were highly intelligent. Three children became Salvation Army officers.

One left during World War II to serve in the Navy. Eventually he became head of the brass department of the Navy School of Music. Later, with a Master's degree, he served as a schoolteacher until he retired.

The daughter and her officer-husband left to enter the education field, both earning Master's degrees and spending their lives as teachers.

The "two-year-old," a lifetime Salvationist, became vice-president of a major investment firm, all the while serving faithfully in the Chicago Staff Band.

The son yet unborn in 1938 is now head of the department of anesthesiology at a major hospital and a faithful soldier in a Chicago-area corps.

The middle child is Commissioner Harold Shoults, who retired after serving as territorial commander of the Central Territory.

I Know That Song!

The story of how The Salvation Army began in Canada is probably well-known in its sketchy form. Jack Addie heard a virtual stranger humming or whistling an Army song, and thus they "discovered" each other, perhaps the only two Salvationists in Canada at that time: 1881. Or so the story went. The best source for the whole story seems to be in *They Blazed the Trail*, a book by Lt. Colonel Herbert

P. Wood, with a foreword by Commissioner W. Wycliffe Booth, a grandson of the Founder.

As Wood tells it, the young men's mutual discovery was not quite so casual as we might think, but it was remarkable nonetheless. It all goes back to John Addie, known practically always as Jack.

Jack was a young Scotsman whose family had to moved to Britain's city of Newcastle. When he attended a meeting led by Gypsy Smith, his Presbyterian parents looked askance at their son's enthusiasm for this "newfangled religion" and tried to discourage him from attending Salvation Army meetings. But he wouldn't be dissuaded; that was where he had been truly saved. When he expressed a desire to become an officer, that was the limit. Perhaps if they moved to Canada, where there was no Salvation Army, Jack might forget. So they emigrated, settling on a farm near London, Ontario. Jack, who in England had been apprenticed to the dry goods business, soon found a job in the largest store in town. So complete was his change of heart that, far from being weaned away from his new-found faith, he looked for the closest thing to the "Army spirit" he could find, which turned out to be a Methodist Church which had just passed through a revival campaign and was keeping the "fire burning" by means of cottage meetings. The minister, noting Jack's evident zeal, put him and a youth named Cathcart in charge of the meetings. For a time Addie found all he needed in stirring up the faith of the converts of the revival. One night a young stranger entered the meeting. Jack hardly noticed him. After an opening song and prayer, Jack called for testimonies, and the stranger rose. But the youth did not speak, he sang. With the words of the song Jack felt a thrill. It was a song he had in heard in one place only: Salvation Army meetings in England. As soon as the newcomer, Joe Ludgate, stopped singing, Jack completely forgot he was leading a meeting and burst out with "Where did you learn that song?" Surprised at being singled out so unexpectedly in the midst of strangers, he answered, "In The Salvation Army in England." Addie's excitement overflowed. He left his place at the front of the room and threw his arms around Ludgate. "I, too, am a Salvationist!"

The upshot? The two of them became officers and began the Army's work in Canada. Addie's co-worker, Cathcart, too, became a life-long Salvation Army officer.

Colonel Jack Addie

Colonel Jack Addie, the co-founder of The Army's work in Canada, spiced up many messages with a song he'd written to drive home a point. He didn't claim they were classic poetry, but when sung to some well-known tune, their point was unmistakable. Some were strongly evangelistic, while others, written for officers' councils, dealt with how to run an effective corps. He even wrote them when he was a divisional commander and field secretary.

In "Squeaky Things" he favored being quietly diplomatic, gentle in speech, and demonstrating practical Christian love in action. Both songs given here were sung to "The Wearin' of the Green":

> *(1)* While riding on a trolley-car, upon a city street, I saw a little incident, a lesson so complete; A man, a can, a squeaky door, the simplest of all tricks—There are so many squeaky things a little oil will fix. (*Chorus*) A little oil will fix, a little oil will fix, There are so many squeaky things a little oil will fix. *(2)* A little hitch 'twixt man and man, Say both are in the right, A molehill seems a mountain, and like dogs they bark and bite. An answer soft turns wrath away, It looks bad throwing bricks, There are so many squeaky things a little oil will fix. *(3)* A band perchance can't understand, why this or that should be! The Captain sometimes with a club, starts out to make them see, The oil can is a better plan than beating men with sticks; There are so many squeaky things a little oil will fix. *(4)* I knew a corps that once was sore, The soldiers out of gear, Because of fancied grievances, they acted strange and queer; Oil calmed the troubled waters then, for though they never mix, There are so many squeaky things a little oil will fix.

"The Bee that Gets the Honey"

(1) Did you ever see a bee-hive look deserted and alone—
The only life around the thing, the queen bee and the drone?
Though seeming dead the chances are 'twas very much alive,
For the bee that gets the honey doesn't hang around the
hive. *(2)* In every Army corps you'll find the workers and
the drones; the latter sitting in the hall to rest their weary
bones; The workers in the open-air, where soldiers live and
thrive—For the bee that gets the honey doesn't hang around
the hive. *(3)* I know an Army Captain who succeeds at
every corps; He visits saints and sinners as he goes from
door to door. You wouldn't find him at his home—he's
never there till five; for the bee that gets the honey doesn't
hang around the hive. *(4)* Now money is, we all concede,
the sinew of this war—you cannot fight without it; fact it's
costing more and more; But there's plenty in the country
if you'll hustle, work and strive, for the bee that gets the
honey doesn't hang around the hive.

You and I may smile at the quaintness of these songs but there is
no question that the words got his point across.

Colonel Jack Addie, Truly an Original

Joshua 24:12 "And I sent the hornet before you which drove them
out before you, even the two kings of the Amorites; but not with thy
sword nor with thy bow." In other words, it was entirely the Lord's
doing, not anything which the Israelites accomplished on their own.
Nor had there been need for bloodshed.

Here is Colonel Addie's "poetic" version which, after being sung,
he would apply it in one of his own unique sermons.

(1) When the Canaanites hardened their hearts against
God, and grieved Him because of their sin, He sent along
hornets to bring them to time and helped His own people

212

to win. The hornets persuaded them that it was best to hasten, and not to be slow; They did not compel them to 'gainst their will, they just made them willing to go. *(Chorus)* [last two lines of each verse] *(2)* If a nest of live hornets were brought to this room, and the creatures allowed to go free, You would not need urging to make yourself scarce— You'd want to get out, don't you see? They would not lay hold and by dint of their strength, throw you out of the window, no, no! They would not compel you to go 'gainst your will—They'd just make you willing to go. *(3)* When Jonah was sent to start Nineveh Corps, the outlook was not very bright. He never had done such a hard thing before, so he flunked and ran off from the fight. He was caught and imprisoned inside of a whale. (The story I'm sure you all know.) God did not compel him to go 'gainst his will—He just made him willing to go. *(4)* When Balaam was sent with the Princess of Moab, he wanted things run his own way; But his ass ever faithful spoke at the right time, made him willing God's voice to obey. God can use any man, since He used Balaam's ass, for He is almighty, you know. You need not compel folks to go 'gainst their will—you just make them willing to go.

Of course the point is that the Lord can accomplish His purposes by means which are beyond anything we could do or even imagine.

On a personal level, there are two or three motivations which lead me to dedicate some space to this highly original pioneer officer. John Addie and his comrade-in-arms, Joe Ludgate, began the Army's work in Canada in 1883. One of those who was saved in those earliest days was my grandfather, who became an officer in 1885. Naturally they were great friends, and both carried on highly effective ministries. But less than ten years later My grandfather was farewelled to the U.S.A., serving as provincial commander in five of the provinces (in the days before divisions) in the course of his career. During many of his years of service, Evangeline Booth served as National Commander until she became General. Grandpa never would have dreamed of holding that office, but later one of his sons, and later a grandson did. Colonel Addie, in his later years, served in the U.S. When he died, his family chose to bury him in Glen Oak Cemetery, the Army's section near Chicago. Needless to say, his memorial service was quite an inspiring experience for teenagers like me. Yes, I was there.

A Song, and Sudden Death

At first I had planned to limit this series on Colonel John Addie to two or possibly three articles. But printing a few more of his songs may help to show the scope of his ability to compress practical lessons into folksy doggerel. Then he would use well-known tunes, either spiritual or secular, depending on the content of the message being conveyed, so his hearers could join in singing the words on the spot; no need to struggle with new or unfamiliar music! Hopefully, the lesson of the day would "stick" in many minds when the meeting was over. (If you are interested in more material from this unique collection, the Central Territory Archives has no less than 41 of these songs which Commissioner McIntyre chose to have published in a booklet. The archives staff will be happy to photocopy any of the material for you.)

Before I finish this series, I want to tell you a very somber story. Since it is too "dark" for a happy series finale, I'll tell it now. Just before Mrs. Commissioner Emma Booth-Tucker boarded a train for an extended trip, she asked Colonel Addie what new songs he had for use in connection with his special soul-saving campaign. "Something," she said, "that will arrest people's attention, arouse them, stop them, and make them think." The Colonel spoke of a song (part of which is given below) which he had used with good results in his Texas campaign. "Sing it to me," she said. He sang it. (Tune: "You never can tell.")

> (1) Bony fingers and pale faces plainly tell you you're near the last; But with none of those death traces, many now are dying fast. (Chorus) You never can tell when the death bell's tolling, You never can tell when your end will be; Cast your

poor soul in the sin-cleansing Fountain, Come and get saved and happy be. *(2)* The pale horse will overtake you, You can't escape, Death knows your name; If your sins are unforgiven, You will have yourself to blame. *(3)* Time and place will cease to know you, Men and things will pass away; You'll be moving on tomorrow, You are only here today.

The last verse particularly struck her. She asked him to sing it again. The third time she joined in the singing the solemn words, little dreaming how strangely true they were of herself—that she was "only here today." (She was killed in a train accident three hours later.)

Granted this would have been a very solemn conclusion to my short series on Addie, but it gives an indication of the wide variety of the songs he used to emphasize his messages and to impress them on the memory of his hearers. In my first two installments I might have given the impression that this officer, with his sunny disposition, was a sort of entertainer, using his funny songs to enliven his meetings. That's because of the songs which I chose to reprint for your "personal file." But there were others which were simply a retelling of incidents straight from the Bible, such as the one about hornets (Joshua 24:12). He also wrote some very down-to-earth verse about conscientious pastoral care and visitation.

Suddenly, There Was Jack Addie!

The title of the following song by Colonel Jack Addie could have been "Priorities," but it isn't. It's a poem about a fictional officer who is held up as a horrible example.

(Remember: many of Addie's poems were written to be used in officers' councils.) It was set to an old tune which the Colonel often found useful: "The Wearing of the Green."

"A Busy Man"

(1) Our Captain is a busy man, as busy as can be. His mind is exercised 'bout things too deep for you and me. He

deals with facts and figures, for he's business through and through; He's busy thinking up the things Headquarters ought to do. *(Chorus)* He's business through and through, He's business through and through, He's busy thinking up the things Headquarters ought to do. *(2)* He'll tell you why he can't do this, and why he can't do that, the difficulties barring him—He's got them all down pat. He says the remedy's beyond such folks as me and you, So he's busy thinking up the things Headquarters ought to do.

Colonel Addie reminds us that it is easy enough to blame "circumstances beyond our control" for anything that does not work out the way we had hoped or planned; In other words, "If the wind had blown the other way."

Then there's the chorus of another of his songs which could remind us that appointments don't last forever, or on a more serious side, considering our lives, "We'll be gone tomorrow, We're only here today."

He also wrote an encouraging song, "All things work together for good," based on the familiar words in Romans 8:28.

Another question: Does everything seem dark and gloomy to you? Then he reminds us, "There's a bright side somewhere." Don't rest till you find it.

The title and chorus: "Easter morning" needs no explaining.

He cobbled together a dozen good, old-time secular songs, interspersed with Army choruses, closing with the words, "But I've learned to sing far better songs than those of long ago."(This could be quite a song session.)

One song that was still used by a noteworthy evangelist many years later was "A mighty revival is coming this way."

Not surprisingly, he wrote a song that voices approval for the old Army custom of clapping hands while singing.

His paraphrase of Psalms 107:2 exhorts all of us to testify as we sing to the tune of "Over Jordan": "Let him say so."

Don't think he assumed that Salvationists shouldn't have a serious bone in their body. Consider the moving words in his meditative song, "In the shadow of the Cross."

All in all, Colonel Addie must have been "a man for all people." When you imagine a group of officers or a huge crowd of listeners singing one of his songs, whether rollicking or meditative, we'd have a hard time imagining a better choice of a pioneer to begin the Army's work in Canada. Yet at the time it began it seemed to have happened purely by accident!

IN a HOLIDAY MOOD

Reformation or Regeneration?

Strange as it may seem, the great pagan temple in Rome, the Pantheon, had a part in bringing us Halloween. When the Emperor Phocas gave the ancient temple to Pope Boniface IV as a church, a feast was held. The temple formerly had been dedicated to all the gods (as *pan-theon* means), or at least all gods of a certain category. What could be more suitable than to keep the "pan" idea and commemorate all Christian martyrs? So May 13, 610 A.D. was the first Feast of All Holy Martyrs. Later the feast became All Saints Day, to honor all saints, regardless of how they died.

About November 1, pagan Rome held a feast in honor of Pomona, goddess of fruit trees. In Britain the Druids celebrated a festival at the same time which included giving thanks for harvest. Among the Britons the two festivals seem to have become one. Meanwhile the church calendar officially set aside November 1 as All Saints Day (or All Hallows Day).

Pagan and Christian celebrations converged but did not merge. The holy day was soon preceded by a most unholy night, called All Hallows Even, All Hallow E'en, Hallowe'en and finally Halloween. The night has lost most of its pagan overtones, but behind it still lurks the theme that demons and goblins and all sorts of hellish creatures kick up their heels until the sun rises on a day of such virtue and solemnity that they must scurry for cover.

Disbelief in the existence of such creatures has never kept fractious human beings from joining the mythical ménage in wreaking havoc on the neighborhood. The demands for decorous demeanor on the next day, a holy day, only spurred them to make hay in the moonlight. The same thing has happened with Lent. It is no accident that Mardi Gras and Fat Tuesday precede Ash Wednesday with goings-on that are the very antithesis of the six weeks of self-denial which follow.

Halloween and Mardi Gras may have counterparts in human reformation. In choosing to reform, one may change because of health or other considerations. But often there are looks of longing toward those habits now forsaken. And there may be one last big bash before "taking the pledge."

In his book *My 58 Years*, Commissioner Edward J. Parker says his early idea of becoming a Christian was "to join the Church, read the Bible for a while, and then drop off bad habits by degrees." He soon learned through the conversion of a wild friend that it's not like that. When Christ enters a life, there is no "one last night to howl." There is no desire to do so. Regeneration brings transformation. We are changed, not rearranged.

For Football Fans

These days there is such a surfeit of sports on TV that some true sports fans have been "turned off" by the whole thing. It is true that the kind of salaries being paid to players would not be possible without the TV royalties, thanks to sponsors who pay enormous amounts for a 30-second spot. It is also true that scheduling is carefully orchestrated so one game can follow another smoothly, often in different parts of the country. And as for the timeouts that make space for the advertisements—well, you'll have to be the judge.

Not so long ago Saturday afternoon collegiate football games did not seem so numerous, and you could only watch one, and then only if you were actually in a stadium.

Bill Stern, one of the most famous sportscasters and writers of the time, stated unequivocally, "The traditional Army-Navy classic will always be the year's greatest football game—in glamour." The first football game between the two schools was in 1890, at which time West Point did not even have a real team; just a scrub team put together for that one game. In 1894 the bloodiest and bitterest of their games was fought, and during halftime, numerous fights broke out in the stands among the spectators. As a result of the game one retired rear-admiral and an aging brigadier-general actually fought a duel. Some feared that the acrimonious spirit would so infect the two armed services that they might be incapable of working together smoothly in case of war. It went so far that the President of the United States, Grover Cleveland, barred the Army-Navy game as too rough, and the ban held for five years.

The games were resumed, but in the 1920s, relations between the two teams became strained over a difference in rules, and they refused to play their games in 1928 and 1929. Would they have renewed the contest later, even without the request of Evangeline Booth of The Salvation Army? No one knows, of course, but we do know that it was she who got them going again. The reason was not so trivial as hating to miss seeing a good football game. In fact many Christians considered such games so worldly and frivolous that they would not attend one.

But there was an urgent need involving a lot of hungry people, and such a game seemed to provide at least a temporary solution to the problem. The Great Depression had gripped the country, and the government had not yet seen fit to offer substantial aid to the suffering. Private organizations were doing all they could, and The Salvation Army had been in the forefront in setting up feeding stations and providing other relief. But with resources stretched to the limit, Commander Booth talked to New York's Mayor Walker to see what he thought about asking the Army and Navy to play a benefit game for The Salvation Army, even though they had forsaken their annual contest. He urged her to go ahead.

When approached, both schools agreed to do it. Grover A. Whalen accepted the chairmanship of the game. Ticket prices ranged from $5 to $50, and Junior League members offered to be ushers. The gate was over $600,000 and Salvationists were able to provide a lot of emergency care until government agencies began to catch up. As for the game, the *New York Times* declared that "it took place in a setting of glittering color and excitement such as football, at least in this city, has never seen."

Perhaps it may seem frivolous to use this page to tell how the Army-Navy games were reinstituted through the influence of The Salvation Army, but it is hoped that you will see the something of Evangeline Booth's imaginative approach to problem solving. It is also hoped that you'll enjoy learning of our part in reviving a tradition which has now passed the century-mark.

Our First "Christmas Effort"

Miss Jane Short, an early member of the Christian Mission and long a paying boarder in the Booth home, described for Harold Begbie the last of the "normal" Christmases ever observed by the Founder and his family. That was in 1867.

One cannot fully understand what lay behind the events of that year without knowing something of the temperament of the Founder. "You could not meet a man," said Miss Short, "whose nerves were more tortured by the spectacle of suffering. Pain, the sight of pain in others, made him wretched. He would turn away from it, quite sick and dizzy. People will never know what he endured in the slums of great cities.

"The General," she continued, "had determined that the children should have a thoroughly happy old-fashioned Christmas, and for a week beforehand every preparation was made for a great family festival. The children were full of excitement, their father entered into the spirit of the thing, and I really thought it would be a day of purest happiness.

"But when the General returned from his preaching in Whitechapel on Christmas morning, he was pale, haggard, and morose. He did his best to enter into the children's fun and frolic, but it was no use; he kept relapsing into silence and gloom. He looked dreadfully white and drawn, just as if he were ill or harassed by some grievous worry.

"And then suddenly he burst out, 'I'll never have a Christmas Day like this again!' And, getting on his feet and walking up and down the room like a caged lion, he told us of the sights he had seen that morning in Whitechapel, indignantly saying, 'The poor have nothing but the public-house—nothing but the public-house.'

"That Christmas Day was the last the Booth family ever spent together. On the following Christmas Day we were scattered in the slums distributing plum-puddings. I remember that we thought the Mission a very great affair because we gave away 150 puddings! How little any of us foresaw the future. All the same, our little gift of 150, many of them made in the Booths' home kitchen, was the beginning of The Salvation Army's Christmas Day."

To this Miss Short added, "The General said to me one day after a prayer meeting, at which some of the recipients had been blessed, 'Sister Jane, the Lord accepted our puddings.'"

Those Angels and Shepherds

Perhaps there are many Christians who are a bit uneasy about factuality when they hear the account in Luke's gospel which begins with the words: "And there were in the same country shepherds abiding in the field, keeping watch over their flock by night."

One may ask in all fairness, how did Luke, the longtime traveler on Paul's missionary journeys, find time for the painstaking research and interviewing needed for his gospel? Secondly, where could he have found, in his travels in the pagan world, Christians who had known Jesus from the beginning of His ministry (Luke 1:1-4)? Did he *have* to have met them in his travels? And thirdly, who could have told him in such detail of the remarkable events which he described in his first three chapters?

Basically, the answers to the first two questions are found in Luke's companion volume, in Acts 21-26. As for the time and opportunity to conduct his research, Luke found himself with two years of enforced idleness during which he probably lived in Jerusalem, perhaps with visits to Antioch, that great center of the early Christian church. As for gathering his material in the pagan world, that is what the second question implies, but obviously that is not how it happened.

Now read on. Paul's arrest on the temple grounds in Jerusalem, on trumped-up charges having to do with Jewish law, led to his being imprisoned in Caesarea. Due to a series of delays, he remained there for two whole years.

But what of Luke? Until shortly before Paul's temple visit, he said "we" did this and "we" did that in his narration. Since he was a Gentile, he could not accompany Paul to the temple; thus the word "we" is not used regarding Paul's temple visit, his arrest, nor his imprisonment. Luke was not there! He tells of these things in the third person, saying nothing of himself. Actually, he was forced to live elsewhere, waiting to rejoin Paul when that became possible. When the apostle finally set sail for Rome, where his case was to be heard by Caesar, Luke was able to rejoin him for the voyage. They were together again, and Luke resumes using "we."

How did Luke use his time during those two years? As I have said, he almost certainly stayed on in Jerusalem, researching his gospel. He had access to the older Jerusalem-based Christians whom he needed for questioning.

Now what about those angels? Who could have told him the events given in Luke chapters one through three? The answer? A man whom Paul came to know and respect at the Council of Jerusalem some years earlier, and whom Luke later came to know very well (Acts 21:18). His informant was James.

This James had not been a disciple but rather was James the Elder, the beloved and revered church leader, the same James mentioned much earlier in the gospels as Jesus' brother. He had had great difficulty during Jesus' lifetime believing that the true Messiah was living in his house, eating at the same table and sharing in the same chores. As a youth at home, Jesus probably seemed so ordinary. What would *you* have thought?

The resurrected Jesus knew of his beloved brother's troubled frame of mind and what was needed to nudge him over into becoming a true believer. Thus we have the post-resurrection appearance mentioned in I Corinthians 15:7. It was this same James, the James who had been so slow to believe, who became the revered leader of the church in Jerusalem.

Regardless of his lingering reservations about his brother's being the Son of God and the promised Messiah, James grew up as a member of the family, doubtless hearing again and again from Mary's own lips of the wonderful happenings surrounding the birth of her firstborn. Would James know in detail of these things? Would he share them with a scholarly person like Luke, a man who was to guarantee their preservation for posterity? Of course he would! There is no reason to wonder how they found their was into his gospel.

Hear and believe without uncertainty on these points—and never let your Christmas joy be marred by habitual head shakers and chronic doubters!

The Greatest Gift

One way to begin to grasp the magnitude of the gift given by God's Son is to look outside the four Gospels for clues as to what really went on behind that scene—the well-known but vaguely understood manger scene. The true gift of Christmas, of course, was that God's Son willingly gave Himself, "Who, being in very nature God, did not consider equality with God something to be grasped, but made himself nothing, taking the very nature of a servant, being made in human likeness" (Philippians 2:6-7 NIV).

The very first step in taking on human form was to begin as human beings begin: as a helpless baby, unable to take care of even His most basic physical needs. What a come-down for God! What had He given up? "He who descended is the very one who ascended higher than all the heavens, in order to fill the whole universe" (Ephesians 4:16). All too often we fail to realize that Christ was the agent of creation and a continuing force in that universe. "For by him all things were created: things in heaven and on earth, visible and invisible, whether thrones or powers or rulers or authorities; all things were created by him and for him. He is before all things, and in him all things hold together" (Colossians 1:16-17).

What He gave up to come to earth is beyond our comprehension. His gift was Himself. Likewise, the gift we as Christians are most often asked to give is ourselves. (It isn't much, but it's all we have!)

227

Let me tell a story from many years ago. A man condemned to death in a Berlin prison requested a visit at Christmas time from a Salvationist. Brigadier Heinrich Tebbe was as busy and hard-pressed as any Salvationist at that season of the year. He could have sent a volunteer or a junior officer. But his love for the poorest and the most distressed people led him to go. With him went his wife. Mrs. Tebbe took along a branch of fir, Yule candles, some "goodies," and a New Testament. She sang carols, read the Bible, and presented the gifts.

That Christmas Eve the man found the Savior in his cell. The story might be expected to end with the man facing his execution peacefully and bravely, knowing that he would go to be with Jesus. But in the spirit of Christmas, the ending was so much better. The sentence was commuted to life imprisonment, and with violin and a song book, the new Christian continued a valued ministry of music to his fellow prisoners down through the years.

For Christians, gift-giving need not be limited to Christmas, especially the giving of oneself. May we all find some way to help another person through the giving of ourselves.

Keeping the Kettle Boiling

Since some bits of Army history seem hard to find when we want them, it may help to make them available by including them in a book, where they will always be accessible when needed. The origin of The Salvation Army's Christmas kettles seems to qualify as one of those items.

Captain Joseph McFee in San Francisco resolved in December 1891 to provide a free Christmas dinner for the area's poor. But how would he pay for the food? The question nagged at him as he went about his duties. Suddenly he recalled his days as a sailor in Liverpool, England. On the stage landing there had been a large pot called "Simpson's pot" into which passers-by threw donations for charity. Why not use the idea in San Francisco?

The next morning he secured permission from the authorities to place a similar pot at the Oakland ferry landing, at the foot of Market

Street. Wasting no time, he obtained such a pot and set it up where it could be seen by all. In addition, a brass urn was placed on a stand in the waiting room for the same purpose. With no thought beyond the pressing need of the moment, the captain had launched a tradition which would encircle the world

By Christmas 1895 the kettle was used by 30 Salvation Army corps in West Coast states. The *Sacramento Bee* that year carried a description of the Army's activities and mentioned the contributions to street corner kettles. Shortly afterward, two young officers who had been among the first to use kettles, William A. McIntyre and N.J. Lewis, were transferred to the East. Knowing a good idea when they saw it, they incorporated the kettle into their Christmas plans. In Boston, McIntyre's fellow officers refused to cooperate for fear of "making spectacles of themselves." So McIntyre, his wife and his sister set up three kettles on Washington Street in the heart of the city. That year the kettle effort in Boston and other locations nationwide resulted in 150,000 Christmas dinners for the needy.

In 1898 the *New York World* hailed the Salvation Army kettles as "the newest and most novel device for collecting money." The same article also noted, "There is a man in charge to see that contributions are not stolen."

In 1901 New York City's kettles contributions provided funds for the first mammoth sit-down dinner in Madison Square Garden, a custom that continued for many years. Today, however, families are given grocery checks so they can buy and prepare their own dinners at home. The homeless are still invited to share holiday dinners and festivities at hundreds of Salvation Army centers.

Kettles are now used in such distant lands as Korea, Japan and Chile, and in many European countries. Everywhere, public contributions to the kettles enable the Army to bring the spirit of Christmas to those who would otherwise be forgotten: to the aged and lonely, the ill, the poor and unfortunate, to prison inmates (through "Operation Toylift") and to those in other institutions. In the United States, The

Salvation Army annually aids hundreds of thousands at Thanksgiving and Christmas.

Have kettles changed since the first utilitarian cauldron was set up in San Francisco? For the most part, not much. A cheery "thank you" and sincere "God bless you" are more appreciated than such "streamlined" devices as self-ringing bells and canned music on today's noisy streets. But whatever the method, the message is the same: "Sharing Is Caring."

Saint Nicholas Revisited

The true story of the Saint Nicholas of history has been so dimmed by the centuries that we know very little about him. His reputed acts of generosity seem to have some factual basis, however, and they became the foundation for the European St. Nick of Christmas tradition, a tall, thin old man with a wispy beard.

That image was greatly changed in America by a poem tossed off in 1822 by Clement Clarke Moore, professor of Oriental and Greek Literature at the General Theological Seminary in New York, which stood on land he himself had donated. A biblical scholar of some stature, he was the compiler of a Hebrew lexicon as well as author of a book on a phase of European history.

Moore never intended that his uncharacteristic bit of frivolity be published; it was written simply for the entertainment of his children. In that lighthearted spirit he had altered nearly everything about the jolly distributor of gifts, but he never intended to tamper with the public's image of St. Nicholas. The next year his poem showed up, to his embarrassment, as an anonymous contribution in a local newspaper, the *Troy Sentinal*, resulting in a flood of letters from delighted readers clamoring to know the identity of its author. The editor held true to his promise to keep the author's name a secret, but by public demand, reprinted the poem the next year and for years to follow. In 1827, when it was anthologized in The *New York Book of Poetry*, Moore agreed to let his name be revealed.

My lines below are intended to be read with "A Visit from St. Nicholas" in mind. Remember: it was Moore who in 1822 provided the ascetic old saint with airborne transportation, and who transformed him into the fat, jolly, pipe-smoking Santa of today.

When the saints go marching in,
There is one whose impish grin,
Belly-laugh and roguish wink,
Face an un-ascetic pink,
Set him off from all the rest;
Make one wonder by what test
   He was canonized.
He's a strange one in that crowd,
Scarce with saintly mien endowed:
Clothing smudged from head to foot,
Stained with ash and chimney-soot,
Tarnished crimson plush—how quaint
Does this garb look on a saint!
Breaking reverential hush,
Suddenly he makes a rush
For his waiting sleigh and deer!
(Once more it's that time of year.)
With a wave and "Ho-ho-ho"
He whistles for the deer to go
   Back to Earth's environs.
Say, old saint with cherry nose
(One shade brighter than your clothes),
Stubby pipe 'twixt bow-shaped lips,
Nicotine-stained fingertips,
Pipe-smoke circling 'round your head,
Wreathing you in halo's stead;
Anyone so overweight
Seems less saint than profligate.

Sainthood speaks of those who knew,
In their lives, how to subdue
    Desire and appetite.
How'd they ever canonize
A fat old rogue with winking eyes?
When your record was reviewed,
I'm surprised you weren't eschewed.
Who, before, had ever heard
Of an elf-saint? How absurd!
Isn't it preposterous?
An elf upon the roster as
A member of that saintly throng!
Somehow, you don't quite belong.
Tell me: do you favor Earth,
With its blend of grief and mirth,
    More than Paradise?
Reader, surely you've surmised
That St. Nick's been Germanized,
    Anglicized,
    Americanized,
    Modernized,
    Publicized,
    Commercialized,
And, by some, now ostracized;
Yet by youngsters idolized.
If in him there's incongruity,
Legend, myth and superfluity
With regard to Christmas Truth,
Let me make it clear: forsooth,
Mark my word, O dearest friend,
That it's our fault in the end.
This good saint of ancient vintage
Has been remade in our image.
    And we've acquiesced.

A New Year's "Sea Story"

There is nothing arbitrary about the length of our day. It is the time it takes the earth to turn once on its axis. A year is the time required to revolve once around the sun: 365 days, five hours, forty-eight minutes and forty-six seconds. To make up for the extra hours, we add a day every fourth year except in century years that are not divisible by 400. Thus there was no Leap Year in 1900 and won't be in 2100, but we did observe Leap Year in 2000.

Although the year and day are tied to real events, the beginning and ending of a year are a matter of choice. The Chinese and Jewish New Year celebrations have as much reason for being as ours. Watch Night meetings, New Year's resolutions, factory whistles and fireworks—the whole rigmarole—none of it has anything to do with an actual break or demarcation in an ongoing celestial phenomenon. It's just an arbitrary dividing line in our man-made calendar.

This point was unforgettably emphasized for me after World War II. Our troopship left the Philippines in late December and was at sea as 1945 slipped quietly into January 1, 1946. The troops aboard ship were mostly quiet, doubtless thinking about the vastly different experiences the new, peacetime year would hold.

At 10 a.m. January 1, we crossed the International Date Line and found ourselves in midmorning of December 31. But in that unique situation, it was not just the day before, but the year before! Again we were looking forward to New Year's Eve and another entry into 1946.

The intriguing thing was the reality of our two New Year's Eves. Both were firmly tied to local time, and there was nothing unreal about either one. But no matter how real, it was clear there was something arbitrary about a system that would plunge us into a new year of peace, then yank us back into a year that would go down in history for its world-shaking events, then only fourteen hours later catapult us for a second time into that "new" year we had visited so briefly! Alice in Wonderland had nothing on us.

This is not to say that New Year's resolutions are nonsense. Good resolutions are praiseworthy, but they can be made at any time. There is nothing magical about January first; no particular power to enable us to "turn over a new leaf." In the truest sense, a slate wiped clean comes only through Christ's cleansing power, and the strength to carry out good resolutions is also from Him.

Let's be sure our resolutions are not just our thinking but His will; then we can rely on His help.

Easter Revisited

If a creative writer were to set his hand to compose a dramatic fictional version of the events of that weekend, he might have Jesus bursting forth from the tomb, leaving the grave clothes in disarray and speeding straight to the Temple grounds, (or wherever He found the biggest crowds) to proclaim His triumph over death, and to confound the Jewish leaders. Instead, He chose to appear without fanfare to three small groups of His grieving followers: the three women who went to the tomb early in the morning; two men on the road to Emmaus, and ten of His disciples—all except Thomas—in a room behind a locked door.

Now think back for a moment to Jesus' temptation in the wilderness before His public ministry even began. Satan suggested that Jesus make a huge impression by leaping from the pinnacle of the Temple and landing unhurt on the pavement below, thus establishing His reputation as the Son of God. Jesus refused, just as He refused to confound the crowds after His resurrection by demonstrating that He had conquered death itself.

There is also the question of Jesus' scarred body. If we believe that Jesus was restored completely after His crucifixion, why did He still have scars? These were not wounds that were still healing; otherwise Jesus would not have told Thomas to put his finger into the nail prints and his hand into His side. These marks were unmistakable identifiers. His followers could see immediately that it was not someone who looked like Him. The prints gave incontestable evidence that it was the

Savior Himself. This was what prompted Jesus to say, "Reach hither thy finger, Thomas, and behold my hands; and reach hither thy hand, and thrust it into my side; and be not faithless, but believing." To which Thomas answered, "My Lord and my God".

This irrefutable, living evidence called forth the strongest of declarations.

STRICTLY MISCELLANEOUS

You Don't Say!

We get some fascinating insights into the minds of the four gospel writers by observing the things they said, and the things they did not say. We find clues as to how the power of the Holy Spirit can change the very character of the people He indwells.

For a proper understanding of what follows, three things should be clearly understood. First, the best explanations of the inspiration of Scripture (the word translated "inspired" meaning literally "God-breathed" in Greek) invariably point out that God did not have to resort to dictating to His chosen "reporters" word-for-word. He worked through their thinking so that what they told was accurate, yet was given in their own words, reflecting their own personality and cultural background. To limit God to some sort of dictation theory is to pose the problem of why four gospels were necessary, and to raise the question of why all four were not identical in wording if dictated by God and faithfully written down by those receiving this dictation (even it if was a sort of "inward" dictation). No; their personalities and backgrounds do show, and when we make verse-by-verse comparisons we gain some interesting insights.

Secondly, the early church fathers agreed that Mark, who had begun that first missionary journey with Paul but had abandoned his friends early on, later traveled with Barnabas, and later still with Simon Peter, who by that time was a most effective and courageous evangelist. In their considerable time together, Peter told Mark a great deal about Jesus and His ministry, miracles and teachings. The church fathers, such as Papias and Eusebius, said that the people of Italy, where Peter ministered for quite a while, clamored for someone to preserve in writing all the wonderful things Peter was telling them. Mark organized this wealth of information and it became a major component of his gospel. Thus, Mark's gospel can be, to a large extent, considered Peter's gospel as well.

Thirdly, when Luke later brought together the recollections of many eyewitnesses and used whatever trustworthy sources were available for his longer and more comprehensive gospel, he incorporated much of Mark's material into his own. We must bear in mind that these gospel writers were not writing "books" for publication in our modern-day sense, but were endeavoring to preserve for future Christians an accurate record of the life of Jesus. Thus there was no thought of "copying" or of plagiarism in their using one another's writings as source material. Luke in his prologue (1:1-4) clearly declared that he used many dependable sources in compiling his gospel.

It should be added that later, probably after Peter's death, Mark rejoined Paul to give him his assistance. (This we know from greetings in the epistles. Note also Paul's urgent request in II Timothy that Mark be brought once again, because he was "profitable" to Paul.)

In Mark's gospel, his brief explanations and translations of Jewish terms show that he was probably writing with Italian (or if you prefer, Roman) Gentiles in mind. When Luke wrote, he had a wider audience in mind: the whole Greek-speaking world. Thus neither gospel duplicated the other, either in purpose or audience.

In case you have ever wondered how Luke could have gotten hold of Mark's record of Jesus' life to use as source material, and whether Mark approved of his utilizing much of it in his larger and more comprehensive gospel, it must be remembered that the two men knew one another well, that they had traveled together and suffered the same privations together, that they were obviously good friends, and that there is scriptural evidence of this. Read Colossians 4:10, 14; II Timothy 4:11; and Philemon 24. In these places they are named together as fellow missionaries, sending greetings by means of Paul's letters.

Here is an interesting observation about Matthew when he spoke of himself and about his hospitality. After Matthew (Levi) was called by Jesus, he gave, says Luke, a "great feast" in his house. But Matthew modestly avoids calling it either great or a feast, saying only that they sat at meat.

As Mark was compiling his gospel, Peter must have said several times, when he felt the spotlight was focused too much on himself, "I'd much prefer that you leave that part out." For example, after Peter started to walk on water in the storm, he began to sink. But he had done what no mere mortal ever did before or since: he walked on water! Jesus' walking on water is described by Matthew, Mark and Luke, but Mark, evidently reporting only what Peter allowed him to tell, says not a word about Peter's remarkable feat. Luke, using Mark as his source, says nothing of it either. But Matthew, an eyewitness, wanted the whole story to be told, so it is only through him that we know what Peter did.

Mark, telling us of the woman who had been afflicted for twelve years with the issue of blood, bluntly tells us that she suffered many things of many physicians, and had spent all that she had, yet was nothing better, but rather grew worse. Luke, the "beloved physician," acknowledged she had spent all her money upon physicians, who had been unable to help her, but he was kind enough not to say she had suffered many things of them, or that she actually grew worse. Some things, he felt, are better left unsaid!

There are many more examples, but perhaps these are sufficient to make us ask: Do we, in the name of "truth," sometimes boast or say more than is necessary, more than is kind, more than is Christlike?

Transformed!

Probably most Christians feel they know a good deal about Simon Peter, the disciple who boldly asserted that he would rather die than deny Jesus, yet who, before that night was over, had sworn three times that he never knew Him. The word "impetuous" has been overworked in characterizing this man, in whom Jesus saw such potential, but whose weaknesses often seemed to undo the good that he did—or that he intended to do.

But what of Peter after Pentecost? There are several "windows" on his life which enable us to see what the Holy Spirit can do in a person.

One such "window" is the book of Acts, which tells of a "new" Peter who was absolutely fearless in the face of danger, and who preached tirelessly for many years, from the very hour that he emerged from that prayer room after the Holy Spirit had descended upon the 120. He, as portrayed in Acts, may not seem to you or to me an attainable example of a Spirit-filled Christian for us to emulate. Peter became a veritable lion of a man; very few of us even come close! But there is more to study in his life.

Through the "windows" of Mark's gospel we catch glimpses of Peter before Pentecost, a man who, it must be acknowledged, seems at that time to have had a tendency to boast. Another "window" provides a picture of a man whose boasting gave way to humility. This window consists of a handful of accounts about those earliest years of the church. Five or six church fathers told of Peter's major contribution to Mark's gospel. It happened like this: Mark, in his mature years, had joined Peter on his missionary tours and had become an invaluable helper. Peter even referred to him in his first epistle as "my son Mark" (I Peter 5:13).

Mark seems to have recorded all of the apostle's public preaching about Jesus' ministry; but he also wrote down many more of Peter's personal recollections, probably in more detailed form than those oft-told public statements which, by constant repetition, had been reduced to the least possible words. Up to the point in Mark's gospel where Jesus and His disciples left the Upper Room for Gethsemane, Peter seems to have been the main source of information. But from that point onward, Mark's eyewitness reporting predominates.

We can imagine Peter telling Mark of incidents which certainly seemed to set him apart as someone special, but adding, "I'm telling you this so you'll have all the facts, but you've got to promise not to put it in your book." Mark promised.

When Mark told of Jesus' walking on water before He stilled the storm, he said not a word about Peter's starting toward Jesus across those waves. It was Matthew who told of Peter's daring act, and although Peter's faith gave way to fear, that faith prevailed for a glorious moment.

Matthew also told of Peter's remarkable catching of the fish with the coin in its mouth, and of his paying the temple tax. As for this incident which certainly "stars" Peter, Mark says nothing.

And what of Peter's "great confession"? Mark makes little of it, quoting just four of Peter's words and telling nothing of Jesus' high praise. The rest we learn from Matthew, including Jesus' remarkable statements about the "rock" and the "keys of the kingdom."

In his preaching, Peter exalted Christ, not himself. One authority declares that in Mark's gospel Peter is never mentioned alone except in connection with his being rebuked by Jesus.

That's not quite the man we usually think of when Peter is mentioned, is it? Quite a testimony to the transforming work of the Holy Spirit.

To what extent have you and I been transformed?

Discovered in a Wastebasket

Alfred J. Gilliard, at that time a major, first appeared in Chicago in 1947 as an aide to General Albert Orsborn. Two decades later Gilliard, by then the senior commissioner in the world, returned to Chicago as editor-in-chief of National Publications. In the meantime he had worked in the Literary Department at IHQ alongside Frederick Coutts, the future General. Later, among other things, he served as a chief secretary, as territorial commander in New Zealand, then as principal of the International College for Officers.

A humble, easy-to-know friend to all on the *War Cry* staff, he sometimes recounted incidents from his more youthful days at International Headquarters that would bring a chuckle.

One might assume his favorite anecdotes would have involved rubbing shoulders with the high and the mighty. Not so. The things which seemed to give the him most pleasure were his contacts with young people, particularly his directing of plays in corps wherever his appointments took him. He saw in drama a way for shy kids to discover they had something to offer.

I suspect he liked to think of himself in one instance as "God's talent scout" —although he never quite said that. Back in the 1920s Salvationists inundated the British *War Cry* with unsolicited manuscripts, mostly handwritten, many of them simply not usable. *War Cry* space was very limited. Clerical help was scarce; consequently, writers whose work was not published did not even receive an acknowledgment for their efforts. With no one to give encouragement, most writers would quit submitting things after a few tries.

Young Gilliard, then on the staff, was talking to the editor when his eye fell on a page on top of the pile in the wastebasket. The bold, angular pen strokes caught his eye, seeming to suggest a strong personality behind the pen. "Do you mind if I have a look at that piece?" He asked. "Go ahead; read it if you'd like," said the editor. Gilliard read it with interest. The subject as presented was not really something *The War Cry* could use, but the writer had incorporated in the article a vivid description of a kind of fog that sometimes formed in coal mines and would creep along the passageways. He made the fog almost palpable.

Gilliard was excited. The officer who wrote it was obviously not an educated man, but he showed great descriptive powers. Would the editor mind, he asked, if he wrote to him, encouraging him and offering some simple suggestions? By all means write, said the editor, always happy to find new talent.

It turned out that the aspiring writer had gone to work in the coal mines before he was fourteen years of age. He had been a miner until he entered Training College at age nineteen, and he was serving as a corps officer. It was true that he had very little formal education, but it was clear that he had a great deal of talent just waiting to be developed.

The young man was Bernard Watson, destined to become one of the Army's most gifted writers. Over the years he edited three of the Army's journals and two of its newspapers, and wrote a number of books, including *A Hundred Years' War* and *Soldier Saint,* the biography of George Scott Railton.

Finding and encouraging talent was a great source of joy to Commissioner Gilliard. I'll never forget his enthusiasm when he said of Lt. Colonel Watson, "You might say, I discovered him in a wastebasket."

May we all find joy in helping others discover their God-given talents, never feeling a pang of jealousy if those we "discover" go on to surpass us in ability and accomplishments!

Her Sufficiency Was in Christ

Let me tell you two little stories. First, ever since the song "In the Love of Jesus" was published, it has occupied a particular spot in my heart. True, the beauty of Ivy Mawby's poetry is greatly enhanced by the music. It begins, you may recall, with a sort of semi-recitative, followed by a chorus containing a soaring melodic line and several wide intervals. To say simply that it is effective falls short of the mark.

But aside from the merits of the music, the words are lovely. One might wonder what kind of a person could write such poetry, and what idyllic life could nurture such thoughts. The truth is that a lot of people who have shared the poet's experience would not feel inclined to praise the Lord for what He had allowed to happen. Ivy Mawby and her husband became Salvation Army officers in 1933. Ten years later he was dead. Whether he died in a bombing raid or from illness I don't know, but she was undeniably young to be a widow. Although she certainly must have grieved, she never railed at God nor bemoaned her fate. She never remarried, but in a life lived alone she found a companionship and communion with her Lord which sustained her.

When I place the two facts side-by-side—her many years of widowhood and the mind which could give expression to such thoughts—I can only marvel at Ivy Mawby's ability to accept her lot in life so graciously as God's plan, and to express her love for Christ in a way that all of us can share.

Now for a second story. Many years ago I read a very moving account in *All the World* about a young French wife who, suffering from severe depression, was sent to a Salvation Army convalescent home.

I cannot begin to tell you the story without ruining it, since it would require more space than is available. Suffice it to say that the outcome was truly one of God's miracles, bringing together as it did circumstances beyond human planning or foresight, and the young woman's consequent spiritual healing. It remained in my memory for 40 years, to the extent that I could even recall in detail the picture on the cover of that issue of the magazine, since it illustrated the story itself.

Recently I decided to search through the archives for it, knowing that it had to be there. Finally I found it! It was then that I discovered why it was so etched in my memory. It was because it was so beautifully written, by an unnamed writer who had obviously poured her soul into it. In those days at least, the authors of most of the articles in *All the World* were not named, but in an inconspicuous corner at the end of the article their initials would appear. The initials were not primarily to give them credit; they were there as a reference in case some question arose about the content of an article. It was a matter of editorial responsibility. The letters I.M. meant nothing to me in 1956, but now they do. I.M. was Ivy Mawby; a bit of checking bore that out.

Colonel Mawby, like many others, did not let virtual anonymity keep her from giving her best. This has been true of a host of "invisible" Salvationists. Nor did she allow alone-ness to give rise to bitterness. With Christ as her sufficiency, she could say with the Psalmist, "Lord, you have assigned my portion and my cup; you have made my lot secure. The boundary lines have fallen for me in pleasant places; surely I have a delightful inheritance" (Psalms 16:5, 6 NIV).

You Can Never Be Sure

At the beginning of the 1950s one of our smaller divisions, with little to spend on property improvements, had a camp located on a river. The river's flow made it too dangerous for swimming, so water was pumped into what can only be described as an "old swimming hole," not a proper pool, but more of a pond, complete with muddy bottom and a lot of green algae. The kids at camp didn't seem to mind, but it would have given any strict health inspector a heart attack.

The campgrounds, considerably longer than wide, fronted on the river, bounded on its other side by an unpaved road. The road led to a piece of property upriver which the Army did not own. This property was roughly triangular in shape and inaccessible except for the road that bordered the camp from end to end. After that land had stood empty and undeveloped for years, the owner decided to sell it, causing our divisional staff to fear that someone might buy it and build something which could lead to a lot of traffic on the dusty road. The parcel of land was not large, and the asking price was only $1,500. That sum, however, didn't seem so small in those days, especially when there were no reserve funds for such a purchase.

As the quickest way to meet the immediate need, the officers decided on a quiet "asking campaign" among a few companies which could easily donate a few hundred dollars apiece. A hotel chain owner, who could at times appear to be an "old bear," asked the officers to outline their long-range plans for the camp.

What were needed most after buying the crucial triangle of land, they said, were a number of new cabins for more adequate and comfortable housing of the poor mothers and children. These would be built as money became available. In truth, there really was not much to the camp except a very nice dining hall (which had been a previous owner's dance pavilion) and a very few cabins with limited capacity. A lot needed to be done, but the acquisition of that piece of land seemed the most urgent item because of its possible impact on the camp's future.

The owner of the hotel chain didn't say yes, nor did he say no. He told them to come back soon, naming a date a few days off. That would give time, he said, for a couple of his men to have a look at the camp.

When the officers returned, the owner said in his gruff voice, "The trouble with you people is that, with your limited funds, by the time you finally get your camp built, the first buildings will already be old and dilapidated. You'll never have a really good camp."

Then came a surprise. The kindly "old bear" continued, "My engineers have been out to look over the place. If you will allow them, with their experience, to design and install a really adequate water supply system, provide good swimming facilities, design comfortable cottages, and lay out the entire camp, I'll open a bank account immediately for the camp's construction and start it out with $300,000, with more to be added as needed."

Thus the little camp, which had hardly filled the bill as a divisional camp until that time, became almost overnight a lovely retreat for poor mothers and children from the nearby big city.

When Salvationists ask for contributions to a worthy cause, sometimes they may get the door slammed in their faces, but not always!

Safe Among Christians

When my wife and I were corps officers in a small Nebraska town in the mid-1950s, we sometimes had a seventy-two-year-old woman baby-sit with our two small children. She was born about 1882, which now seems like an awfully long time ago. She recalled seeing the covered wagons laboring along on their way west, following the Oregon Trail. Even at that time it seemed almost beyond belief that a person we knew as a neighbor and friend could have watched the great western migration at first hand. But it took nothing more than simple arithmetic to show that her statement was true. For example, in 1894, when she was twelve years old, the Oregon Trail was still in constant use, and a youngster such as she would have watched with great interest the sight of covered wagons making the long trek past her house, heading for a new home in the West.

If the Oregon Trail itself seems remote and a bit story bookish to you, I must point out that it crossed the two-lane highway which led to Fairbury, twenty-six miles or so west of our corps town. Whenever we went to Fairbury, either to sell special issues of *The War Cry* or for other business, we would pass a small official highway marker which noted the fact that the Oregon Trail had crossed the highway at that point. We could actually see the broad indentation in the ground made when wagon wheels by the thousands had dug into the dirt and gradually pushed it to the sides, thus hollowing out a clearly-defined depression that could still be distinctly seen. There were no actual wagon tracks left, of course. The whole thing was covered with green grass, like a dry, shallow river bed angling off to the northwest. As a matter of fact, it is probably just about as visible today as in the '50s.

Another friend, a retiree, was a member of our corps. He recalled when, as a young man, he had traveled by himself, looking for work, in a part of Nebraska where one could go for miles without seeing a soul. He was traveling by horseback, carrying all of his belongings, including money of course, with him. Since there were no towns within reach, he did what many people did when evening came; he stopped at a farm and asked if they could put him up for the night.

The father and his grown sons were a big and burly threesome, striking him as rough looking. Too late he began to realize they could easily do away with him, bury his remains some where on their farmland, take his money, his belongings and his horse, and no one would ever know. Such things did happen in the old west. No one in his own family had any clear idea of where he was, and absolutely no one knew he was in this house, surrounded by men stronger than he. His horse was out of sight in the barn, and there were no communications. He could be in grave danger!

But then he joined the family at the dinner table. They all bowed their heads while the father asked the Lord's blessing on the food. It was so naturally done, he could see it was a part of their lives. At once he knew there was nothing to fear. In outward appearance they looked rough. But they were Christians!

It has always been true, hasn't it? Just knowing we are among fellow-believers makes all the difference.

A Different Man

A man complained loudly and vehemently that, no matter where he poked himself, he had suddenly begun to experience sharp pain—a lot of pain. Contrary to what you might suspect, this was not because he was poking himself with a pin or a sharp metal object; no, he was simply poking with his finger. After he had demonstrated this malady to a number of his friends, one of them persuaded him to go to a doctor to see if he could solve the mystery.

So the man went through the rigmarole again for the doctor. "See, when I poke my shoulder, it really hurts. Ouch!" And so it went, as he poked his knee, his thigh, his chest, his face, the top of his head, all with yelps of real pain.

The doctor tried poking the same places, but the man didn't register any discomfort at all. After a bit of thought, the doctor recommended an x-ray; not a series of x-rays or a body scan, just a single little x-ray. And sure enough, he found the problem. The man had fractured his index finger!

Isn't that ridiculous? It's one of the things that makes jokes funny: the ridiculous, the unexpected, the illogical. Our mind is led in a certain way by the storyteller. Like a magician, he employs misdirection. Suddenly we are zapped with the punch line, which in a crazy way has a logic of its own. Of course! In this story we hadn't thought about the "pointer" itself. Such latitude is the privilege of the joke-teller. But in the story is hidden a lesson: fix the "pointer" and the pain is gone.

It is not quite so funny in real life. It's all too easy to point at people, at family members, at organizations and at our corps and find a lot of things wrong. But when seemingly everything is wrong, we begin to wonder about the one who does the pointing— the "pointer."

So often there is need for spiritual healing. When that healing occurs, the erstwhile complainer suddenly finds the world a remarkably better place, even though it hasn't changed a bit; he or she is seeing it through new eyes.

I remember a testimony of someone who had found a great deal wrong with the Bible. This man questioned statement after statement, incident after incident, finding them inconsistent, irrelevant, and so on. But when, through the counsel of a friend, the critic accepted Christ into his life, he found that his doubts had shriveled and fallen away. The Bible was no longer a stumbling block to belief, but glowed with light and truth. He wasn't just sweeping his doubts "under the rug," so to speak. They were gone! His outlook was changed.

The same holds true with regard to one's attitude toward people. When we become a true Christian, the world is a different place. In "Take Over Bid" a character sings, "I'm a different man." The odd thing—the wonderful thing—is that, for the convert in so many cases, everyone else is changed, too!

The Great Commission Still Stands

In 1893, a Congress of Religions was held in Chicago, timed to coincide with the Columbian Exposition, the city's first World's Fair. The Congress was an attempt to bring together representatives of the world's great religions, with the intention of promoting a spirit of human brotherhood among men of all faiths and of sharing the important and distinctive truths held and taught by each religion. The organizers hoped to promote a permanent international peace through better understanding among the nations of the world. As you doubtless know, the Exposition and the Congress of Religions took place in a period of great optimism. As men were to learn, that optimism was ill-founded.

In the final session of this Congress, a representative of each religion was assigned to outline the leading features of his own creed and practice and, without "putting down" the beliefs of others, to show why his particular faith merited belief. After all, if each and every speaker did not sincerely believe that his was the only true religion, why did he cling to it rather than switching to something more worthy of his loyalty and commitment?

It goes without saying that the assignment was a very delicate and tricky one. The time allotted to each speaker was not long; everyone naturally would set forth his own views in the most favorable terms possible. Yet, how to do this without coming right out and saying, "I'm right and all of you are wrong"? Such a declaration would be tactless, without a doubt totally ineffective, and entirely foreign to the spirit of the occasion.

What would you have done? How could you be faithful to the Great Commission of Jesus and yet not appear to be a bigot, seemingly lacking in Christian grace and compassion? It was a time for great diplomacy and high intelligence in witnessing for the Master. The man speaking for Christianity had to stay within the guidelines of the conference. He could hardly hope to win any converts on the spot, but he certainly could give them something to think about—something to take back home with them and to consider very seriously.

So he gave them one fact, the unique fact of Christianity, and he wrapped it up in a "package" so it would have the greatest possible effect on his listeners' minds. With the utmost tact and respect he referred to the great reverence for the mortal remains of the founders of other faiths; of how their tombs were so sacred to their followers. "That is what is different about Christianity," he said. "Jesus left no body to which we can pay homage, no relics to venerate, no burial place at which we can pour out our adoration. He rose from the dead, leaving behind an empty tomb." With great effect he emphasized the point. "We do not strive to keep alive the memory of a leader long since departed. Jesus is alive! Who among you can say that of your leader?" Of course no one else could.

There is a lot of talk today about religious tolerance. Some would even say that we must be willing to acknowledge that others' religions are as good as ours, that Christian evangelism is dangerously close to bigotry. But while we as Christians should be tolerant and generous-spirited, we must never forget: Jesus' Great Commission still stands. That is not to say that we are to "argue religion" with non-Christians in a carping or critical manner which is ultimately fruitless. Our essential message, the message which the Holy Spirit can use to bear fruit, is the crucified and risen Christ—the living Christ.